THE
GUNPOWDER
PLOT

For Martin Travers 1945–2018.
A lover of history and of literature

THE
GUNPOWDER
PLOT

TERROR IN SHAKESPEARE'S ENGLAND

JAMES TRAVERS

AMBERLEY

First published 2019

Amberley Publishing
The Hill, Stroud
Gloucestershire, GL5 4EP

www.amberley-books.com

Copyright © James Travers, 2019

The right of James Travers to be identified as
the Author of this work has been asserted in
accordance with the Copyrights, Designs and
Patents Act 1988.

ISBN 978 1 4456 8467 3 (hardback)
ISBN 978 1 4456 8468 0 (ebook)

British Library Cataloguing in Publication Data.
A catalogue record for this book is available
from the British Library.

Typesetting by Aura Technology and Software
Services, India.
Printed in the UK.

CONTENTS

FOREWORD

Guy Fawkes is back. Adopted by the hacktivist internet group Anonymous, Guido Fawkes has become the face of political disaffection once again. Thanks to his popularity as a mask, he has reclaimed some of the original mystique and the nightmare quality associated with him; the 'unknown face' of the Plot, prized by the well-known and well-connected plotters as a man who could pass unnoticed in Westminster, even as he went to destroy the Houses of Parliament.

In 2005, to coincide with the 400th anniversary of the discovery of the Gunpowder Plot, I was asked by The National Archives to write a book that would bring its indispensable Plot documents out of the footnotes and on to centre stage. Then it seemed an almost nostalgic project. Bonfire Night appeared an ageing and increasingly marginalised tradition, losing out inexorably, it seemed, to the commercial might of Halloween. Now Fawkes has returned as a Halloween figure in his own right, subversive, disconcertingly historical and yet familiar, amid the fake horror and candy.

Gunpowder: The Players Behind the Plot followed on naturally from *James I: The Masque of Monarchy*, my 2003 book about the Scottish king in England. It took a literary approach, looking closely at the language of key documents through transcription and analysis. This new approach let the story of the Plot unfold like a novel without the benefit of hindsight, allowing readers make their own judgements based on the evidence. This dramatic treatment proved attractive to television production companies and other broadcasters looking to tell the story of the Plot in an accessible way.

Thanks to the media interest in the Plot since 2005, the key aim of the original book has been accomplished to a much greater extent than I could have dared hope. The documents of the government's investigation of the Plot, previously seen by a small group of scholars and enthusiasts, have now become familiar objects to millions. BBC2's 2014 documentary drama *Gunpowder 5/11: The Greatest Terror Plot* drew on the book's approach, and I was the programme's historical consultant. In it, we saw the documents being written, read and even burned; we saw the flames curling around Robert Wintour's desperately worded letter pleading for help to his father-in-law, as the Midlands rebellion led by the plotters failed around him. A couple of weeks after the 2014 programme was first broadcast, coming back from a November fireworks display, I overheard the Midlands rebellion and the letter being discussed as a given part of the Plot story for the first time.

Going back to the story and its sources for television has led me to further insights and discoveries, which seemed a good reason to revisit the story in book form. Other elements have come to the fore. The opposition to James VI & I's vision of England and Scotland uniting politically as Great Britain, so central to the motivation of the Gunpowder Plotters, then seemed a parochial and forgotten part of the Plot's context. Now it appears more topical and relevant because the entity created by the Act of Union in 1707, that ultimately successful Stuart project, seems under threat.

The 2005 book set the action in three acts. The core plot was in London, but there were two much less well known elements: the ill-fated attempt to raise a rebellion in the Midlands in the days after the discovery, and the investigation by the government to discover the 'great man' and other forces behind the Plot. The investigation went on intensively well into 1606, until the execution of Father Henry Garnet in May. Loose threads were followed for years afterwards. The documentary drama in its 60-minute broadcast version included the rebellion but took the story only as far as the plotters' executions in January 1606. The investigation into the director of the Plot, into the involvement of missionary priests and the network of Catholic households that sheltered them, could not be included in the broadcast version.

Gunpowder 5/11 was originally titled *Gunpowder Plotters in their Own Words* and it drew on the language of the plotters as set down in documents. The show proved what the book had only contended; that thanks to the massive and far-reaching government investigation, the story of the Plot could be told through genuine recorded original dialogue with a level of detail and accuracy perhaps greater than any other event of the period.

Working on the drama made me look at the archival sources more closely and more widely. In its many draft versions, the television programme suggested new scenes which the book only reported. The original book aimed to bring out the richness and layers of meaning in official documents, which had divided historians ever since they became publicly available. The limits of the traditional narrative were clear. There was, for example, a need to suppress evidence of the humanity of the plotters and the role of any of their circle in the discovery of the Plot. Then there was the attempt to present Lord Monteagle and his warning letter as miraculous agents of deliverance and to suppress his many links to the plotters and other plots. And there was the desire to portray the Jesuits as drivers of the Plot rather than a source of restraint. This official narrative naturally had no place for the complexity of the role of the Jesuits and the courage of the network of Catholic women who protected them; I have tried to redress this balance using other sources.

All this suggested a new book incorporating new lines of enquiry; and the new evidence that has emerged or gained importance since the original publication includes that relating to the torture of Guy Fawkes. Prompted by Mark Nicholls' excellent *Investigating Gunpowder Plot*, I looked again at the documents of the official investigation; in particular, at the questioning, trial and imprisonment of the earl of Northumberland, which offered new possibilities to explore the depth and breadth of the conspiracy and drew in unlikely figures, from Sir Walter Raleigh to Inigo Jones. It also shed new light on questions that had nagged at the back of my mind for years – such as Shakespeare's apparent disinclination to travel overseas, unlike most of his literary rivals.

There is another pressing reason to return to the story of the Plot and its sources. The 2005 book helped alert broadcasters to the dramatic possibilities of the Plot, but sadly, the drama has begun to leave

Plotter engraving produced in the wake of the plot's discovery. (British Library)

the evidence behind again. Now that the documents have become a common currency, and famous in their own right, it is very common for dramatisations to use original documents in their opening credits for atmosphere, but then promptly leave them behind for extended scenes of invented character and situation. It is time to present the Plot once more in a way the plotters and those who hunted them might recognise.

The thing that strikes you about the famous group engraving of the Gunpowder Plotters (above) is their social ease. True, there is a certain amount of whispering and passing of notes, but overall they look like a group of men and at a wine and cheese party whose only conspiracy has been not to invite their wives so that they can tell risqué jokes. Are they simply being represented as bad plotters, too good-humoured and gregarious to keep treason to themselves? Or is there a hidden truth in this image about the nature of the Plot, one that helps explain its unending controversy? This book looks at these men not as automata driven by inexorable historical forces discernible only with hindsight, but as social beings whose fates rested on key moments, which we can reconstruct from documents held at The National Archives, at Hatfield House and elsewhere.

It also presents a wider perspective on the Gunpowder Plot and the individuals it enveloped. It follows the small group of plotters pictured here beyond the whispering London world where the conspiracy to blow up the House of Lords was hatched to a house on the borders of Worcestershire and Staffordshire where they accidentally blew themselves up with their own gunpowder. It traces the rippling repercussions of the Plot from local loyalties and law enforcement in England to the grand stage of international politics.

The engraving shows the core plotters, including three who dominated and drove the scheme forward: Robert Catesby, gentleman of Ashby St Ledgers, Northamptonshire, who was its mastermind; Thomas Percy, gentleman, constable of Alnwick Castle, member of the king's bodyguard and the group's means of access to Parliament and the royal family; and Thomas Wintour, gentleman, soldier and scholar, its diplomatic arm, who in Flanders had recruited Guy Fawkes, a skilled soldier who had served the Spanish forces abroad for so long that his face was conveniently unknown in England. John Wright, a schoolfellow of Fawkes in York, is shown listening, while Catesby and Percy talk simultaneously. He seems to have been the strong silent type. Both Wright and Thomas Wintour recruited their brothers as extra manpower and both are depicted towards the edge of the group. Robert Wintour, the elder brother who had inherited the family estate in Worcestershire, is shown passing a note to Catesby's servant Thomas Bate. Characteristically, he is looking outside the group to his responsibilities beyond.

The engraving re-created for *Gunpowder 5/11: The Greatest Terror Plot*, 2014. (Courtesy of Aenon Productions)

The second image (previous page) shows the actors in the drama recreating the poses of the plotters in the original engraving. In the modern version, the gaudiness of Catesby's clothes marks him out as a leader and a defier of convention. Thomas Wintour, behind him, seems a sober, restraining influence, while Guy Fawkes is silent in the centre. Thomas Percy is holding forth, convincing the group of his own importance, perhaps reminding them of the personal nature of his betrayal by the king, an argument they appear to have heard before. They look rather younger than the men in the engraving, perhaps a closer reflection of their actual age and aspect. Catesby was in his early thirties when the Plot was hatched. Here was a new kind of 'dramatic' evidence, which took us wider and deeper into the language of the documents. Watching the plotters interact, their words supporting or undermined by their actions, the actors' interpretations suggested new lines of enquiry and possibilities that had not been obvious from my original reading of the sources on the page.

Many more of those involved in the Plot lurk in the shadows around this social circle. Wealthy late recruits Sir Everard Digby, Ambrose Rookwood and Francis Tresham are all still to arrive at the party – indeed, they claimed Catesby barely had time to introduce them to the others before the Plot was discovered. Lord Monteagle, Tresham's brother-in-law, hailed as the saviour of his nation for disclosing to the government an anonymous letter warning of the Plot, had employed Thomas Wintour as his secretary and had been in plotters' circles for years. Henry Percy, earl of Northumberland, Thomas Percy's cousin, who had appointed the plotter to the king's bodyguard, was reportedly already dissatisfied with the Scottish king he had done so much to bring to the English throne. Henry Garnet, Father Superior of the English Jesuit Province, was close to the core plotters, but was he a restraining influence or the arch-plotter himself? To what extent did other Jesuits in the English mission accept and act on his authority? What encouragement or restraint to the Plot did they offer independently? What role, deeper in the shadows, was played by the state? Was this happy group monitored and manipulated by their intended victims, Secretary of State Robert Cecil, earl of Salisbury, and the king himself?

In the writing of a history of something as controversial as the Gunpowder Plot, characters can swiftly become polarised on ideological grounds. Original documents generally depict them more ambiguously. Certainly, the conspirators appear with a more human face than the official version of events would allow, but this also makes them more difficult to excuse or dismiss as mere pawns in a fabrication. The great ideological divide between religious groups is real and ever-present, but as you study a key moment in the Plot, it is often unclear exactly where each character stands in relation to this great divide, and still less clear whether a character's position remains constant. The ambiguity and playfulness with language that makes Shakespeare's 'position' on almost any subject notoriously difficult to establish was not confined to him, though perhaps he did it with greatest skill. Many of his contemporaries, including the prominent figures involved in the Plot and its investigation, used language in this way even in extremis. Generally, there are more interpretations possible than historians usually admit. Contemporaries described the Gunpowder Plot as a tragedy, but it is one made all the more tense, exciting and terrible by the fact that the dead bodies on the stage at the end of the final act are real.

Unlike the well-crafted drama of the period, with its inexorable dramatic irony, real events unfolded in a fragmentary way without modern bureaucracy or reportage to inform or co-ordinate. We shall see the government use torture to gain information that had already been gleaned by others a hundred miles away. For much of the first week after the discovery of the Plot, the official investigation was a frantic attempt to gain information about a rebellion that was over almost before they knew of it. Local information could be accurate as far as it went but was often overlooked, or even superseded before it was known. The government was reliant for law enforcement on local gentry, characters who in rank and education were not dissimilar to the plotters themselves, so there was always the possibility that royal proclamations would go unheeded because local loyalties would obstruct the monarch's purpose.

The scenes of the Plot divide naturally into the three acts mentioned in connection with my previous book: the plotters' final preparations and the discovery of Fawkes with the gunpowder in London; the plotters' failed attempt to foment rebellion in the Midlands; and the more composed government investigation trying to make sense of the Plot, which flushed out and teased evidence from those in the wings and in hiding, much of it embarrassing for the government. A chronology detailing the events in their proper order appears at the end of the book. It gives us the luxury of seeing events in the orderly fashion they rarely assumed for participants at the time.

Where possible, I have avoided the use of footnotes and instead put references to documents alongside their use in the text. This is intended to stress the accessibility of the documents to all of us, not just to the community of scholars who deal in footnotes. The majority of domestic state papers have now been digitised and are available online; the originals are stored in a former salt mine in Cheshire. A great many of the other documents I use are still produced in their original forms for anyone with a reader's ticket who wishes to consult them. There is only one thing better than books and drama to bring the voices of those behind the Plot to our ears, and that is to see the originals for ourselves.

PROLOGUE

'A Muse of Fire'

The three acts of the Gunpowder Plot are full of dramatic elements. The plotters were self-conscious performers, donning special clothes and props for their part as martyrs – scarves embroidered with exhortations and swords engraved with Christ's passion. There were also theatrical aspects to the Plot: anonymous letters, prophecies and a suitably ironic moment when the plotters, making their last stand, were blown up with their own gunpowder. Drama was also important in shaping how people at the time viewed these events. The plotters and their contemporaries were the original audience of William Shakespeare's history plays; they could see played out in them the machinations of the court, the intrigues of the succession and the historical role of the eminent families who still retained their traditional power to make and unmake kings.

Plays could be 'occasional' in the sense of dealing with specific events. *Macbeth* was first performed in the months following the Gunpowder Plot, and its author could not resist articulating some of the malcontents' sentiments at the accession of the new Scots king to the English throne. In addition, what writer could forbear to comment on the doctrine of equivocation – the poet's theological device, which allowed you to say two things at once? When we look at the Plot's background in the light of Jacobean theatre, we begin to appreciate it through the eyes and ears of the people who lived through the Plot, Shakespeare's first audience.

'Here Cousin, seize the Crown': James VI & I and the lessons of history

With the succession of James VI of Scotland to the English throne in 1603, the stage was set for intrigue and incident. As king, James might be expected to sit above the unfolding of Gunpowder Plot looking down in splendid detachment on the machinations below. But in his own favourite form of drama, the court masque, he was more central and involved, enthroned on stage while the courtiers performed around him. James was very much one of the characters of the Plot, and the players around him appear in a variety of guises, their roles often changing with circumstances or dependent on the audience. He was already an experienced survivor of plots and an expert at making political capital from their discovery; he was also a plotter himself, having intrigued with factions in England before his predecessor Elizabeth I's death. Much of the air of conspiracy, the odd closeness of the plotters to the king and government, can be traced the king's own plotting before 1603. As the investigation of the Plot continued, it became evident just how close James and his government were to the plotters.

Early in his reign, James had restored to favour families who had supported and intrigued on behalf of his mother, Mary, Queen of Scots, against Queen Elizabeth, rewarding their loyalty to his dynasty during adversity. He had fostered links with the earl of Essex as the strongest English advocate of his claim to succeed to the English throne, drawing back just far enough not to be implicated in the earl's ill-fated rebellion in 1601. The night before the rebellion saw a specially commissioned performance of Shakespeare's *Richard II*, which seemed, at least to some degree, to justify the deposition of the reigning monarch. Those imprisoned and questioned after the failure of the Essex rebellion give a reasonable initial cast list for the characters behind the Gunpowder Plot: Lord Monteagle, Francis Tresham, Robert Catesby, John and Christopher Wright and the earl of Northumberland's brothers Charles and Jocelyn Percy. Shakespeare and King James were able to talk their way out of it.

The real lesson of *Richard II*, especially in the context of the plays that follow, is that the usurper has set a precedent that then undermines his own position. He who lives by the plot will die by the plot. James was too committed a plotter to be deterred by this lesson, but years of plotting and counter-plotting in Scotland meant he was all too aware of the risks. He had engaged in shadowy secret correspondence with various groups in England before 1603, and conveyed words of comfort to English Catholics. Unfortunately for James, those who plotted on behalf of his mother had done so not merely out of loyalty to his family but out of a desire to replace a Protestant monarch with a Catholic one. The motley assortment of malcontents who rallied to Essex in 1601 remained predictably discontented during James's reign.

In King James the English Catholics found themselves confronted by a monarch who was not only as convinced a Protestant as Elizabeth had been, but also one who wrote and spoke about theology and derided the 'superstitions' of Catholics more openly and more often. It was only natural that the new king should try and extend his patronage to those who had suffered under Elizabeth, but it is still constantly striking how many of the people involved in the treason designed to blow him up in November 1605 had been engaged before 1603 in treason, designed to assure his place on the throne. How broad and deep was the support for the new foreign monarch? Who could he really rely on among these former plotters, and who was simply waiting for the chance to replace him?

James's succession to the throne was a plot in itself, the product of an extraordinary secret correspondence with Queen Elizabeth's Principal Secretary of State, the then Sir Robert Cecil, later rewarded by James with the earldom of Salisbury. The trusted councillor and his prospective monarch corresponded using code numbers to disguise their identity, involving a few trusted noblemen in a benign conspiracy behind the queen's back to ensure a smooth succession in the event of her death. James was still playfully using the code numbers of this secret correspondence in the autumn of 1605. It was a bond between him and his fellow former conspirators, who had now become the government. While James and his new councillors enjoyed playing at intrigue from comfortable positions of power, a whole host of shadowy figures, plotters and place-hunters who had not gained what James had promised or hinted at while wooing interest groups south of the border came trailing in his wake in search of belated reward or revenge. One of these was a man who had heard the verbal assurances given by the king to English Catholics and exaggerated them to emphasise his own importance: Thomas Percy.

Francis Bacon, lawyer, philosopher, poet and courtier, was also one of those who took a variety of paths on the rocky road to advancement. Bacon had been a dependant of the earl of Essex but was instrumental in his trial after the earl's rebellion, in which so many of the plotters and their allies were involved. He also drew up 'A Declaration of the Practises and Treasons attempted and committed by Robert late Earl of Essex'. Was this unscrupulous betrayal or good judgement? Bacon's movement towards the now dominant Cecil was rapid. Cecil helped him with his already impressive debts and must have regarded Bacon as a clever man, better to have on your side than against you, but not entirely trustworthy.

Having recommended himself by annoying Queen Elizabeth with his parliamentary speeches, Bacon held out hope of office under the new king. In a letter of 1603 to the earl of Northumberland, Bacon praised the king's even-handed if rather indiscriminate bestowal of honours on the royal progress south. Bacon soon found himself a beneficiary, but, as he might have anticipated, it was hardly the individual recognition he was looking for; he was knighted in a batch of three hundred on 23 July. High office in keeping with his talents continued to evade him.

Many of James's councillors happily followed their monarch in plotting throughout these years. The most consummate plotting councillor was Henry Howard, created earl of Northampton in 1604. The involvement of the Howard family with the plotting and intrigue surrounding Mary, Queen of Scots blighted Henry's political prospects under Elizabeth, despite his attempts to maintain court favour through flattering scholarly addresses. By 1595, Henry had hitched his star to the young favourite, the earl of Essex, with whom he shared an elevated and self-congratulatory view of the importance of noble birth. Howard was too canny to involve himself in Essex's revolt in 1601, and immediately after it, he, like Francis Bacon, moved smoothly to the victorious Cecil faction at court. Sir Robert Cecil might have had reason to be suspicious of him, but Howard's well-established contact with James VI of Scotland was too valuable to overlook, as James emerged as the likely successor to the English throne. In the secret coded correspondence with the king, the 'long approved and trusty' Howard was one of those plotting to ensure the smooth transfer of power after the death of Elizabeth. Plotting James's succession, Howard lost no time in elevating his own place in affairs, warning James against other English courtiers, particularly Lord Cobham and Sir Walter Raleigh, both of whom were conveniently implicated in plots against James in 1603.

What was the nature of James's promise to Catholics in England before his accession? It has been endlessly debated. That which was committed to paper was ambiguous. In March 1603, Queen Elizabeth's illness seemed sufficiently grave for the earl of Northumberland to resume his correspondence with the Scottish king. On the day of Queen Elizabeth's death, James wrote a reply from Holyrood, as yet unaware of her death and his own succession, still intent on smoothing his way with the principal Catholics in England: 'I will neither persecute any that will be quiet and give outward obedience to the law; neither will I spare to advance any of them that will by good service worthily deserve it.'[1]

This sounded fair and equitable, but obeying the law meant accepting the penal laws against Catholics and impossibility of practising their faith. What level of service would they be allowed to achieve in order to deserve that advancement? That would be very much at the king's discretion.

The Gunpowder Percys

In Shakespeare's play on the subject, those who had done most to help Henry IV take King Richard's crown, and who later reproached him for his ingratitude, were the Percys, earls of Northumberland. Indeed, the audience of Shakespeare's history plays could watch Percys rebelling and making and unmaking kings, generation after generation, every night. Too close for comfort, and beyond the chronology of his plays, Shakespeare's audiences would know that the Percys had continued to fill this role on the national stage in the recent past. The seventh earl urged the excommunication of Elizabeth I and prompted the papal bull *Regnans in excelsis*, by which Pius V freed Catholics from their allegiance to her. He led a rebel force in the North, threatening to release Mary, Queen of Scots from her captivity. He was attainted and executed in 1572. The eighth earl, though loyal to Elizabeth rather than to his brother on that occasion, was later fined and confined to his house at Petworth after his own involvement in plots to free Mary, and was eventually imprisoned in the Tower and shot, apparently by his own hand. This script, or versions of it, seemed to be handed to each successive head of the family, and a paying audience might feel they had every right to expect rebellion from the latest incumbent.

Intelligence reports in 1592 suggested that 'the Earl of Northumberland that now is, doth stand very well affected to the see of Rome and ... he continueth much discontented from his father's death'. Overseas it was suggested he could come under the influence of the Jesuits, who might 'secure him from his allegiance to his Prince and his country as too many of that most honourable house already have been'.[2] This was Henry, ninth earl of Northumberland, head of one of England's great Catholic families, though he professed not to be a Catholic himself. In the same year, Northumberland was inevitably in a list of those whom English rebels overseas, hoping for a Spanish invasion, looked to for support and horses in England. 'Being discontented that they were not advanced nor preferred as they happly expected [they] would easily be moved to follow the Spaniard who would promise largely and put them in places of authority if he should possess this land.'[3]

The suggestion that the ninth earl was prone to be influenced by strong personalities around him would be made repeatedly in the years to come. He could still play the courtier, though. Whatever Elizabeth's spies reported of him abroad, he was soon comfortably back in favour with Elizabeth, earning remission of his father's fines imposed in Star Chamber.[4] There seemed to be so many facets to his character. The things that made him useful also made him potentially dangerous. One of these was an interest in military tactics. Ever since the first performance of *The First Part of Henry IV* around 1597, audiences had heard Northumberland's interests in artillery and ordnance articulated by his ancestor Harry Hotspur, and would remember Falstaff's tremulous, 'Zounds! I am afraid of this gunpowder Percy though he be dead.'

The earl therefore came from a background steeped in rebellion against the English Crown and hostility towards the Scots, but he became instrumental in the accession of England's new Scottish king and was restored to favour under him. Were his military interests directed to defending the new king, or replacing him? Controversy has raged about the real extent of Northumberland's loyalty to King James and his complicity in the Gunpowder Plot through his cousin Thomas Percy. His pleas of innocence were not helped by the ambiguity of his language; his letters betray a nobleman biding his time. The earl appeared in so many guises: was he the real power behind the Plot, one of its intended victims, or, as he insisted himself, a man of private life who liked gardening and arcane scientific experiments and who had no interest in power? Sometimes it seemed he did not have sufficient power to control his own poor relation Thomas Percy.

While Northumberland's brothers Jocelyn and Charles were involved in the earl of Essex's rebellion in 1601, Northumberland stayed aloof and secured their release from the Fleet prison. In the Low Countries in 1601 and 1602, he spent spectacular sums on horses and books, learning military tactics and making contacts among scholars and military commanders. Often in his company was his kinsman Thomas Percy. Later, in the light of the Gunpowder Plot and its discovery, it would be asked whether Thomas was simply following his master or directing him. Retrospectively, this activity could be interpreted in at least three ways. Northumberland maintained he was pursuing intellectual, academic interests and that arms and horses were necessary to maintain his strength in the North, which would help ease the smooth succession of the Scottish king to his English throne when the time came. Alternatively, he could have been gaining the necessary experience to assume a military command of the English forces fighting Spain, since he felt they lacked commanders of sufficient ability. But in the light of the Plot, it was suggested that the horses were intended to support a Spanish invasion of England following the explosion, all part of Thomas Percy's plan.

Thomas Percy was one of those who did not undertake his master's prudent shift in religious belief but who felt relatively at ease as a practising Catholic in the earl's service. Northumberland himself admitted he had followers set in their ways 'with oars in that boat'. It was also an environment in which the occasional anti-Scots rant was perfectly acceptable. Nonetheless, Northumberland was a major figure in the secret correspondence with James in Scotland before the death of Queen Elizabeth. As his messenger, the earl selected Thomas Percy, and through him he sought toleration for English Catholics.

Northumberland's carefully phrased, heavily qualified prose style seemed well adapted to the secret correspondence with James before his accession. Apparently speaking for the Catholics in England, introducing and retracting ideas in case they were distasteful, like Iago to Othello he suggested that 'it were pity to lose so good a kingdom for the not tolerating of a mass in a corner, if upon that it resteth'.[5] But did it?

The Scottish recipients of Northumberland's letters hastily copied them to Cecil and Henry Howard; they had no desire to entertain two channels of communication that might contradict or compromise one another. It was quite clear whom they regarded as the true and reliable figure. Northumberland asked to stop writing to the king in 1602, and their correspondence only revived when the path was clearer and all declared allies would need to be brought together for practical assistance.

Though the succession was in the end remarkable for its smoothness, this was not the view held by those left out of the secret negotiations. Sir John Carey, writing to Sir Robert Cecil on 16 March 1603 from Berwick, a stronghold that was soon to lose considerable strategic importance, felt the situation was far from clear. Was he to resist or welcome the Scottish invader?

> What should I do here not knowing how or for whom to keep this place, being only in the devil's mouth, a place that will be first assailed and I not being instructed what course to hold, either for the good of my country or to continue myself an honest man.[6]

Later, in March 1603, when Elizabeth lay dying, Northumberland was asked to join the council to oversee the transition, and there seems to have been a suggestion that the earl should act as protector of the realm while James made his way south. This was not required in the end, but it may have sowed a seed of ambition in the earl, and doubt in the minds of the council. Having suggested Northumberland for this role themselves, it is little wonder the authorities took seriously the suggestion that the Gunpowder Plotters might have expected the earl to act in the same capacity after the death of the king. It was Robert Carey who famously rode north to bring James the news of Elizabeth's death, but the official news came from Northumberland's brother Sir Charles Percy, together with Thomas Somerset.

Northumberland continued fruitlessly to urge some form of toleration for Catholics once James was on the throne, and foreign ambassadors began to report that the earl was disillusioned with James and his Scottish entourage. Nonetheless, the earl gained office in keeping with his rank. He was sworn in as a member of the Privy Council in April 1603 and was appointed captain of the gentleman pensioners, the official royal bodyguard, in May, recruiting Thomas Percy.

In November 1603, in the midst of the trial of Sir Walter Raleigh and the pleas for mercy of Lord Cobham and George Brooke, Northumberland chose to recommend Thomas Percy to his king and remind James of Percy's past service in a letter about plots. The earl congratulated the king on his escape from the plots that surrounded his accession earlier in the year, themselves an indication that, though James is rightly said to have come to the throne almost unopposed, there were a great number of well-connected individuals who were malcontents or potential malcontents. Even those who worked most conscientiously to bring James to the throne could be opportunists as much as they were loyalists.

As always with Northumberland, much in the letter could be read in two ways, recommending mercy as well as justice to the two barons among the plotters of 1603, who found themselves in a similar position to that suffered by members of his own family in the recent past, as if being implicated in treasonable plots were a harmless occupational hazard of noblemen. Northumberland reminded the king of the plot they were both involved in before his accession. It was as if he was saying, 'While we are on the subject of plots, remember my servant Thomas Percy who was essential to the cloak and dagger negotiations for your succession, he would like to see you again.' No wonder suspicion hung over Northumberland. His rhetoric about the plots of 1603 implicates him in the anti-Scots language of which Thomas Percy and indeed Guy Fawkes himself were all too fond. The treason uncovered in 1603, he admits, 'carries with it a taint to all of us as we are English'. The letter is heavily crossed through, as if Northumberland struggled to find the right phrases. They are the careful words of a great man treading a fine line, rather than the joyous outpourings of a loyal subject.

This ancient Mercury of mine, my cousin Percy, who could not before time look you in the face but by owl-light, would be glad to see your majesty by day light, poor men may have as great

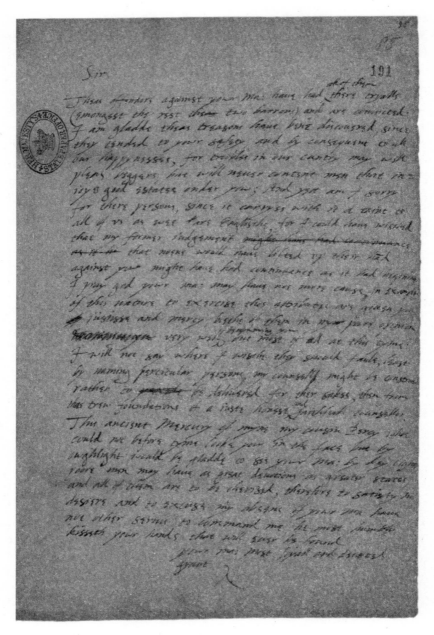

Northumberland's letter to the king calendared 18 November 1603. He congratulated the king on his escape from the plots of 1603, and then invited him to meet a core Gunpowder Plotter, his kinsman Thomas Percy. (The National Archives SP 14/4/85)

devotions as greater states, and all of them are to be cherished, therefore to satisfy his desire and to excuse my absence if your majesty have not other service to command me, he most humbly kisseth your hands, that will ever be found your majesty's most loyal and devoted servant, N.

There is some ambiguity about the 'he' referred to here, whether Northumberland is talking of himself in the third person, or of Percy, acting for him or in his absence. Either way, Northumberland seems to equate his loyalty with Percy's, five months before the latter took a vow to blow the king up. In retrospect, the king might well ask how great that loyalty was. There was also a contradiction in the letter, which cast doubt on Percy's devotion as a poor man. Earlier, in congratulating James on his escape from the Main and Bye plots, the earl had contrasted the attitudes of rich and poor to the thwarted treason: '... troubles in our country may well please beggars but will never content men that enjoy good estates under you'. So are poor men as devoted to the king as rich ones, or not? Northumberland then presents Percy as a poor man suing for favour. Is the implication that if Percy is not rewarded with an estate of his own for his crepuscular service he might join the ranks of 'beggars' looking for trouble, and the king might be at fault if his meanness leads to more malcontents? Is he counselling the king to bribe suspected malcontents to ensure their loyalty in his new kingdom? No wonder Northumberland struggled to find the right phrases. Might the letter be a veiled warning that Northumberland knew Percy's loyalty was at best in the balance and that some timely patronage might secure him?

The letter was certainly seen as an unfortunate attempt at an introduction in the light of subsequent events. Percy's death before the authorities had a chance to cross-examine him has robbed us of valuable evidence of the speed and depth of his disillusionment. While Father Henry Garnet's later evidence, suppressed by the king himself, suggests many of those behind the Plot found the king 'odious', of all the plotters Percy seemed most motivated by a personal dislike of James, perhaps because he knew him so well.

Percy's too sanguine reporting of James's relentlessly ambiguous diplomatic language bore some responsibility for the 'disappointment' of Catholics in James's supposed broken promises of toleration.

Percy felt the king had deceived him. What were the feelings of Thomas Percy at the time in November 1603 when Northumberland suggested to the king that Percy would like to meet him openly after years as a secret go-between? Was he a man eager to accept his due reward now James was established on the throne, like so many others who emerged from the shadows on James's accession, in the expectation of better times ahead? On the other hand, was he of the same mind as the Thomas Percy who only five months later was sitting in the Strand with Catesby, Thomas Wintour, Fawkes and John Wright devising the Gunpowder Plot? Perhaps the difference between these two versions of Percy is not, after all, that great, and Northumberland's 'misjudgement' of his loyalty is more understandable than it appeared to the authorities.

The difference between the loyal Percy of the owl-light and the dangerous one of the daylight was not necessarily the result of a great shift in ideology, but rather vanity and personal pique. He had helped put James in power, had boasted of his influence, but had not got what he wanted. Perhaps Percy's position was not that different to Northumberland's own.

'Will the line stretch out to the crack of doom?' Robert Catesby and Banquo's ghost

Robert Catesby's death alongside Thomas Percy at the siege of Holbeach robbed the Plot of its most charming and motivated advocate, and this allowed him to be eclipsed in history by Guido Fawkes as the central figure. Had he survived to give evidence we might burn Roberts instead of Guys on bonfire night, or perhaps Robins, since this was the name by which his many friends, both among the plotters and their intended victims, knew Catesby.

Robert was the son of Sir William Catesby of Lapworth, Warwickshire, and his wife, Anne, daughter of Sir Robert Throckmorton of Coughton, the very house that Sir Everard Digby would rent from the Throckmortons as his base for Catesby's rebellion. He was a descendant of the William Catesby who appeared as Richard III's 'cat' in the rhyme 'The cat the rat and Lovell our dog, ruleth all England under a hog'. It is almost tempting in this context to see the Gunpowder Plot as a last Yorkist rebellion of disenfranchised country gentlemen who blamed the Tudors and their successors for planting and nurturing an alien religion in England and who wished a return to pre-Reformation English piety. There were plenty of plotters and priests in Catesby's circle with Yorkshire and Yorkist connections, and Catesby's generation, as the first audience for Shakespeare's history plays, was certainly expected to take a long view of history and understand that poetic justice could be played out over a period of centuries.

Catesby's father was one of Jesuit Edmund Campion's hosts on the mission to England that ended in Campion's martyrdom. Many of the conspirators in the Midlands or their families were converted or confirmed in their faith by Campion or the other Jesuits. Catesby certainly believed that there was a hard core of Catholic families there who would follow a strong leader, that many others had adopted the new religion superficially in the hope of advancement rather than out of deep spiritual conviction, and that they would revert if the political climate changed.

Catesby seemed to be embarking on a conventional career, but the loss of his elder son and his wife in quick succession seems to have intensified both his general discontentment with the world and his lack of care for his own safety. His part in the Essex rebellion saw him wounded, imprisoned and fined. With his fellow Essex rebels and future Gunpowder Plotters John and Christopher Wright, Catesby was placed under arrest on the death of Queen Elizabeth.

With the accession of King James, the unstable atmosphere prevailing since the Reformation, in which a change of regime and religion was only an assassin's bullet away, suddenly seemed to come to an end. As long as the excommunicated Queen Elizabeth could be displaced by Spanish invasion, there was some prospect that a Catholic government was possible. Now there was a Protestant royal dynasty with a Cecil dynasty to serve it, an unending succession like the vision of Banquo's progeny in Shakespeare's *Macbeth*, first performed in the months following the discovery of the Gunpowder Plot. 'What!' cries Macbeth, 'Will the line stretch out till the crack of doom?' (iv.i.117) You can hear a touch of Catesby's anguish in this cry, as it seemed to hold the prospect of the lot of Catholic families deteriorating forever. Ill-omened though Macbeth's attempt to interfere with the succession appears on the stage, might not a sudden blow by Catesby alter that course for England, allowing them to return to the true religion and escape the rule of the Scots? There seemed now to be many more obstacles to the restoration of the Catholic faith in England than there had been under the reign of Elizabeth, but how deep was loyalty to the new king?

'Faith, here's an equivocator': Father Henry Garnet and Catholic rebellion, 1603–1605

Henry Garnet, Father Superior of the English Jesuit Province, was perhaps the most influential individual interrogated by the commissioners investigating the Plot, and the one who caused them the most difficulty. He advanced two contradictory defences of his conduct in relation to the Plot: that he was ignorant of it, and that he had done all he could to prevent it. His evidence was difficult to evaluate, and he infuriated his examiners, not least because they suspected, probably correctly, that he was smarter than them. His social ease with his questioners annoyed them too, and popular rumour flourished about the priest who drank wine liberally, sang to the lute and inspired love in the women who protected him.

The authorities alternated the threat of torture with theological debate, at which he triumphed continually, almost monotonously. Worse still, he interpreted the seal of the confessional so broadly that he felt able to conceal from the authorities almost anything told to him in confidence. Thanks to the doctrine of equivocation, which Garnet himself wrote about at length, he felt able to lie with calm religious conviction in a good cause. Though it cannot have been the first time that the authorities were aware that a suspect was telling them less than the truth, Garnet's equivocations seem to have enraged them, threatening to undermine the whole basis of gathering and accrediting evidence on which the investigation was based. Equivocation achieved some celebrity and made its way into the foul mouth of the porter in *Macbeth*. 'Faith, here's an equivocator, that could swear in both scales against either scale, who committed treason enough for God's sake, yet could not equivocate to heaven.'(II iii 9-13.)

It may not be a coincidence that this remark is introduced with a joke playing on one of Garnet's many pseudonyms and his fate: 'Here's a farmer that hanged himself upon the expectation of plenty.' Perhaps Garnet, alias Darcy, alias Whalley, alias Measley, alias Farmer, like a true martyr, welcomed his own hanging on the expectation of a place in heaven.

Equivocation appears again in a serious context later in the play. The ambiguity of the witches' prophecy becomes 'the equivocation of the fiend' when Birnam Wood does come to Dunsinane. As always with Shakespeare, there is more than one way these lines can be read. Is the treason for God's sake? Will heaven see through the equivocator's lies, or is he simply too devout to lie to heaven? Is equivocation devilish or is this simply a tyrant's view of a prophecy telling him the truth? Perhaps in their ability to say two things at once the playwright and the priest had much in common.

A scholar and musician at Winchester College, Garnet did not make the expected transition to New College, Oxford, going instead to London. Here, he contemplated a legal career and befriended Sir John Popham, who as Lord Chief Justice would supply much of the information on the Catholic underground in London as one of the investigators of the Gunpowder Plot. In 1575 he travelled to Portugal, and then Rome to join the Society of Jesus, becoming ordained around 1582. There was some doubt among his superiors as to whether the scholarly and contemplative Garnet was suited to the dangers and deceptions of the English Jesuit mission.

Garnet arrived in England at the time of the Babington plot, which had seen London too full of spies and suspicion to be safe. Garnet began to use and expand the network of Catholic country houses that would shelter him in the wake of the Gunpowder Plot and the failed Midlands rebellion. After Garnet had been in England for less than a month, Father William Weston was captured by the authorities. Garnet was now head of the English Jesuit Province.

Garnet was enthusiastic about Catholic prospects upon the accession of James I, writing on 16 April 1603: 'Great hope [there] is of toleration: and so general a consent of Catholics in the [king's] proclaiming [that] it seemeth God will work much.' Expectation quickly turned to disappointment and anger. Rumours of Catholic plots and conspiracies even reached Rome, and Garnet was instructed to do everything he could to prevent Catholics from resorting to violence. In June and July, Garnet corresponded in Latin with the head of the Jesuits detailing his attempts to restrain Catholic insurrection and gain time by persuading the plotters to seek papal guidance. Then, on 25 July 1605, in confession, Garnet learned of a plot from the Jesuit Oswald Tesimond. In the late summer of 1605, Garnet led a pilgrimage to Wales in a party including plotters, their families and friends, which passed through the plotters' houses, where preparations for something momentous were evident. Was this a last attempt at dissuasion, an attempt to distance himself, a bestowal of blessing on the enterprise or a simple act of devotion unconnected with the Plot?

Much of Garnet's evidence might be dismissed as unreliable, but it remains controversial, and he himself has attracted vilification and vindication in equal measure. Despite Sir Edward Coke's attempt to turn the Gunpowder Plot into 'The Jesuit's Treason', there is little evidence to suggest that Garnet had anything to do with planning the Plot, though he knew of it, was ineffectual in his attempts to stop it, and did nothing to alert the authorities. It is perhaps a tribute to Garnet's symbolic importance as well as his evasions that so much evidence was taken from him and so much interpretation was placed on it. Whenever we are tempted to think of the Plot in straightforward religious terms, it is always worth recalling the ambiguity of Garnet's role.

The evidence of the witnesses to the Plot is often ambiguous, heavily qualified, even playful in its language. This is not just the influence of the doctrine of equivocation, which allowed the concealment of meaning in a good cause. More simply it was because the raw material at their disposal when planning the Plot, or pleading in desperation during a doomed rebellion, or in hoping to evade the gallows or ruinous fines, was the language of Shakespeare's contemporaries and audience. They were not consciously composing literary texts, but overwhelmingly the plotters were literate, and might be expected to understand him without too much glossing.

We have evidence that some of the plotters attended Shakespeare's plays. Do carefully selected quotations from contemporary letters, notes and reports really tell us in convenient soundbites what we need to know about a character's convictions in relation to the Plot? Can we pigeonhole them comfortably on ideological grounds on that basis? So much evidence was taken so quickly from those in the streets of London and in the houses of the educated gentry in Warwickshire. The Gunpowder Plot offers us the largest single snapshot of people forced to offer testimony to describe a single event, under pressure and often in fear of their lives. The voices of four centuries past do speak to us through the documents, but to interpret their significance we need a fuller understanding of their world. When approaching the copious and fascinating legacy of the investigation, to paraphrase the great Elizabethan teacher and scholar Roger Ascham, we need to care for words as well as hunting after matter.

ACT I

BRIMSTONE AND TREASON
1603 TO 6 NOVEMBER 1605

Cast List

JAMES VI AND I, King of England, Scotland and Ireland, 'odious to all sorts'

HENRY PERCY, earl of Northumberland, captain of the king's bodyguard, 'The Wizard Earl'

HENRY HOWARD, earl of Northampton, privy councillor, 'Conjuror of priests and devils'

ROBERT CECIL, earl of Salisbury, Principal Secretary of State, 'The Little Beagle'

WILLIAM PARKER, Baron Monteagle, defender of Catholics in Parliament, recipient of the 'Monteagle letter'

ANTHONY MARIA BROWNE, Viscount Montague, nobleman, employer of Guy Fawkes

SIR JOHN POPHAM, Lord Chief Justice, sometime friend of Henry Garnet

SIR EDWARD COKE, Attorney General, prosecutor and conspiracist

SIR FRANCIS BACON, lawyer and essayist

FRANCIS TRESHAM, gentleman of Rushton Hall, Northamptonshire, brother-in-law to Lord Monteagle

ROBERT CATESBY, gentleman of Ashby St Ledgers, Northamptonshire

THOMAS WINTOUR, gentleman, soldier and scholar, secretary to Lord Monteagle

THOMAS PERCY, gentleman, member of the king's bodyguard, kinsman to the earl of Northumberland

GUIDO FAWKES, alias Guy Fawkes, alias John Johnson, gentleman soldier

I

ACTING ALONE: GUY FAWKES AND THE GREAT BLOW

We think of the Gunpowder Plot as a metropolitan drama unravelling within the iconic walls and cellars of the nation's political heart. Though the Plot centred on London, many of the parties concerned showed a marked reluctance to go there. Luckily for us, this led to a great deal of correspondence, since there was no other way, short of bonfires, of communicating at a distance. We have letters from the king, hunting at his favourite base at Royston, to those councillors remaining in London, and others from plotters reluctant to leave the security of their network of family and friends in the country for the world of heretical careerists and informers in the capital. The plotters were almost as keen as the king himself on hunting, with its blend of skill and fortune. Both sides knew London as a place of political machination and backstabbing, where fortunes and position could be won and lost in a moment, where the ambitious coveted the position and favour of others, and where a misplaced letter could turn a predator into prey.

In a letter written while hunting in October 1605, James apologised to Lord Salisbury for his 'lack of matter' and confessed that, aside from his habitual financial embarrassments, 'I was never so void of care'. In the letter, the earl of Northampton's Catholicism is treated not as a threat, but as a bit of a joke, an eccentricity that only highlights his loyalty. Using his and Northampton's code numbers from their secret correspondence, James wrote to Salisbury,

> Ask of 3 how he thinks a priest can both make a god and eat a god and lodge both God and the Devil within him *simul et semel*. But I am sure that 3 loves so dearly his old 30 as he spares not to conjure both priests and devils for his master's service.[1]

Here James jokingly continues to use his and Northampton's code numbers (30 and 3 respectively) from the secret correspondence before his accession – a shared intrigue in the past strengthening bonds in the present.

In October 1605, Northampton was involved in the preparations for the opening of Parliament and reported Jesuit moves in the Low Countries to have the king excommunicated. He was also one of the councillors engaged in the king's great domestic struggle with his finances, and again conducted the reform of household expenses in secret, as if it were a plot. He repeatedly reminded the king to burn his letters, not trusting the grooms of the chamber, who might read them, remarking that 'letters are a prey which many hunt after'. Old habits die hard, and the new government still betrayed some of the fear and caution of plotters.

When he was not 'void of care', James was famously nervous of assassination attempts and plots. London, with its anonymous crowds, seemed a dangerous place. He preferred the feudal security of the hunt. He was hunting when the Monteagle letter was delivered, warning of a 'great blow' to be given to Parliament, and hunting again as soon as the immediate threat of the Plot had diminished. Nonetheless, he seemed to have less cause to be nervous in England than he had in Scotland, where noblemen lived in proper fortified castles and thought little of kidnapping and imprisoning their king until their demands were met. In England, his councillors lived in domestic security in houses whose crenellations were just affectations. There were, however, landed Catholic families who lived in true medieval fashion under real fear of siege, behind moats and drawbridges, their houses full of gothic features that served as hiding places for missionary priests, ever wary of the periodic searches and confiscations of pursuivants. What was the real nature of their loyalty to the king? For James and his councillors, their status and treatment were a conundrum. Were they really as passive and conservative as they seemed, or might they break out and turn on their oppressor? James seemed to be continually in two minds about the Catholics, deriding their 'superstition' but cultivating and advancing those such as Northampton who conformed outwardly.

While the king hunted at Royston under the watchful eye of Robert Catesby – who often shadowed the royal party from his house in Hillingdon in Middlesex – the plotters planned their own hunting party. Catesby and his companions conceived of a gathering at Dunchurch in Warwickshire, which would use the cover of a hunt to disguise a rebellious uprising. In the course of it, James's elder daughter, Elizabeth, would be kidnapped from Coombe Abbey following the death of her father and brothers in the London explosion. The conspirators' notes at this time show an element of bravado, rather than the fatalism that emerges from the official evidence reconstructing the Plot after its failure. The time for action was near, and the plotters relished the occasion; the mood of their correspondence appears jauntier even than the king's coded notes, and less nervous than Northampton's restless desire to have his letters to his master burnt.

The intended victims and the plotters directly concerned with the gunpowder end of the operation slowly converged, with varying degrees of reluctance, on London. Their suspicion of the city was widely shared. Ben Jonson, the poet and playwright who had his own murky role as a player behind the Plot, was well acquainted with the saying of John Hoskyns – whom he called his 'father' in literary style – that 'all those that came to London were either carrion or crows'. In Jonson's comedy *Volpone, or The Fox*, his theatrical response to the Plot, the merchant Corvino – 'the crow' – is seen on stage alongside other predatory birds and animals; as in the real plot, however, the roles of predator and prey change from scene to scene.

Jonson emerges from the events of the Gunpowder Plot as an ambiguous and shadowy figure. He presents a number of images of himself through his poems, plays and recollections. He was the former soldier and convivial but dangerous drinking companion who killed another poet in a duel. He was the meticulous classical playwright, critical of Shakespeare's lack of editing, and the comic dramatist celebrating the tricksters who thrived amid London's greed and duplicity. Yet simultaneously Jonson appeared to hesitate in the wings as the great drama of the Plot unfolded, seemingly determined to play as small and invisible a role as possible. In the summer of 1605 he had been imprisoned, voluntarily in his telling, in solidarity with his fellow playwrights, for a play called *Eastward Ho!*, a collaboration between Jonson, John Marston and George Chapman, performed by the Children of Her Majesty's Revels at Blackfriars. The play satirised the king's liberality in bestowing knighthoods on his Scottish followers, and, worse still, their accents. The threat of mutilation as libellers hung over the three men, but in the event they were released unmolested. This could simply be an example of James's indulgence towards Jonson, who was already writing regularly for the King's Men, the king's own company of players; on the other hand, it might also be that the authorities expected something in return.

2

PLANS AND PREPARATIONS

Much of what we know of the events leading up to the discovery of the Gunpowder Plot and the version of the story that is usually told is reconstructed from the examinations and declarations of the principal surviving plotters, in particular those of Thomas Wintour and Guy Fawkes, with additional information about the mind and motivation of Robert Catesby from Robert Keyes and Ambrose Rookwood. Whatever our view of this evidence, one thing about it is clear: it was written in the full knowledge of the failure of the Plot and the near certainty of the men's executions. It tends to paint a rather fatalistic picture, in which the chances of success seem absurdly remote and the whole attempt so flawed that even given Catesby's powers of inspiration and magnetism seem insufficient to sustain it.

Documents written by the plotters at the time have a very different tone. Yes, they have been abandoned by Spain, and the Protestant succession stands as an immovable barrier to their prospects and prosperity, but their resolution to act alone has come as a relief. No more secret diplomacy and disappointment; their fate is in their own hands. If not at ease in wider society, they are content in their own circle. The Catholicism that marks them among their own countrymen as something to be scorned or feared is among themselves a badge to be flaunted. They liked to show themselves as something apart from their fellow men: Thomas Wintour's reading matter was exotic and his dress flamboyant, while Ambrose Rookwood's flashy riding waistcoat, 'unfit for his degree', showed his pride in his horses but also an unwillingness to be constrained by an uncongenial society's idea of what he should wear. Even Guido Fawkes's choice in rendering his Christian name was a challenge to the narrow isolation of Protestant England.

Anything outside their narrow circle was suspect. Catesby and his fellow conspirators seem in truth to have been singularly unimpressed by many of the forces the authorities believed might be assisting their rebellion. They admired the Jesuits for their courage, but were impatient about the sophistications of their theology; they courted Spain as a source of patronage, but showed no surprise when it failed them; they consistently maintained a genuine hostility to 'foreign princes', among whom they counted the Scottish king himself. They must, it was thought, be reliant on a 'great man' for patronage and support, but Catesby's contempt for the nobility was consistent and scathing. Even the famed network of Catholic women who sheltered the missionary priests and nurtured the faith in their households do not seem to have interested the conspirators, who excluded their wives and families as much as was possible. 'The people' as a whole seem barely to have entered the plotters' thoughts as a political force, it being assumed they would rally to a new monarch under whichever protector Robert Catesby saw fit to proclaim with the same docility with which they had accepted King James. If the plotters were distrustful of all these groups, it is difficult to see from where they expected to draw their support. The answer, presumably, was other gentlemen like themselves, who so far had done nothing but talk.

Even within the ranks of the conspirators, there were differing degrees of trust. Ambrose Rookwood, Sir Everard Digby and Francis Tresham seem not to have been in Catesby's confidence, but were rather seen as good-hearted rich men who could be used and remain loyal. Tresham, at least, was as crafty and conscious of his own interests as Catesby himself, and this misjudgement of character by Catesby proved fatal to the 'project of the powder'. Digby perhaps had the most to lose. Tall and handsome, he naturally drew attention, and exploited his charisma successfully. He was appointed to household office at the court of Queen Elizabeth and knighted by King James at Belvoir Castle on 24 April 1603, during the king's journey south to

London. Four days afterwards, he appeared as a gentleman pensioner extraordinary at the queen's funeral.

Digby could have lived a comfortable life despite his religion, but the convert felt the plight of his fellow English Catholics keenly. Little more than two years after his knighthood, his friend Robert Catesby was able to persuade him that he had a vital role to play in improving their lot by destroying James's government. Subsequent documents suggest that persuading Digby of his own importance and of the rightness of Catesby's plot was not too difficult.

Much of the detail of the plotters' preparations comes from Thomas Wintour's evidence, given after his capture. As Catesby's lieutenant, he was the best informed of the surviving plotters who came into the hands of the authorities. Luckily, the scholarly and rather witty Wintour also wrote some intriguing notes to his fellow conspirators at the time, which give us an impression of their mood and motivations without the distorting screen of hindsight.

As late as December 1603, Thomas Wintour was still doing his bit for the Catholic cause by fighting with the Spanish forces in Flanders. On 4 December, he wrote a witty letter to his brother-in-law and later fellow plotter John Grant about the uncertainty of news, the accidental turns of history on such things as the weather, and the social rounds of Lord and Lady Montague:

> Though I have bin at the fountain of news, yet can I learn little to [the] purpose, only a supply is expected by the Spaniards, some forty were taken in a little castle, which was surprised by our Lord Deputy, they confess that the rest are in some distress, having no store of victuals nor almost wood at all, and little artillery. Count Maurice is risen from Sitemgambes, some report with loss of 1500 men and most of his great ordnance, others say he was raised only by frost and hard weather, so tis uncertain whether [it] is true. Ostend is hardly pressed and likely to be won either by the Duke or by the Sea. This is all our news.
>
> Commend me to your mother and my sister, tell your sister Mary that my Lady Montague is in the country, but I will shortly make a voyage thither on purpose, in her behalf.
>
> So fare you well – this 4 of December your loving brother Tho: Wintour.

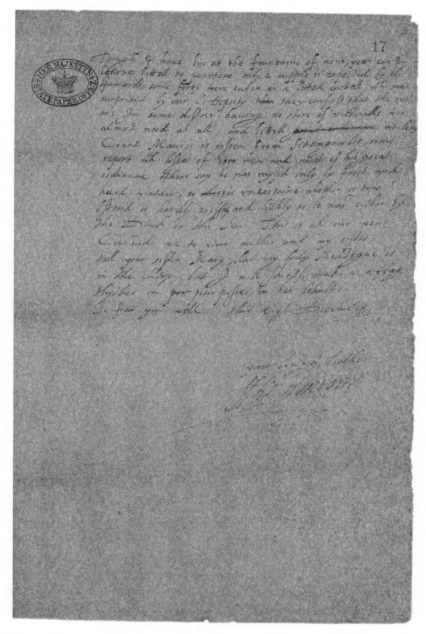

Thomas Wintour to John Grant, 4 December 1603. Wintour could be dispassionate and witty in describing the bloody religious conflict in the Low Counties. Some of the style of such letters survives in his confessions after the Plot's discovery. (TNA SP 14/5/6)

The letter is written with some detachment. He appears to be on the opposite side from 'our' Lord Deputy. The 'Duke' is Archduke Albert, who led the Spanish forces besieging Ostend while Prince Maurice of Nassau was leading the Dutch revolt against Spain. It would be difficult for anyone unfamiliar with the campaign to follow which side is which. Cold weather and high seas seem as likely to affect the outcome as human action, but these God-driven forces do not favour one side or the other. The Spanish cause was at once theirs yet not theirs, Catholic but foreign. As Spain moved towards peace with King James in 1604, it became clear that the real work for the Catholic cause would have to be done at home. Wintour was devout, but had a practical soldier's view of the workings of providence in the affairs of men. They would have to act for themselves.

It was early in 1604 at the still besieged Ostend that Wintour met Guido Fawkes, the latter's particular skills no doubt being useful to the Spanish attempt to drive a mine under the walls of the city while Wintour made his latest effort to ascertain if practical support from Spain could still be expected. In further conversation at Dunkirk, Wintour told Fawkes that he and some friends were set upon a resolution to 'do somewhat in England if the peace with Spain helped us not'. Thus Catesby, Wright and Wintour disclosed the Plot to Fawkes and Thomas Percy. They did so early in May 1604 at Catesby's lodging in the Strand in London, the five men having first received communion from Father John Gerard. Fawkes, 'because his face was the most unknown', adopted the name John Johnson and pretended to be Percy's servant.

As was revealed in Wintour's later declarations, corroborated by Fawkes and others, they originally planned to drive a mine under the lords' chamber in Parliament. Progress was slow because of the thickness of the wall, the interruptions of their plans by the prorogations of Parliament and the decision of the commissioners considering the abortive union of England and Scotland to use Thomas Percy's chamber next to Parliament for their deliberations.

They needed to recruit more conspirators to speed the work. Around this time, Thomas Wintour wrote to his favourite correspondent, John Grant, to lure him closer into the plotters' circle:

If I may with my sister's good leave, let me entreat you brother, to come over Saturday next to us at Chastleton, I can assure of

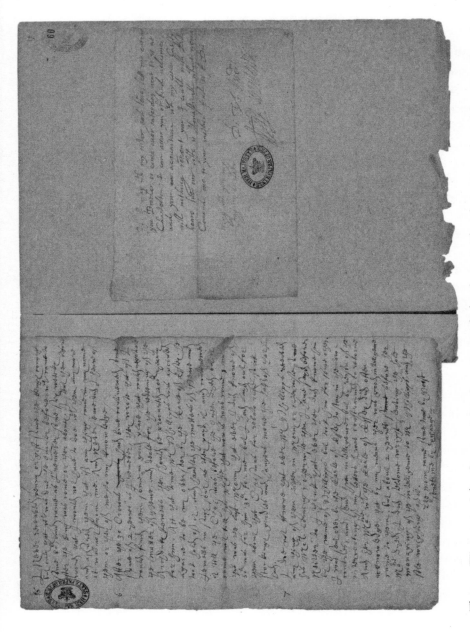

Thomas Wintour to John Grant, 26 January 1605 (right-hand page). The plotters were bound by more than the conspiracy itself; ties of family, religion and culture made Wintour view them as 'monastical' – withdrawn from the mainstream of English life. (TNA SP 14/12/39)

kind welcome and your acquaintance with my cousin Catesby will nothing repent you, I could wish Doll here, but our life is monastical, without women.

'Doll' is Wintour's sister Dorothy, Grant's wife. Wintour jokes about their 'monastic' life and their not entirely successful attempts to conceal their business from their families, but there is also a genuine religious content to the letter; they often referred to the Plot in religious terms as an act in God's cause, with their religious devotion taking the form of a plot to blow up the government. The letter is conspiratorial not just in its secrecy and what it does not say but also in its Latin tags and Italian books; our conversation and culture, it asserts, is different to that of our fellow Englishmen. There is a footnote: 'Bring with you my Ragion di Statto (Reason of State)', suggesting there was still the need for Jesuit authorities to give written intellectual support to their actions, as well as the imperative to recruit more conspirators and get on with the practical business. Keeping women out of the way was obviously a preoccupation of the unmarried Wintour. He wrote to John Grant again in August asking him to clear his house of co-conspirator Henry Morgan 'and his she-mate'.

Jack, certain friends of mine will be with you on Monday night or Tuesday at the uttermost, I pray you, void your house of Morgan and his she mate, or other company whatsoever they be, for all your house will scarce lodge the company. The Jerkin man is come but your robe of durance as yet not finished, I have sent you ten pounds, which I wonder at myself for doing, having neither kine nor corn to sell as you have, but a cloak to lay to pawn or so when I want money.[1]

This passage, playing as it does with ornate, romantic language, clothes and credit echoes Shakespeare's *The Second Part of Henry IV* Act 1 Scene 2, specifically the line, 'Is not a buff Jerkin a most sweet robe of durance?' In that scene, Prince Hal is mocking Falstaff's language in praise of Mistress Quickly, so Wintour's quotation, if that is what it is, sustains his joke about excluding women and readying themselves instead for masculine martial pursuits, since the 'robe of durance' would protect Grant in the fighting that would come in the aftermath of the Plot. This is aruably an early and interesting example of correspondents quoting Shakespeare, confident that the reader would get the joke. It is quite possible that Wintour and Grant had seen the play together. Perhaps the Church authorities were not wrong to suspect playhouses were meeting places for Catholics as well as a breeding ground for vice.

Yet not all the plotters shared this view of women or pretended the same indifference to social ties and responsibilities. Family man Robert Wintour did not feel the same detachment from his fate as his bachelor brother Thomas, the widower Catesby or the suspected bigamist Thomas Percy. It also became clear that the network of Catholic women who sheltered their families and missionary priests from the authorities were quite alert, and sensitive enough to realise that something was being planned.

In fact, even Thomas Wintour, Thomas Percy and Guy Fawkes were not as 'monastical' and withdrawn from society as they could have been. It later emerged that Fawkes had not kept as low a profile in London as might be expected of the man with the 'unknown face', and that he attended the wedding of Philip Herbert, later earl of Montgomery, on 27 December 1604 along with Thomas Wintour, Thomas Percy and Lord Monteagle. Naturally, the king and Principal Secretary Robert Cecil, later earl of Salisbury, were there too, the king taking a prominent role in the ceremony. Fawkes would later be questioned as to why, having access to his sword, he did not take advantage of the opportunity to assassinate the king, to which he answered simply that there was no evil intended that day. Presumably, there would have been no hope of escape and the attack would not have had the destructive effect of the intended explosion.

Even so, we are left with an extraordinary scene: some of the core plotters – Fawkes, Wintour and Percy – with their various noble entourages joining the throng of their intended victims watching the king, the principal target and the prime object of their religious disappointment and personal hatred, playing at priesthood in a marriage ceremony. What a chance for the 'ancient mercury' and his fellow plotters to see James in the daylight a year after Northumberland's letter and at a time when their preparations were well underway. On that occasion, it seems, it suited their purposes to eat, drink and make polite conversation while the ceremony played out before them. Yet this was not an isolated coincidence of plotters meeting their intended victims.

In August, a royal progress took James to Harrowden Hall, the house in Northamptonshire where Eliza Vaux harboured missionary priests and where several of the plotters made their own progress only weeks later as part of preparations for a rising of Catholic families in the Midlands. James was consistent in cultivating Catholics of rank who were willing to take their place in the important business of facilitating royal pomp and ceremony. Despite his conviction that those who could not pray with him could not love him, James depended on those who showed loyalty despite their faith. It allowed him to build new allegiances, particularly with those who had suffered under Elizabeth or who had sought to protect James's mother from the English queen's vengeance, but it left him vulnerable to those like Thomas Percy, whose show of loyalty was just that – show.

Soon after the new recruits arrived, the vault beneath the chamber they had attempted to mine became available and the need for extra manpower disappeared. The group had grown, however, and although Robert Wintour, John Grant and Christopher Wright were all trusty relations of the original conspirators, the risk of detection had increased.

Outside the plotters' circle at this stage but not far from it was Francis Tresham. Heir of a leading Catholic family of Northamptonshire, his father's great wealth attracted punitive recusancy fines and stealthy negotiations to avoid them. Francis's character and motivations along with those of his brother-in-law Lord Monteagle have given rise to intense speculation. Like Thomas Wintour, Tresham had received intelligence of English Catholic disillusionment with Spain. On 26 September 1605, William Tresham wrote gloomily from Antwerp to his brother Francis about the losses incurred by English Catholic forces who had successfully stormed Bergen op Zoom only to be let down by their German allies. He then returned to a subject that had occupied Francis in an earlier letter: the career prospects of English captains in the army of Spain.

For to be in a Spanish company one reason is for to learn the language, the other for sooner preferment, for the language, I do

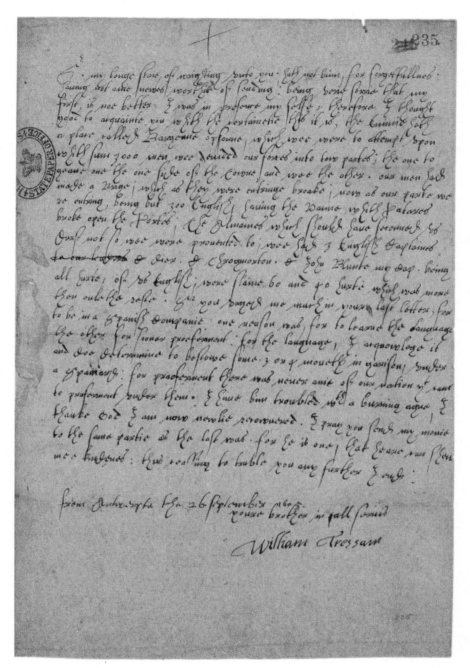

William to Francis Tresham from Antwerp, 26 September 1605. The military patronage of Spain could not be relied upon. (TNA SP 77/7 f. 235)

acknowledge it and do determine to bestow some 3 or 4 months in the garrison under a Spaniard. For preferment, there was never any of our nation that came to preferment under them. I have been troubled with a burning ague, I thank God I am now newly recovered.

The letter, directed to Francis Tresham 'at Sir Thomas Tresham's house at Hoxton near London', is annotated, 'This man is not at home.' Francis Tresham was always difficult to pin down, more so at this point because early that month Sir Thomas Tresham had died of a painful disease and Francis had succeeded to his debts as well as his massive estates. By the end of the year, he too would be killed by disease. A month after this letter, the house at Hoxton was occupied by Lord Monteagle. It would have a pivotal role in the discovery of the Plot.

Unlike Thomas Wintour, Tresham did not believe the response to the abandonment of the English Catholics by Spain was to put faith in Robert Catesby. On 18 February, Francis Tresham had written to his father 'in my cousin Catesby's promises there is little assurance'. Now, however, Catesby needed him. He was somebody who could raise large amounts of money quickly, an attractive prospect for Catesby, who had emptied his own pockets to fund the Plot. Along with Ambrose Rookwood and Sir Everard Digby, Tresham was to be exploited for his wealth, but, unlike them, was too wary of Catesby to fall under his spell. He would use his money to try to buy the plotters off rather than forward their enterprise.

On 12 October 1605, Thomas Wintour wrote to Robert Catesby pleading poverty but claiming he was in good spirits in the easy atmosphere of their Midlands stronghold:

Though all you malefactors flock to London as birds in winter to a dunghill, yet do I, honest man, freely possess the sweet country air, and to say truth would fain be amongst you but cannot as yet get money to come up. I was at Ashby to have met you, but you were newly gone, my business and your uncertain stay made me hunt no further.[2]

London was enemy territory, to be infiltrated but not dwelt in longer than necessary. When the decisive blow had been struck in Parliament, the next stage of the Plot would take place in the relative safety of a network of Catholic households in the Midlands.

Though the details and evolution of Catesby's plan only emerged later, it seems always to have focussed on the Lords' Chamber. There was a divine or poetic justice in this for Catesby, as it was there the anti-Catholic legislation had been passed. From an ideological point of view, the choice made perfect sense. Catesby was ready to attempt to save 'nobles that were Catholics' provided they did not jeapordise the Plot: '... rather than the project should not take effect, if they were as dear to him as his own son ... they should be also blown up'. The peers were 'atheists, fools and cowards' almost by definition for taking part in the heretic government, though some sympathy was reserved for those who used their position to oppose anti-Catholic legislation in Parliament.

Looked at from the perspective of the plotters' social connections, things were less clear-cut. For all Catesby's sweeping statements, the House of Lords was well stocked with patrons, friends and family of the plotters, not least Catesby himself. Lord Monteagle had been a stout defender of the Catholic cause in Parliament, had been involved with Thomas Wintour and Guy Fawkes in their negotiations with Spain, owed money to Thomas Percy and perhaps other plotters, and was Francis Tresham's brother-in-law. Catesby seemed to be on close terms with Lord Montague and Lord Mordaunt. When Robert Keyes asked that Mordaunt might be warned against attending Parliament, Catesby promised that he would 'put a trick upon him, but would not for the chamber full of diamonds acquaint him with the secret for that he knew he could not keep it'. If they were bright enough to take Catesby's hint, they would survive; otherwise, they would die. Some of the plotters understandably thought the hints might need supplementing.

Sir Everard Digby was not part of Catesby's original group of trusted plotters but was brought in on account of his wealth, horses and connections. He was not to be part of the gunpowder end of the operation but of the rising that was to follow it. Sworn to secrecy, Digby questioned the proposed deaths of so many people, especially

Catholic friends and allies in the House of Lords, but believed Catesby when he said he could trick their friends into staying away from the opening. 'Assure your selfe,' said Catesby, 'that such of the nobility as are worth the saving shall be preserved and yet know not of the matter.' Unbeknownst to Digby, that group might number fewer than ten; it might not even exist.

3

'THEY SHALL NOT SEE
WHO HURTS THEM'

On 14 October came the fateful recruitment of Francis Tresham. Twelve days later, on 26 October 1605, Lord Monteagle made the sudden decision to visit his house at Hoxton for the first time in several weeks, and ordered supper to be prepared. A 'reasonable tall' stranger, his features fortuitously concealed by the twilight, left a letter with a servant of the house who happened to be outside. This was passed to another servant, whom Monteagle asked to read it aloud while he ate. This has been taken as evidence both of Monteagle's innocence and his complicity. The letter contained a thinly disguised warning of some explosive enterprise against the opening of Parliament. The letter was oddly worded and disguised by an artful illiteracy, but the meaning was clear enough:

My lord, out of the love I bear to some of your friends, I have a care of your preservation, therefore I would advise you as you tender your life to devise some excuse to shift of your attendance at this parliament, for God and man hath concurred to punish the wickedness of this time, and think not slightly of this advertisement, but retire yourself into your country, where you may expect the event in safety, for though there be no appearance of any stir, yet I say they shall receive a terrible blow this parliament and yet they shall not see who hurts them, this counsel is not to be condemned because it may do you good and can do you no harm, for the danger is past as soon as you have burnt the letter and I hope God will give you the grace to make good use of it, to whose holy protection I commend you.

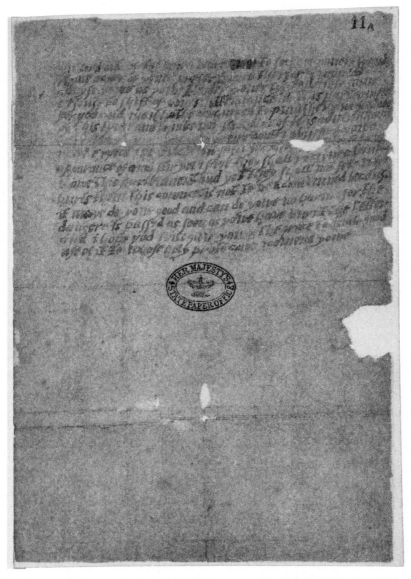

The Monteagle Letter, disclosed 26 October 1605. Lord Monteagle left his own supper at Hoxton to find a group of Privy Councillors still dining in Whitehall. (TNA SP 14/216/2)

Luckily for us, Monteagle did not follow instructions and burn the letter.

The letter's authorship has provoked great debate. The plotters themselves identified the author as Francis Tresham, Monteagle's brother-in-law and the owner of the house in Hoxton, the lukewarm plotter who had offered Catesby money to forget the whole thing. Among others ingeniously supposed to have written the letter was the earl of Salisbury himself, keen to show off the efficiency of his intelligence network by inventing a plot for it to uncover. The heavily disguised and archly illiterate letter certainly suggests a writer known to Monteagle, one who wished to conceal his identity, though it has been suggested that Thomas Phelippes, Francis Walsingham's chief decipherer and the annotator of the 'Gallows Letter' which helped send James' mother, Mary, Queen of Scots to her death, might have been the man to concoct it. Perhaps only Francis Tresham knew his man well enough to know precisely what Monteagle would do with the information it contained, and knew too that the warning would need to be disguised because Monteagle was too careful of his own newfound credit with the government not to tell them the identity of the messenger.

Tresham's moral and practical position in relation to the Plot was rather like that of his brother-in-law Monteagle. He was of the plotters' circle and associated with previous plots, but he had dissociated himself from the Gunpowder Plot as soon as he heard of it and done all he could to prevent it beside direct betrayal, which would have put him at the mercy of the plotters and the authorities. The letter was a lame compromise, but it worked and was as brave to concoct as it was for Monteagle to reveal it. Tresham never got the recognition and protection of the authorities, who did not show any great curiosity about the identity of the author of the letter. Perhaps to identify the source, since it must have come from one close to the Plot, would risk giving the conspiracy a human face. We have no surviving evidence that Tresham claimed authorship of the letter to try to gain favour with the authorities, which is about the only evidence against his having written it, but since Salisbury's object was to preserve Monteagle as the sole loyal figure, the lack of written confirmation of Tresham's authorship is hardly surprising.

Monteagle took his letter to Whitehall, where he found some of the most prominent members of the Privy Council at supper. Salisbury's initial reaction to the letter seems to have been sceptical. In the official account of events, King James, in his Old Testament wisdom as a prophet Joseph or a Daniel, returned from hunting at Royston, was shown the letter and immediately grasped its significance, to the admiration of his hitherto mystified councillors. This is not quite as incredible as it sounds; James's father had been killed in a gunpowder explosion, and James was always sensitive to the possibilities of assassination.

The substance was quickly passed on to the plotters and indeed it may have been read aloud for that purpose. Thomas Wintour was, after all, well known in the Monteagle household; he had served Monteagle as a secretary of some sort for several years, and had attended the prorogation of Parliament on 3 October 1605 in Monteagle's entourage. Wintour gave the news to Catesby, counselling discretion, if not emigration, but Catesby had another card up his sleeve. As Wintour later reported, 'He told me he would see further yet and resolved to send Mr Fawkes to try the uttermost, protesting if the part belonged to myself, he would try the same adventure. On Wednesday Mr Fawkes went and returned at night, of which we were very glad.' Fawkes went out in ignorance of the peril he was in, to see if anything were amiss, once more the 'unknown face' being most likely to escape detection. Fawkes later stated that he would have gone in any case, even if he had known of the letter.

Father John Gerard, who had converted Sir Everard and Mary Digby to Catholicism, was at Gayhurst for the feast of All Souls. He discovered Sir Everard moving his household to Coughton Court. He did not know it was done on Catesby's instructions, but the upheaval and preparations raised suspicions that an act of rebellion in the name of the Catholic cause was planned. As later recounted in Gerard's letters to members of the Privy Council and to Digby himself, it was an uncomfortable encounter between the convert and his confessor. Digby could not bring himself to lie directly to his ghostly father but was bound by his oath not to reveal what was planned. Gerard was well known to the authorities, who assumed he was central to the planning of the Plot. In his evidence establishing his innocence of any complicity, it was nonetheless clear that he could spot and was familiar with preparations for rebellion.

On the following day, armed with their knowledge of the warning given to Monteagle and what he had done with it, Thomas Wintour and Catesby confronted Francis Tresham at Barnet. They accused him of betrayal. He denied it, trying again to deflect their purpose, offering them money to return to Flanders. A surviving document indicates Tresham's fear but also his sincerity in wanting to export the plotters and himself at this time – a licence granted to him to 'pass beyond the seas' for two years.

A licence for Francis Tresham of Rushton in the county of Northampton Esq. to travel beyond the seas with two servants, three horses or geldings and £50 in money with other his necessaries and there to remain two years after his departure with provisions usual, dated the second of November, procured by Sir Thomas Lake.

Tresham never made his escape. Perhaps he was under too much pressure from the plotters, who wanted him where they could see him. Perhaps he felt he must stay and do all he could to prevent the ruin that he felt would follow the discovery of the Plot, wherever he was. There is some evidence that he joined the militia, mobilised to search for the plotters after the discovery, perhaps hoping they had already made their escape.

Information about other plots was still landing on Salisbury's desk all the time, a reminder that the Monteagle letter was only one of a number of possible plots to be pursued. On 2 November, a letter partly in cipher about a possible assassination attempt landed on Salisbury's desk having been found in the street, describing the participants as the 'actors' and desiring to see 'the tyrannous heretic [King James] confounded in his cruel pleasures'.[1]

On the evening of 3 November, Thomas Wintour and Robert Catesby met Thomas Percy, who had recently arrived from the north 'on the King's own especial service'. Percy stiffened their resolve and offered to go to Syon House to dine with the earl of Northumberland to try to gauge the level knowledge of the Plot. After the dinner, he was able to reassure them that there was no sign of the Plot having been discovered. So Fawkes took up his station in the vault, with a slow match, and a watch sent to him by Percy via Robert Keyes, 'because he should know how the time went away'.

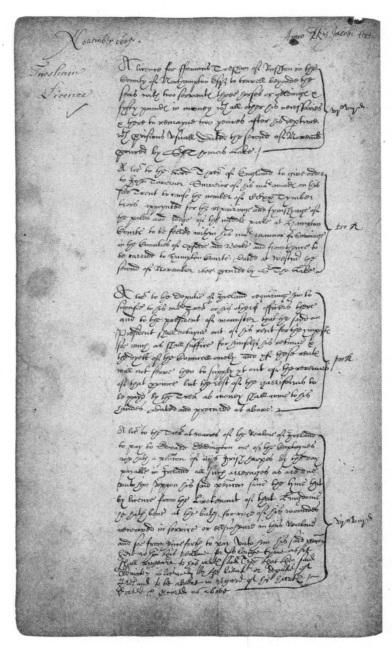

Passport for Francis Tresham, 2 November 1605. Rather than fund the plot Tresham thought instead to use his money to persuade Catesby to abandon it and leave England. (TNA SO 3/3)

Meanwhile the Privy Council was treading carefully. To allow the Plot to ripen, nothing further was done until 4 November. James hoped that, as the plan progressed, not merely those who were involved in its mechanics but also those in power who were supporting them would be revealed. An initial tour by the earl of Suffolk – as Lord Chamberlain he was responsible for preparations for the new session of Parliament – accompanied by Monteagle provided the authorities with all the evidence they could have hoped for. They found Fawkes overseeing a large quantity of firewood in a vault rented by his master Thomas Percy. Monteagle made a few pointed remarks to Suffolk as they returned, about being previously unaware of Percy, a known Catholic, renting a cellar in Westminster. Fawkes was arrested and the gunpowder discovered.

At about 5 a.m. on Tuesday 5 November, Christopher Wright came to Thomas Wintour with news of the discovery of the Plot. Wintour coolly walked to the court and then to the parliament house, but found both heavily guarded and the discovery of the Plot being discussed. Wintour rode off in pursuit of Catesby and Percy who had left London the previous evening. The authorities only really began to suspect him the next day. Wintour rode to his brother's house at Huddington and from there to Catesby's house at Ashby. There he received a message to meet Catesby in the fields away from the house and the news he already knew: 'Mr Fawkes is taken and the whole plot discovered.'

With the discovery of the Plot came an explosion of official documents. The secretive letters of the plotters and the shadowy notes from Salisbury's more or less unreliable informers give way to the bombardment of an official investigation involving many of the principal officers of state and lasting eight months. For the first two months, the investigation of the Plot seemed to absorb almost all the resources of government to the exclusion of other business.

While Salisbury composed the official version of events, the court newsmonger John Chamberlain wrote to Dudley Carleton enclosing a copy of the Monteagle letter and reporting the now familiar celebrations that had greeted the discovery of the Plot. 'On Tuesday [5 November] at night we had great ringing and as great store of bonfires as I ever I think was seen.'[2] Carleton was a diplomat whose correspondence with Chamberlain in London gives a valuable insight into the rumour and gossip of Jacobean court life. The Gunpowder Plot however turned Carleton from a detached ironic observer of events to one of the figures at the centre of the greatest sensation of the reign. For weeks, his career and future prospects hung in the balance because of his connections with the lease of Thomas Percy's house and of the vault below Parliament. There were fears that the celebrations could lead to attacks on Catholic diplomats in London, particularly the Spanish Ambassador, for whom William Waad, Lieutenant of the Tower, advised protection. In a related direction from the Privy Council to the Lord Mayor of London, the council felt obliged to make it clear to the mayor that the ambassador was beyond suspicion and would have died in the explosion. 'He having desired to be present this day to see the form of Parliament and this being granted unto him was in the same condition and fortune as all the rest to have been destroyed.'[3]

Guy Fawkes in the vault below the House of Lords with his dark beard, dark lantern and barrels of gunpowder is the abiding image of the Plot and the focus of the 5 November celebrations. For some time the authorities knew him only by the alias he gave, 'John Johnson', and for a long week after the discovery of the Plot he was questioned alone in the Tower of London, the authorities' only direct source of information. By the end of the week, it was clear that he was far from acting alone, but his status as the lone face of the Plot was established. Documents show his humanity, steadfastness and lack of repentance, making him a figure difficult to hate but also difficult to defend.

The examinations of 'John Johnson', though largely formulaic, give a clear indication of the character of the man. The wit and style of his replies, his stubbornness and contempt for his examiners, and his distrust of foreigners – 'upon his soul ... neither he nor any other with whom he had conferred would have spared the last drop of their blood to have resisted any foreign prince whatsoever' – are all consistent. His examiners wrote grudgingly of his fortitude, his 'roman' resolution. Confronted with a barrage of questions, he refused to implicate his colleagues, apart from Percy, whose identity was part of Fawkes's own cover and would be clear to anyone who investigated the ownership of the vault. Fawkes admitted having recently travelled to Flanders, but when pressed for a reason the

Spanish soldier mocked his examiners, declaring that he had set out 'to see the country and to pass away the time'. When he did speak plainly, it was to castigate the Scots, an attitude evident when he had predicted English discontent with King James's accession in his reports to the Spanish Crown in 1603, to complain of the foolishness of the warning given to Monteagle and to express incredulity that he should even be asked to betray the other plotters. What the authorities received from the 'desperate fellow' with the unlikely pseudonym was a noticeably calm enunciation of the Plot and its intentions.

Fawkes's early interrogations show the same pride in and carefully observed knowledge of the Catholic world across the English Channel as did Thomas Wintour's witty, literary diplomatic notes. It was a world over which his interrogators had no control. 'Johnson' described the well-trodden path of Catholic gentlemen in France and the Spanish Low Countries, through the theological colleges at St Omer and Douai to the Imperial court at Brussels. He made no attempt to conceal his Catholicism and Catholic connections even at his first interrogation and was happy to implicate Hugh Owen, perhaps the man Cecil's intelligence networks most wanted to silence, in the comfortable knowledge he was safe in Brussels. Owen the Welsh 'intelligencer' was suspected of fomenting plots against England's Protestant succession over many years and his dislike of the new Scottish king seemed to be as visceral and instinctive as was that of Fawkes the Yorkshireman. Surrounded and alone though he was, Fawkes's evidence retains something of the confident language evident in Thomas Wintour's conspiratorial notes. He is able to taunt his persecutors with the limitations of their knowledge of and influence over the Catholic world. It is almost as if a government installed by Catesby and other patriotic Catholic Englishmen is the best England can hope for. Then at least they would have some self-determination alongside the much greater power of the Hapsburg Empire and the Papacy, which must otherwise, someday, overwhelm them as an invading force.

C. And confesseth that when the King had come to the parliament house this present day, and the upper house had been sitting, he meant to have fired the match and have fled for his own safety

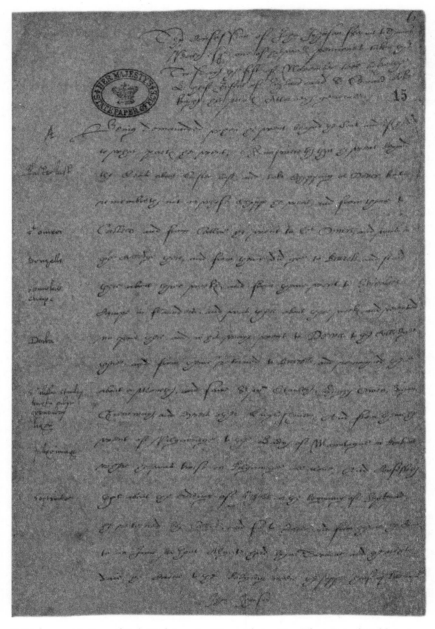

Initial examination of 'John Johnson', 5 November 1605. The wit and stubbornness of Fawkes under questioning impressed and frustrated his examiners. His replies were more anti-Scottish than anti-Protestant. (TNA SP 14/216/6)

before the Powder had taken fire, And confesseth that if he had not been apprehended this last night, he had blown up the upper house, when the King, Lords, Bishops and others had been there...

E. And being demanded if his purpose had taken effect, what would have been done with the Queen's Majesty and her royal issue, saith that if they had been there he would not have helped them.

F. And being demanded if the King and his royal issue had been all taken away whom would have been published or elected King, Saith Percy never entered into that consultation.

G. And being demanded when the King, his royal issue, the Nobles Bishops, Judges, and of the principal of the Commons, were all destroyed what government would have been, Answereth we were not grown to any determination therein, and being but a fewe of them they could not enter into such conversation, but that the people of themselves would decide a head...

K. And confesseth that when this act had been done they meant to have satisfied the Catholics that it was done for restitution of religion, And would have drawn others by publishing that it was done to prevent the Union that was sought to be published at this parliament...

P. Being demanded what was the main intent and purpose of his going beyond sea as is aforesaid, Answereth that his purpose was to see the country and to pass away the time.

There were hints here of a wider conspiracy, though as yet the authorities had no firm evidence of it. No one could quite believe that the plotters had intended to sweep away the entire government without the support of powerful forces either foreign or domestic, or without any clear idea of the regime that was to come next. The man to find a conspiracy, even where none existed, was Sir Edward Coke, the Attorney General, who searched assiduously for a wider conspiracy behind the Plot and greater men than the central plotters themselves to bring to trial. Sometimes in his zeal he exceeded the remit of investigation set by the king and the earl of Salisbury and the results could be as embarrassing to the government as they were enlightening. We have Coke's initial thoughts on the early examinations of 'Johnson', entitled 'my notes', in Coke's hand. Surprisingly to modern eyes, Coke was keen to pick up references to prophecy and astrology relating to the Plot, something perhaps to explain the confidence of a group with such apparently narrow support. 'Johnson' was carrying a letter addressed to 'Mr Fawkes' (an alias, the prisoner explained), which contained the following riddle: 'fast and pray that the purpose may come to pass and that Tottenham shall be turned French.' The fulfilment of so great a change as Tottenham turning French, which Coke interpreted as referring to a return to Catholicism in England, showed the Catholics falling back on prophecy where the practical help of Spain had failed them.

To make the prophecy come true needed more than a few gentlemen plotters. In Coke's mind, a 'great man' was indispensable to such an enterprise and he already had some names handy, among them the unlikely figure of Sir Walter Raleigh, already imprisoned in the Tower. In their quest for information about the whereabouts of the plotters, the authorities turned to Simon Forman, astrologer and physician. Though locating lost and sought-after people and objects was a standard part of Forman's trade, it is probable that his knowledge of the lives of his patients rather than his powers of divination were the real reason why Forman was consulted. He was known to have strong Catholic connections; the patients who consulted him most frequently and confidentially were the wives of London Catholics, who came to him, if we are to believe his diary, for his particular and unethical brand of fertility treatment.

James, too, was fascinated by prophecies as well as by the plotters and their motives. In a letter framing the questions to be used in the interrogation of 'John Johnson' and authorising his torture, James linked him to the malcontents who had unearthed prophecies to oppose the idea of the creation of 'Great Britain'. In this, he correctly identified Fawkes, who thought the plotters' opposition to the union of England and Scotland would be enough to make their Catholic government popular with non-Catholics.

James did not recognise but half expected to know Fawkes, as he knew Thomas Percy, not just because of his plotting past but also because of the small world of Jacobean court life. Though he posed as a servant, James suspected from his conversation and experience that he was no such thing. His social rank betrayed him as much as his unlikely alias. He saw a class of man familiar to him and vital to the smooth running of the state.

Thomas Wintour as secretary to Lord Monteagle and Fawkes as a member of Lord Montague's household had the entrée to social events close to the king. One of Fawkes's pieces of evidence never to appear in the official version of events was that he had been at the wedding attended by the king at the end of the previous year; even the demon outsider was not that much outside the charmed circle of the court. In setting out the questions he wanted Fawkes to answer, the King shows himself not only personally involved in his interrogation and torture, but also oddly similar to him, ridiculing his Catholic superstitions while brooding on his own.

The examinate would now be made to answer to formal interrogators:

1. As what he is (for I can never yet hear of any man that knows him)?
2. Where was he born?
3. What were his parents' names?
4. What age is he of?
5. Where hath he lived?
6. How he hath lived and by what trade of life?
7. How he received those wounds on his breast?
8. If he was ever in service with any other before Percy, and what they were, and how long?
9. How came he in Percy's service, by what means and at what time?
10. What time was this house hired by his master?
11. And how soon after the possessing of it did he begin his devilish preparations?
12. When and where learned he to speak French?
13. What gentlewoman's letter it was that was found upon him?
14. And wherefore doth she give him another name in it than he gives to himself?

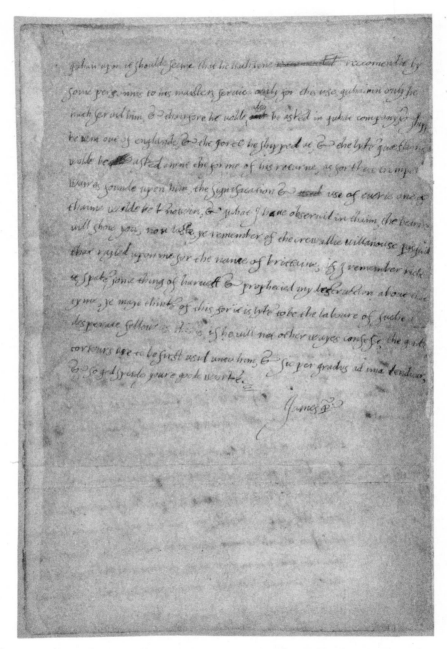

King James's letter authorising the torture of 'Johnson'/Fawkes, 6 November 1605. James seemed to suspect early on that Fawkes was not simply Thomas Percy's servant as he claimed. (TNA SP 14/216/17)

15. If he was ever a papist, and if so who brought him up in it?
16. If otherwise, how was he converted, where, when, and by whom?

The course of his life I am the more desirous to know because I have divers motives leading me to suspect that he hath remained long beyond the seas and either is a priest or hath long served some priest or fugitive abroad, for I can yet (as I said in beginning hereof) meet with no man that knows him. The letter found upon him gives him another name, and those that best know his master can never remember to have seen him in his company, whereupon in should seem that he hath been recommended by persons to his master's service only for this use, wherein only he hath served him. And therefore he would also be asked in what company and ship he went out of England, and the port he shipped at, and the like questions would be asked anent [about] the form of his return. As for these trumpery wares found on him, the signification and use of every one of them would be known. And what I have observed in them the bearer will show you. Now last, ye remember of the cruelly villainous pasquil that railed upon me for the name of Britain. If I remember right, it spake something of harvest and prophesied my destruction about that time. Ye may think of this for it is like to be the labour of such a desperate fellow as this is.

If he will not other ways confess, the gentler tortures are to be first used unto him, et sic per gradus ad ima tenditur [and so by degrees until the ultimate is reached]. And so God speed your good work.

James R.

Some of these questions are straightforward, others more remarkable. James's idea that Fawkes might be a priest does not exactly chime with the popular image of him. Many of the questions, whether remarkable or not, would prompt uncomfortable answers. Fawkes's experience overseas and language skills came as a result of his service in the Spanish forces in Flanders, service which James himself had come to sanction as part of the treaty with Spain in 1604. The gentlewoman whose letter Fawkes carried was Eliza Vaux, a member of one of those Catholic families James had negotiated openly and amicably with over fines for recusancy. It was clear that moves in Parliament towards a union between England and Scotland were at the front of the king's mind as a motivation for disaffected people, as it was in the mind of Thomas Percy. Gradually it would recede in the official account as the Plot came to viewed and remembered as being motivated purely by religious zeal.

The only connection the unknown man would give the authorities was one he could not deny, that he was acting for his master, Thomas Percy. Percy, unlike Fawkes, was well known to the authorities and the proclamation against him, a kind of descriptive 'Wanted!' poster, is not so much a mug shot as an intimate portrait. The 'gentleman pensioner' was at this stage the prime lead as Fawkes's pretended master and the man who had rented the vault beneath the Lords' Chamber. Though they could deduce some probable plotters from known Catholics suddenly absent from London, the authorities were still relying on the Percy connection to reveal the extent of the Plot. It was clear that Percy had regarded his office simply as a vantage point from which to blow up the king. But what of the man who had got him the job? Would he prefer Percy alive or dead?

Whereas one Thomas Percy, a Gentleman Pensioner to his Majesty, is discovered to have been privy to one of the most horrible Treasons that ever was contrived, that is, to have blown up this day, while his Majesty should have been in the upper House of the Parliament, attended with the Queen, the Prince, all his nobility and the Commons, with Gunpowder (for which purpose a great quantity of Powder was conveyed into a Vault under the said Chamber, which is this morning there found) the Chamber where they should be assembled, which Percy is sithens fled:

These are to will and command all our Officers and loving Subjects whatsoever, to do that which we doubt not but they will willingly perform, according to the former experience We have had of their love and zeal towards us, That is, to make all diligent search for the said Percy, and to apprehend him by all possible means, especially to keep him alive, to the end the rest of the Conspirators may be discovered. The said Percy is a

Draft proclamation for the apprehension of Thomas Percy, 5 November 1605 (right-hand page). The earl of Salisbury's draft shows signs of being hurried and revised but drew on accurate information about Percy, who was well known in court circles. (TNA SP 14/16 no 8; printed soon after, SP 14/73 p114)

tall man, with a great broad beard, a good face, the colour of his beard and head mingled with white hairs, but the head more white than the beard, he stoopeth somewhat in the shoulders, well coloured in the face, long footed, small legged.

Given at our Palace of Westminster, the fifth day of November, 1605, in the third year of our reign of Great Britain.

God save the King.

To the government, Percy was not just another Catholic malcontent, but also a betrayer, an insider who had compromised security. Percy's connection with the earl of Northumberland also made him the government's chief lead in investigating the power behind the Plot. The earl, it transpired, had recruited the would-be assassin to guard the king without ensuring he had taken the Oath of Supremacy, which was obligatory for the job. Not only had Northumberland apparently misjudged Percy's loyalty, he had saved him the discomfort of making a statement of it.

Percy's trusted position and aristocratic connections made him more of a story abroad than his fellow conspirators were. To satisfy this international interest, an engraving of him by Crispijn de Passe the Elder was hastily produced and is now preserved at London's National Portrait Gallery. Though it does not show Percy's long feet or his small legs, it does have some intriguing features. His broad beard is duly darker than the hair of his head, both mingled with grey, 'a sable-silver'd' like that of Hamlet's father's ghost. Guy Fawkes appears in two of the corner roundels in a garbled version of his alias as 'Thomas Johnson' and the siege at Holbeach simply as 'Arce' or 'Arx', which is probably just 'refuge' or 'citadel'. In later versions, these details were corrected, suggesting this early version was produced quickly to meet demand in the wake of the discovery.

The adaptability of the artist and his images to meet the occasion was shown five years later when De Passe produced an image of the French King Henri IV's assassin Francois Ravilliac surrounded by gunpowder barrels, faggots and fuses, though he had stabbed the king to death. The base drawing shows the same figure holding keys, which may well be Fawkes with keys to the the vault.

Percy was reported leaving London in all four compass directions on the same day. But he was not a lone conspirator fleeing into hiding, a loose end to be tidied up now the immediate danger had passed. The plot had more to it than that. He was riding as fast as he could to a rendezvous where thousands were expected to join in the next phase of the Plot. Percy, it began to emerge, had used his position as a gentleman pensioner responsible for the king's safety to ask searching questions about the younger royal children and how they were guarded. Then there came reports of horses and arms being stolen close to where the James's eldest daughter the Lady Elizabeth was staying in Warwickshire. Perhaps the Plot had only just begun.

ACT II

DIVINE DISPLEASURE

Cast List

HENRY PERCY, earl of Northumberland, captain of the king's bodyguard, 'The Wizard Earl'

ROBERT CECIL, earl of Salisbury, Principal Secretary of State, 'The Little Beagle'

WILLIAM PARKER, Baron Monteagle, defender of Catholics in Parliament, recipient of the 'Monteagle letter'

ANTHONY MARIA BROWNE, Viscount Montague, employer of Guy Fawkes

SIR EVERARD DIGBY, knight of Stoke Dry, Rutland, courtier

SIR FRANCIS BACON, knight, lawyer and author

SIR ARTHUR GORGES knight, poet, translator

AMBROSE ROOKWOOD, gentleman of Coldham Hall, Suffolk, horseman

FRANCIS TRESHAM, gentleman of Rushton Hall, Northamptonshire, brother-in-law to Lord Monteagle

ROBERT CATESBY, gentleman of Ashby St Ledgers, Northamptonshire

ROBERT WINTOUR, gentleman of Huddington Court, Worcestershire

THOMAS WINTOUR, gentleman, soldier and scholar, sometime secretary to Lord Monteagle

THOMAS PERCY, gentleman, member of the king's bodyguard, kinsman to the earl of Northumberland

HENRY GARNET, alias Walley, alias Farmer, alias Darcy, Father Superior of the English Jesuit Province

OSWALD TESIMOND, alias Greenaway, missionary priest, schoolfellow of Guido Fawkes

EDWARD OLDCORNE, alias Hall, alias Vincent, alias Parker, missionary priest, schoolfellow of Guido Fawkes

BEN JONSON poet, recusant, suspect and informant

4

'THIS LETTER ONLY WERE ENOUGH TO HANG ME'

With the first confused reports of a rising in the Midlands, the focus of the Plot suddenly widened. The court intrigue of a disillusioned gentleman pensioner abetted by a well-connected gentleman posing as his servant suddenly threatened to become a full-scale Catholic rebellion. Percy was not just a bodyguard turned assassin, he had plotted to kidnap and proclaim a puppet Catholic monarch from among King James's younger children after the explosion. Might this part of the plan go ahead though the explosion had been foiled?

The authorities were able to draw up an accurate and lengthy list of Catholics suddenly absent from London, all of them related and based in the Midlands. The earl of Salisbury had to rely on reports two or three days old, some accurate, some wild, of what was going on in the Midlands, while the investigations in London brought copious evidence of the explosion already foiled but little more on a planned rebellion. The pressure on Fawkes increased and the authorisation to torture him was eagerly taken up by interrogators with an urgent new line of enquiry to pursue. The authorities only garnered fuller information when the surviving plotters arrived in London on 12 November, when Fawkes's tortured testimony was suddenly overwhelmed by fresh evidence from these new prisoners. In the week from the discovery of the Plot until this date, all was uncertainty. Luckily, we can share through the surviving documents not only in the atmosphere of suspicion in London but also in the uncertainty of the rebellion itself. The government continued to issue proclamations that lagged limply behind the events they sought to control.

Relying on the Thomas Percy connection, they moved on 7 November to denounce not simply his dereliction of duty as a gentleman pensioner, but the blindness of his Catholic faith and his 'lewd life and insolent disposition'.[1] They added a short but largely accurate list of his fellow conspirators deduced from their knowledge of known Catholics suddenly absent from London rather than any information Fawkes had given them.

One of the most memorable scenes in the drama of the Gunpowder Plot must have been the rendezvous at Dunchurch, where Sir Everard Digby's gallant hunting party of Catholic gentlemen was interrupted by the fleeing conspirators from London. They were exhausted and beaten, but Catesby was still proclaiming the king and Salisbury dead and a Catholic rising well underway. Digby was taken aside by Catesby and told a series of lies about the success of the venture to keep him onside. Catesby said that 'though he hath been disappointed in his first intention yet was there such a pudder brid [commotion bred] in the state by the death of the King and the earl of Salisbury, as the Catholics would now stir'. Digby might at the time have interpreted this special treatment as a sign of his importance. Gradually though, the feeling grew that Catesby was being 'close', and not telling the full truth. Fantasy figures were bandied about, including a force of a thousand men expected to converge at Holbeach House in Staffordshire.

Catesby advised Digby to take a house in Warwickshire or Worcestershire as a base from which to prepare for a hunt on Dunsmore Heath. This was a front for a raiding party to capture the Lady Elizabeth, the 'next heir', who would be would be proclaimed and controlled by the plotters after the death of her father, brothers and Protestant councillors in the explosion in Parliament. Digby borrowed Coughton Court from Catesby's cousins, the Throckmortons. He took his greyhounds, trunks of money and fine clothes and set off to play his role as the reassuring face, the gallant and handsome knight who would calm the fears of the young princess as she was swept up from her captivity at Coombe Abbey near Coventry. She would be borne off on his horse to a new, exciting and romantic life as the puppet queen under a Catholic protector and then a Catholic husband. This pretty illusion overlooked the fact that the princess was as convinced a Protestant as a girl of her age could be, but it fuelled Digby's idea of himself as indispensable, first to the conspirators and then, as we shall see, to Salisbury and the English state.

In the drama of the Gunpowder Plot, Sir Everard Digby appears as something of a leading man in looks, but found himself being led by Robert Catesby. John Aubrey, who wrote a brief life of Digby, called him 'a most gallant gentleman and one of the handsomest men of his time'. The priest John Gerard, who converted him to Catholicism, also describes Digby as a handsome man, as well as being six feet tall, a complete sportsman, horseman and musician. He was just the type of man to court the favour and catch the eye of King James. Yet he was manipulated by Catesby into acts of rashness, which imperilled his family and secured his own destruction.

Digby stayed with Catesby, Percy and their associates, some eighty in all. At eleven on the night of 5 November, the rebels raided Warwick Castle, seizing fresh horses from the stables. Such a drastic move was opposed by Thomas Wintour's elder brother, Robert. While his younger brother Tom intrigued with Spain and advertised the plight of English Catholics, Robert Wintour with his wife Gertrude Talbot did their bit for their faith domestically, turning the family home, Huddington Court in Worcestershire, into a haven for priests. Robert Wintour's letters give us a clear view of a human face among the plotters, from his desperate and unwilling appeal for support to his father-in-law as the Midlands rebellion failed to ignite, to revelations of his nightmares when a fugitive from justice. He was fearful for his wife and children, but happy to think that they would continue the fight after his death.

With an estate and family, Robert had more to lose than his brother did from a Midlands uprising. His uncharacteristic flirtation with adventure came when he was admitted to the Gunpowder Plot in January 1605 at The Catherine Wheel in Oxford, a haunt of Oxford's Catholic martyrs, at the same time as John Grant and Christopher Wright. The adventure was to cost him his life. Robert Wintour's connection to the earldom of Shrewsbury through his marriage was a factor in his recruitment, though Robert himself seems to have been unconvinced of the likelihood of any help from his father-in-law. Sir John Talbot of Grafton had had enough trouble with the authorities and was determined to demonstrate his loyalty to King James. Nonetheless, by June 1605 Robert was sending conspiratorial letters to his sister's husband and fellow plotter John Grant in which Talbot's movements were a preoccupation.

After the discovery of the gunpowder end of the operation, Catesby arrived in the Midlands with all his faith pinned on dreams of assistance from men like Talbot. Robert Wintour had stayed in the Midlands and was not among the initial suspects sought by the authorities, but as they trailed from house to house looking in vain for support, he felt the noose tighten around his neck. He spent 6 November very uncomfortably, bound by faith and family to the plotters but an unwilling figure who objected to the 'great uproar in the country' the horse-stealing raid on Warwick Castle would cause, since it implicated him beyond redemption.

By the time conspirators arrived at Robert Wintour's house he was its master only in name. Catesby assumed command again and with John Wright pressured his host, who had none of Catesby's illusions about support from Talbot, to write for support to his father-in-law. Wintour later protested:

> Mr Catesby and my cousin John Wright took me aside and told me there was no remedy, but I must write to my father [in law] Talbot to see if I could therewith draw him unto us. I flatly refused it saying, 'My masters you know not my Father Talbot so well as I, If I should send him such a letter, he would surely stay my man, for I protest I verily think all the world cannot draw him from his allegiance, besides what friends hath my poor wife and children but him, and therefore satisfy yourselves I will not.' 'Well,' (quoth Catesby) 'you shall write to one Mr Smallpeece that serveth your father-in-law.' So to satisfy their importunity I took paper and writ as he willed me word after word, which done, 'Well Sirs,' (quoth I) 'this letter only were enough to hang me and any he that should conceale it.'[2]

The fatal letter Robert Wintour was forced to write is perhaps a unique survival, being neither a planning letter from before the Plot or evidence generated by the official investigation, but a hurried note written in desperation and under duress during the rising itself.

The possibility that they would all hang preyed on Robert's mind as he wrote, with Catesby dictating and looking critically over his shoulder. Catesby might have reported the incident differently but the fact remains that Robert Wintour did not deliver the letter, which was found on Thomas Wintour at Holbeach after he had tried and failed to gain Talbot's support in person. The letter has sustained some damage to the right-hand margin, possibly a result of the injuries suffered by Thomas Wintour at the siege of the house or even the gunpowder explosion the night before. Although only part of each line survives, the nature and desperation of the plea is very clear.

A letter found upon [Thomas Wintour] in ye house at Holbeach where he was taken, written to Mr Smallpeece in Mr Talbot of Grafton's house.'

Good cousin I hope it will not seem strange to you that...
a good number of resolved Catholics now perform matters of such...
will set the most straight or hang all those that ever...
use your best endeavour to stir up my father Talbot...
which I should much more honourable than to be hanged after...
cousin pray for me, I pray you and send me all such friends as thou hast,
I leave you from Huddington this 6 November[3]

On the same day that Robert Wintour wrote hopelessly to his father-in-law for material aid, Sir Everard Digby wrote to Father Henry Garnet for spiritual support. He was to be equally disappointed. Later Digby would brag to Salisbury of his influence with Garnet, but when Digby wrote to the Father Superior on 6 November, asking for pardon and hoping for his support, he got a lecture instead. Garnet wrote back from Coughton saying that he 'marvelled they would enter into so wicked actions, and not be ruled by the advice of friends'. Digby's wife Mary was also at Coughton at the time, and she came into the room while Garnet and his fellow Jesuit Oswald Tesimond were discussing her husband's fate with the messenger, Thomas Bate. Garnet recorded that Mary burst into tears when she learned what

Digby had done; she knew he was doomed. The delivery of the letter and Garnet's response to it perfectly sums up Garnet's ambivalent position. There is no doubt that Garnet was close to and personally sympathetic to the plotters, such that Digby might *hope*, even if he could not expect, to receive his forgiveness, but Garnet did not give it, indeed his incredulity at their rashness seemed entirely genuine.

Garnet was nevertheless at Coughton. He himself wondered why the authorities were so slow to ask him about this, the strongest piece of circumstantial evidence against him. Why, if he were not involved in the Plot, did he happen to be at the house rented by Sir Everard Digby for the meeting at Dunchurch and the Midlands rising on the day after king and Parliament was supposed to have been destroyed?

Not everyone was engaged in passive wailing and in fuelling the sense of doom, which fills the examinations taken after the event. There were other fighting spirits as well as the core plotters. Oswald Tesimond, who had heard of the Plot in Catesby's confession in July, went to the conspirators on 6 November 1605 at Huddington to give the usual consolations of religion to the conspirators. Fellow Jesuit Edward Oldcorne gave evidence that they had argued when he and Garnet had refused to support the Midlands rebellion, and that Tesimond had stormed off, vowing to stir up rebellion in Lancashire. Certainly, Tesimond may have been less content with Garnet's caution than Oldcorne was, but it may be that Oldcorne was simply making his own life easier in custody by heaping blame on a man he hoped had escaped the authorities. Tesimond did escape, and lived to put his name to an account of the Plot. His narrative, an odd amalgam in his hand but not originated by him, as he appears in it as Greenway in the third person, provides intimate if slightly eulogistic portraits of the core plotters. The avowed purpose of the narrative was to clear the Jesuits of any involvement in the Plot. Tesimond was perhaps an unlikely figure to be associated with it, since other accounts suggest he was more inclined to incite and support rebellion than were many of his fellow missionary priests.

5

THE EYE OF THE STORM

As the rebels travelled with varying and generally shrinking degrees of hope from Robert Wintour's house at Huddington to make their final stand at Holbeach, the earl of Salisbury was drawing up an account of the Plot, to be read alongside Fawkes's confessions, to inform the Privy Council, and then to be published for home and foreign consumption. Piles of documents full of information about the Plot, some of it contradictory, much of it useless, poured onto Salisbury's desk in the week between 5 and 12 November. It came from impecunious aristocrats, ambitious lawyers and those bearing local grudges who took the opportunity to establish their own loyalty and sue for reward. The still unfolding rebellion meant this account was already well out of date before it emerged.

One of those caught up in the political maelstrom was Dudley Carleton, a rising diplomatic star. After a brief period as secretary to Sir Thomas Parry, ambassador to France, Carleton became controller of the household to Henry Percy, earl of Northumberland, and through him found a place a place in the mainstream of court life. At the time Carleton joined Northumberland's household in 1603, the earl – given his role in the succession of James I and his restitution by the new king to political significance as a member the Privy Council and a position of trust as Captain of the Guard – seemed a coming man whose patronage would establish Carleton's own position. By 1605, Carleton was in the earl of Nottingham's embassy for the ratification of the Anglo-Spanish peace treaty and a figure at the centre of political life. With the Gunpowder Plot and the revelation of the earl's connections with prime conspirator Thomas Percy, all that changed. Worse still, Carleton had been personally involved in obtaining the lease for Thomas Percy of his house next to Parliament and the vault in which the gunpowder was stored.

John Chamberlain, the courtier and 'intelligencer' who wrote news reports in the form of letters, wrote his letter about the Plot to Dudley Carleton on the same day that Susan Whynniard, from whom Carleton had helped obtain the lease for Thomas Percy, was examined by the investigating commissioners. He wrote with some sympathetic nervousness about the fate of Carleton's patron the earl of Northumberland, but still with a degree of detachment, apparently innocent of how close his friend was to the eye of the storm. In the same letter that brought news of the first celebratory bonfires, Chamberlain, no doubt trying to be comforting to Carleton, spelt out the circumstantial evidence against the earl on the basis on his connection with the prime suspect, Thomas Percy. It sounded damning: 'nearness of name, blood, long and inward dependence and familiarity'. However, the mildness of the earl's initial treatment – 'he is rather wished than willed to keep his house' – gave grounds for optimism. Chamberlain hinted that Carleton had developed suspicions of Thomas Percy when part of the earl's household: '[Percy] hath verified your judgement but exceeded all degrees of comparison and gone beyond Nero and Caligula that would have all Rome but one head.'

As further news, Chamberlain noted 'Sir Edwin Sandys's books burnt' and 'Sir F. Bacon's new work on learning'.[1] The juxtaposition is perhaps significant. Sir Edwin Sandys was in many ways the king's least favourite man, having been to the fore among those who opposed the Union of England and Scotland in Parliament, and was later prominent in the Virginia Company aiding dissident groups like the Pilgrim Fathers. It is sometimes said that his book, *A Relation of the State of Religion*, was burnt in the wake of the discovery of the Plot because of its tolerant tone towards Catholics, but Chamberlain records that it was burnt in St Paul's Churchyard on the Saturday *before* the discovery of the Plot. Bacon was certainly in a more favoured position than was Sandys and had spoken in favour of the Union, but he was still outside the charmed circle. Portraits of this highly talented man show a mixture of intellect and slyness; he could seem too good at too many things to be trusted. He might praise James in a poem but attack royal policy in the House of Commons, dedicate a great work of philosophy to the king but undermine his position with legal argument composed with an artfulness that would escape censure.

By 1605 Bacon had turned to the consolations of philosophy, and, having found the usual classical sources unhelpful, wrote his own. In the long months of the prorogation between January and October 1605, while the plotters retired to their houses in the country and waited, Bacon wrote the second book of *The Advancement of Learning*. This book, perhaps the most influential single text in the evolution of the scientific method in England, was thought incomprehensible by his hoped-for patron the king, who famously commented that the book was 'like the peace of God which passeth all understanding'. In this, Bacon had something in common with John Donne and so many literary types who hoped for advancement at James's court: 'Give me a proper job close to the centre of power,' they seemed to say, 'or I shall write more of this stuff and dedicate it to you', resorting to that most desperate measure, publishing in English, in order to gain an audience. Bacon believed in retrospect that publishing in English had been a mistake and he later published an expanded version in Latin. In the event, any initial effect *The Advancement of Learning* might otherwise have had was submerged in the excitement of the discovery of the Plot.

It was perhaps incumbent on those thought too clever for their own good to make a conspicuous show of loyalty. On the day following Chamberlain's letter, Friday 8 November, Bacon had found another way to put himself forward; he became part of the earl of Salisbury's network of intelligence. The Inns of Court where Bacon began and ended his career were essential nurseries for the clever lawyers the government needed to present its version of events and prosecute so many peripheral figures on circumstantial evidence, but they were also self-sufficient, independent institutions, said to harbour Catholic priests and sympathisers and seditious rumours. In the frenetic days following the discovery of the Plot it was from here that Bacon got his information and chose to pass it on to Salisbury. He enclosed an explanatory note.

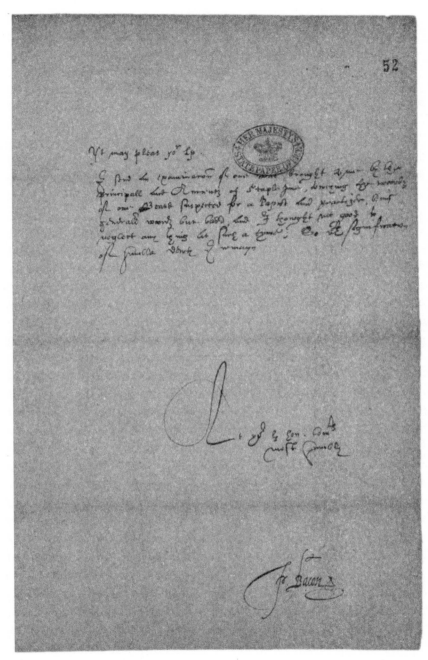

With his note to Salisbury, Francis Bacon supplied evidence of careless talk about the plot on the morning after its discovery. (TNA SP 14/16/29)

I send an examination of one [who] was brought to me by
the principal ... of Staple Inn today, the words of one Beard,
suspected for a papist and practiser, being general words, but
bad and I thought not good to neglect any thing at such a time.

Bacon enclosed with this note a witness statement, which conveys
something of the atmosphere of celebration and suspicion of two
days earlier, the Wednesday morning after the discovery of the Plot.
The searches among London Catholics, which allowed Sir John
Popham to determine the principal conspirators very quickly, created
an atmosphere illustrated here in which a boot-maker turned on a
long-standing customer. Bacon has signed this witness statement,
which was evidently made on the same day as the incident, being 'the
examination of John Drake servant to Thomas Reynolds shoemaker
dwelling in Holborn near Gray's Inn'. Drake went to Mr Beard's
lodging in the house of one Gibson in Fetter Lane (probably Dr Gibson
of Doctors Commons and the Court of Arches, recorded as living
there in the lay subsidy of 1600) to take measurements for a new
pair of boots. Beard asked Drake 'whether there were any watching
and warding abroad' on the streets, to which Drake replied that 'the
night before there was much watching and searching for Papists and
recusants' and named one Percy and that it was the most heinous
treason that ever was. Drake heard Beard mutter under his breath, 'It
had been brave sport, if it had gone forwards.' Drake reported this
was not said 'in any laughing or jesting manner', so presumably satire
on blowing up politicians was something he would recognise. Drake
added that Beard afterwards 'spoke against the [plot] very much',
implying bluster to cover his indiscretion, perhaps sensing Drake's
sense of humour failure.

More witnesses were rapidly found to testify that Beard had
previously lodged with a known recusant who 'hath bought up
recusant children', a still greater offence. No evidence was taken
from Beard himself, who no doubt could expect his own visit from
the authorities. There is perhaps an echo in Beard's remark of Snug's
wish in *A Midsummer Night's Dream* Act IV Scene 2, 'If our sport
had gone forward we had all been made men'; that the mechanicals
would have their fortunes transformed if their play were chosen to
be performed before the marriage of the duke and various lords and

ladies. Almost immediately, they learn from Bottom that it has been chosen. Perhaps in the destruction of the ruler and the lords Beard saw a parallel circumstance in which the fortunes of recusants would be transformed if Catesby's 'sport' had succeeded. Some people believe Francis Bacon wrote the plays ascribed to Shakespeare. If so, Bacon showed no sign of having recognised the line. Bacon's reward for his loyalty was to be made one of the lesser commissioners who investigated the wives and servants of the principal plotters and also the more minor conspirators, while the Lords Commissioners headed by Salisbury himself dealt with the lords, priests and gentlemen. Once again, Bacon had achieved a level of official recognition below his own estimation of his abilities.

Ben Jonson, poet and dramatist, a familiar figure beside Francis Bacon in the literary history of the period, appeared alongside him providing evidence relating to the Plot, which landed on the earl of Salisbury's desk on the same day. Jonson too was giving evidence of a sort about London's Catholics – perhaps the consequence of a deal to obtain his release from prison in the summer of 1605, when he and his fellow playwrights had displeased the king with their satirical play *Eastward Ho!* at Blackfriars.

Whether he was continuing to live on the wrong side of the law, or was on secret government business as an informer, Jonson found himself in the autumn near the heart of the Plot. He attended a supper party on or about 9 October 1605 at William Patrick's house, 'The Irish Boy' in the Strand, along with many of the leading conspirators and suspects who had returned to London in anticipation of the new session of Parliament. They included Robert Catesby, Francis Tresham, Thomas Wintour, Lord Mordaunt and Sir Jocelyn Percy, brother of the earl of Northumberland and yet another participant in Essex's revolt of 1601.

This reminder of Jonson's involvement landed on the earl of Salisbury's crowded desk on 6 November, nearly a month after the event, along with a plethora of half-remembered and possibly invented information from people wishing to ingratiate themselves with the authorities in the wake of the discovery of the Plot. On the next day Jonson received a warrant from the Privy Council allowing him to escort an unnamed priest to visit the lords and give testimony about the conspiracy to members of the council. Jonson was quick but unsuccessful in his work because by Friday 8 November he was reporting his failure to locate this priest, who may have been the Jesuit who converted Jonson some years earlier:

> May it please your Lordship to understand, there hath been no want in me, either in labour or sincerity in the discharge of this business to the satisfaction of your Lordship or the state. And whereas yesterday upon the first mention of it I took the most ready course (to my present thought) by the Venetian Ambassador's chaplain, who not only apprehended it well, but was of mind with me, that no man of conscience or any indifferent love to his country would deny to do it, and withal engaged himself to find out one, absolute in all Numbers, for the purpose, which he willed me (before a gentleman of good credit who is my testimony) to signify to your Lordship in his name. It falls out since that that Party will not be found (for so he returns answer) upon which I have made attempt in other places, but can speak with none in person (all being either removed or so concealed upon this present mischief) but by second means I have received answer of doubts and difficulties, that they will make it a Question to the Archpriest with other such like suspensions: so that to tell your Lordship plainly my heart; I think they are all so enweaved in it as it will make 500 Gentleman less of the Religion within this week if they carry their understanding about them. For myself if I had been a priest I would have put on wings to such an Occasion and have thought it no adventure where I might have done (besides his Majesty and my Country) all Christianity so good service. And so much have I sent to some of them. If it shall please your Lordship I shall yet make further trial and that you cannot in the mean time be provided I do not only with all readiness offer my service, but will perform it with as much integrity as your particular favour, or his Majesty's right in any Subject he hath, can exact.
>
> Your Honour's most perfect servant and
lover Ben Jonson.[2]

It is difficult not to feel that this letter is more ambiguous and opaque than it need be. In essence, Jonson confesses that he has achieved little and will do little more unless Salisbury insists, but he takes a very long time, and lot of qualifying remarks in brackets, to say it. 'The present mischief' might appear to downplay the seriousness of the Plot as far as the earl of Salisbury was concerned, and cast some suspicion on his informant. In the end, perhaps it does say something about the atmosphere among Catholic priests in London and Jonson's own religious position. Theoretically, there were no Catholic priests allowed in London, but it is evident that there were sufficient numbers to merit a network of spies and that before the Plot Salisbury had a number of contacts among them. The government was prepared to deal with 'loyal' priests in return for information and they appeared relatively willing to give it. Jonson's line about consulting the Archpriest implies a degree of confusion among London's frightened and fugitive Catholics about what a good Catholic ought to do in the light of the discovery of the Plot. Characteristically Jonson follows a standard satiric Protestant line about Catholics abandoning their 'politically inconvenient' religion in the wake of the Plot (hardly fair given the actual privations many suffered daily for it) with a thought about how he would behave if he were a priest himself. Evidently, this was not so great an imaginative leap.

Jonson's attitude seems even more ambivalent in the light of events that followed. On 10 January 1606, while Sir Edward Coke was preparing the case against Sir Everard Digby and just a few days after the performance at court of one of Jonson's masques, surely a sign of royal favour, Ben and Anne Jonson were presented before the consistory court on charges of recusancy. Jonson claimed he had not taken communion because of a religious 'scruple' and so was ordered to discuss his theological difficulties with the dean of St Paul's and the Archbishop of Canterbury's chaplain. Their arguments cannot have been too persuasive because in May and June of the same year he and Anne were back in the consistory court to answer the same charges.

Jonson prudently addressed a congratulatory epigram to Lord Monteagle, whom he praised as the 'saver of my country'. Perhaps a more genuine response came in the more ambiguous form of his next play, *Volpone*, in the early months of 1606. Whether or not he was influenced by his negotiations with the Venetian embassy at the time of the Plot, the play is set in Venice. Italian settings, beloved of

Shakespeare and Jonson, always gave an opportunity for playwrights to show their audiences Catholicism as the accepted religion of the country – or to satirise it. In *Volpone*'s Venice, under the influence of St Mark, the patron saint of goldsmiths, the worship of money has long since replaced religion, and his audience might well recognise the governing greed of London underlying this exotic setting. Whatever his religious views, Jonson remained a consistent cat's paw of Stuart patronage, subsisting on royal pensions rarely paid, alternately meagrely rewarded for his wit and imprisoned for his indiscretions.

This mass of London information was all very well, but the authorities also needed to know urgently about the Midlands rising and plans to kidnap and proclaim 'the next heir'. Their only direct source of information was still Guy Fawkes, who was examined again on the same day, Friday 8 November. However, he would not, or perhaps could not, tell them much more than they already knew.

> As they knew not how to seize Prince Charles, they resolved to surprise the Princess Elizabeth, and make her Queen; they prepared, in her name, a proclamation against the Union of the Kingdoms, and in justification of their act, but without any declaration as to religion; they would have taken the Princess Mary, but knew not how.[3]

They also tried to establish the nature of the rebels' plans by examining royal servants who had seen Thomas Percy acting suspiciously and asking questions about the royal children in the days before the discovery of the Plot. Agnes Fortun was able to add information on the same day Fawkes was examined, which shed more light on their inability to 'seize Prince Charles' (later Charles I). She was a servant to Charles and recalled a conversation in which Percy had been keen to know the prince's routine and how he was guarded. Entitled 'A report of a Scottish woman concerning Percy', it sounds unpromising, as if it had has been hastily labelled 'more gossip' by a weary official. It is in fact telling and dramatic evidence of Percy's role in the Plot. Fawkes's and other evidence relating to the 'hunt' at Dunchurch suggests they had settled on 'The Lady Elizabeth' as their puppet monarch, having abandoned the possibility of taking Prince Charles. Perhaps Percy's interview with Agnes Fortun was the final straw before the plan was abandoned. Not only was the prince well protected at all times, but also the staircase by which Percy had hoped to surprise him had recently been blocked to 'make his chamber more private'.[4]

Fortun had offered Percy the chance to stay and see both Charles and the man charged with protecting him, 'if he would stay a bonny while he might see the Duke and Sir Robert Carey both', but Percy declined this offer and left looking hard at the blocked staircase and contemplating a change of plan. The other tactic of the authorities on 8 November was to set rebel against rebel by singling out Percy as the leader and chief offender, offering a reward of 'a thousand pounds at the least' and a pardon to those terrified into rebellion with him for his apprehension. Once again, events in the Midlands were to overtake them.[5]

6

'HOIST BY THEIR OWN PETARD'

After a dispiriting trudge in cold drizzle, which had failed to raise a single supporter but allowed many of those who had rallied at Dunchurch to make their escape, the remaining rebels arrived at Holbeach House, Staffordshire, on the evening of 7 November. They decided to dry their damp – currently useless – gunpowder before the open fire, only for it to explode, leaving Catesby and Rookwood badly burned and John Grant nearly blinded. The others were badly shaken and any remaining confidence was swiftly eroded. This horrific explosion, rich in dramatic irony, finally raised in the minds of the conspirators the idea that God did not, after all, support their scheme. John Wright suggested to Catesby that they might take this signal of divine displeasure as a cue to end their hopeless situation, by blowing themselves up completely with the remaining gunpowder. The suggestion was not followed, but unsurprisingly there were further desertions.

One of the most significant departures was that of Sir Everard Digby. He rode off with two servants early the following morning. Digby's 'desertion' of Holbeach before the siege may have been prompted by the need to escape Catesby's web of words and find out what was actually going on. His instinct was to try to find someone of sufficient rank to surrender to, but he found no one. He tried to hide in a wood, but was tracked by his horse's hoof marks to a dry ditch. The pursuing sheriff's men crowed at their discovery, crying

'Here he is, here he is,' but Digby was too proud and too confident to stay in hiding and rode out to them with a challenge: 'Here he is indeed, what then?' At first, he hoped to break through them, but recognising at last the overwhelming odds, he surrendered. He was taken to London and lodged with the other superior prisoners in the Tower. To begin with he denied all knowledge of the Plot before his conversation with Catesby on 5 November, but confronted with the evidence of Guy Fawkes and Thomas Wintour, he admitted his deeper involvement.

Thomas Wintour's own story is vividly captured in the documents of the investigation, and through his evidence the final, fatal, twists of the Plot fall into place. On the morning of 8 November, carrying his brother Robert's unwilling plea for support, he had ridden to Pepper Hill to call on Sir John Talbot in a vain attempt to recruit backing. Returning from this fruitless mission, he was advised when he was still some distance from the house by Stephen Littleton, the owner of Holbeach, to make good his escape. Wintour later recorded his soldierly response: 'I told him I would first see the body of my friend and bury him, whatsoever befell me.' In his own account, Wintour asked Catesby, Percy, the Wrights, Rookwood, and Grant what they resolved to do. 'They answered we mean here to die, I said again I would take such part as they did.' When the house was besieged by the local militia on the Friday morning Thomas Wintour, Robert Catesby and Thomas Percy – the bachelor, the widower and the bigamist – fought back to back in a last desperate struggle. Only Wintour survived long enough to report their last stand:

> At about eleven of the clock came the company to beset the house and as I walked into the court was shot in the shoulder, which lost me the use of my arm. The next shot was the elder Wright struck dead, after him the younger Mr Wright and fourthly Ambrose Rookwood. Then said Mr Catesby to me standing before the door they were to enter, 'Stand by me Tom and we will die together.' 'Sir', quoth I, 'I have lost the use of my right arm and I fear that will cause me to be taken.' So as we stood close together Mr Catesby Mr Percy and my self they two were shot (as far as I could guess) with one bullet, and then

the company entered upon me, hurt me in belly with a pick and gave me other wounds until one came behind and caught hold of both mine arms.[1]

Documents survive which give us an account of the siege from the point of view of the besieging forces, and also give insight into the nature of local law enforcement. Those who joined specially raised forces might do so through their own loyalty and motivation. Among those who joined Charles Blount, earl of Devonshire's force charged with putting down rebellion was Francis Tresham. There were sometimes disputes among the sheriffs when the action took place, as at Holbeach, on the border of three counties.

Our most dramatic first-hand account of the capture of Thomas Wintour comes from evidence taken from one such argument among local militias. Men under the command of Sir Francis Kettleby and Sir Richard Walsh haggled about who was responsible for taking Thomas Wintour prisoner. One, Thomas Williams, was intent on preserving his life; the other, Thomas Bannister, would have killed him. Both claimed him. The document provides a version of the dialogue of the fight and the strange, to modern ears, deference and social sensitivity of the militia in the presence of gentlemen, albeit treacherous ones.

Interrogatories administered on behalf on the complainant [Williams] to the defendant [Bannister]. 'Did you not see the complainant Williams leap down into the court of Holbeach first and before any man and did you hear the complainant say to Wintour "Gentleman, yield" and did not Wintour say "Kill me and I will kill thee if I can" and did you not thrust at Wintour with your bill and did not the complainant Williams break your thrust with his calliber and say "Oh hurt him not!" and did not you say to some of your friends and acquaintance, that on your conscience you [would have] killed the said Wintour if the complainant Williams had not been there.'[2]

Williams it seems took Wintour's 'damask sword' and handed it to Bannister to free his hands while he secured the prisoner, Bannister later using the sword as evidence that he had taken Wintour prisoner. In an interesting postscript, the same document includes the evidence of Gilbert Wheeler of Droitwich, who describes Thomas Wintour being taken as a prisoner to Worcester and a dispute arising over his spurs:

> Thomas Wintour amongst the other traitors was brought to the Town Hall of Worcester and at that time having a pair of gilt copper spurs on his heels the officers of the town intending to have pulled off his boots would have taken away his spurs as due unto them, but the complainant Williams being there present made open challenge of the said spurs as he said due to him by law of arms.

This was apparently heard in Wintour's presence and Williams's prior claim upheld. This is further minor evidence of the cost and style of the plotters' clothing and arms. At the same time, Sir William Waad was preoccupied with significantly embroidered scarves made for the conspirators and there were also examinations of a cutler who had made them swords engraved with Christ's passion. These might simply be for their protection but they also suggest a group dressed for martyrdom.

While the rebellion was petering out a hundred miles away, Guy Fawkes in the Tower was coming under increasing pressure from the authorities to tell all he knew. He was no longer a source of information merely about a plot whose danger had passed but about what appeared to be an unclear and present danger. Waad wrote to his master the earl of Salisbury with clear indications that at the very least 'the gentler tortures' specified in the king's letter of 6 November were being threatened. The severity of this treatment reflected the scale of the government's anxiety. Wild rumours were still being received about the extent of the Midlands rebellion, suggesting a growing popular uprising, which might threaten the government afresh:

> I have prevailed so much at the length with my prisoner, by plying him with the best persuasions I could use as he hath

William Waad to Salisbury, 9 November 1605. Fawkes seems to have resisted making a written confession. Was there macabre wordplay in Waad's letter, which confirmed that Fawkes had been racked? (TNA SP 14/216/53)

faithfully promised me by narration to discover to your lordship only all the secrets of his heart, but not to be set down in writing. Your lordship will not mislike the exception for when he hath confessed himself to your lordship, I will undertake he shall acknowledge it before such as you shall call, and then he shall not make dainty to set his hand unto it. Therefore, it may please your good lordship, if any of the Lords do come with you, that at first your lordship will deal with him alone. He will conceal no name nor matter from your lordship to whose ears he will unfold his bosom. And I know your lordship will think it the best journey you ever made upon so evil occasion. Thus in haste, I thank God my poor labour hath advanced a service of this importance. From the Tower of London, the 9th of November 1605. At the commandment of your Lordship, W G Waad.

Since the plotters and many of those investigating them, including the king, were of the generation which provided the first audience of Shakespeare's plays, I have always been interested to see how much an education steeped in rhetoric had affected how the plotters and investigators used language to convey and conceal meaning. Some were indeed very well concealed. Looking again at the language of Sir William Waad's letter to the earl of Salisbury, 'at the length' seems to be a veiled reference to racking, suggesting Fawkes was now longer than he was before, and 'best persuasions' echoes the 'gentler tortures' in the king's instructions of 6 November, suggesting that in fact the least gentle had been employed. Reading this, Salisbury would have had no doubt as to what it meant. There are also the careful parallels of 'best' and 'evil', 'poor' and 'importance', which allow Waad to play with the idea that his labour is indeed 'poor' and the torture of Fawkes 'evil' without saying so directly. Anyone who thinks it unlikely that someone would have fun punning and playing with subjects such as torture has never seen or read a Shakespeare tragedy. Perhaps, as in tragedy, there is some catharsis or detachment to be gained in real life in dealing with these things in a literary way.

When Fawkes did set his hand to the declaration that followed, he could barely write. The infamous declaration, with its failing signature, in fact gave the authorities little additional information. Fawkes remained their only direct source of information about the Plot until the survivors of Holbeach arrived in the capital on 12 November. The severity of his treatment reflected this. His torture came at the height of the government's anxiety, when wild rumours about the extent of the Midlands rebellion were still being received. Then it seemed that Fawkes's evidence might be the only way to understand not only the catastrophic destruction of Parliament so narrowly averted but also a growing popular rebellion, which might threaten the government afresh. Ironically, the information Fawkes was able to provide under torture was less than Thomas Wintour, in government hands at Worcester, would already have been able to offer, and was in any case superseded within days by Wintour's arrival in London. The rebellion for which Fawkes had suffered was over before he struggled to write his name.

> The plot was to blow up the King with all the nobility about him in Parliament.
> He confesseth also that there was speech amongst them to draw Sir Walter Raleigh to take part with them, being one that might stand them in good stead as others in like sort were named.

Fawkes also helpfully located White Webbs, the house rented by Ann Vaux as a haven for priests where the conspirators often met, where it lay in relation to Salisbury's vast estate, Theobalds. (Theobalds was so large that everywhere between London and Hertfordshire could be located as either 'this side of Theobalds' or 'the other side of Theobalds'.) This is not only a declaration made to Salisbury but to some extent one made by Salisbury himself – and Coke – reflecting their preoccupations, perhaps a sign that evidence under torture was more likely to affirm the questions put rather than bring anything new. Fawkes's answers reflect the interests of the people who are questioning him and their regard for their own personal safety. Though on the day before Fawkes's confession Waad had identified Francis Tresham, despite his service in the militia, as a Spanish pensioner worth keeping an eye on, only with Fawkes's confession did Tresham become formally implicated in the Plot, albeit as an unwilling figure 'exceeding earnest' to warn Lord Monteagle not to attend Parliament.

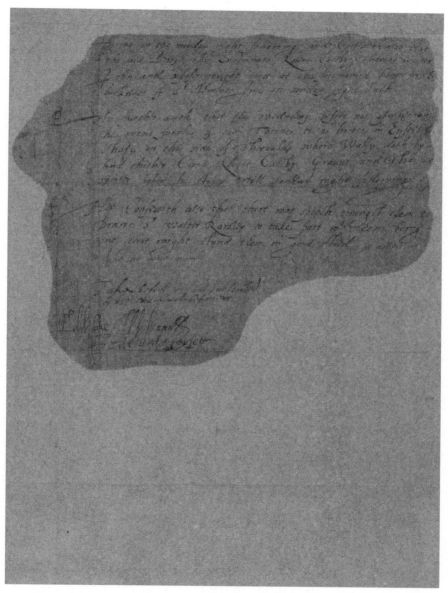

Declaration of Guy Fawkes, 9 November 1605. Fawkes's evidence under torture clearly reflected the nature of the questions asked rather than any deeper truth about the plot. Sir Walter Raleigh, implicated here, barely figures elsewhere, other than in the mind of the Attorney General, Sir Edward Coke. Further evidence of Fawkes's physical deterioration comes from his very faint signature. (TNA SP 14/216/54)

Rumours that Thomas Percy had been taken prisoner at Holbeach reached London far enough in advance of the news of his death that Salisbury had the time to report him 'sore hurt and taken' in a letter to Sir Thomas Edmondes in Brussels. The earl of Northumberland wasted no time in writing a note to the Council dated 'Sunday afternoon' (10 November) that Thomas Percy should be saved from his injuries if possible. Only Percy, if he could be believed, could give the vital evidence that would clear the earl of any complicity. Percy was already dead when the earl wrote this note, his injuries sustained on the eighth exacerbated by ill treatment by 'the baser sort' among the besieging forces, leading to his death on the ninth. It is even possible that Northumberland knew this by the afternoon of the tenth, and took the opportunity to stress his belief in his own innocence in the certain belief that Percy could do nothing to contradict him.

> I hear Mr Percy is taken, if that I hear be true, but withal shot through the shoulder with a musket; our surgeons in this country are not over excellent for a shot, if heat take it, the patient with a fever will soon make an end; none but he can show me clear as the day, or dark as the night, therefore I hope it shall not offend you if I require haste, for now will he tell truly if ever, being ready to make his account to God almighty. Thus with my humble well wishes to your Lordships I rest to do your Lordships service, Northumberland.

As always, Northumberland's note is ambiguous. Perhaps there is an echo too in 'clear as the day or dark as the night' of the 'owl-light'/daylight note about Percy in November 1603. Is Percy being presented as sincere and religious or insincere and superstitious? The line about Percy's readiness to make confession sounds like a standard Protestant joke at the expense of Catholics obsessed with their own religious practices. In the context of the note, though, it is clear that Northumberland himself believes that Percy, despite his treachery, will tell the truth in a deathbed confession. For all his capital temporal offences, Percy will not risk his soul at the last. This sounds more like a ringing endorsement of Catholic religious

Northumberland to the Privy Council, 10 November 1605. Brief and urgent, Northumberland's note about Percy's health is still full of ambiguity. What were his motivations in writing it? (TNA SP 14/216/225) practice, a dangerous position for a man trying to prove he was not the hidden power behind Percy's rebellion.

Salisbury's agents were soon set to uncover evidence of Jesuit involvement in the Plot by showing that a supposed Jesuit teaching, which justified the deposition of heretic kings, had influenced the plotters. The confessions of the plotters themselves seemed to suggest that the desire to 'do somewhat in England' came from a simple desire to improve the lot of English Catholics without complex theological justification, but it was politic for the government to suggest that only poisonous indoctrination stopped all Catholics from being loyal 'Church Papists' like the earl of Northampton.

Accordingly, on 11 November Salisbury received from Thomas Wilson further reports of White Webbs, the 'House on Enfield Chase on this side of Theobald's' of Fawkes's declaration, which was still being used as a safe house for priests including Garnet, not only 'this side of' but also uncomfortably close to Salisbury's Hertfordshire estate.

Guy Fawkes might be losing importance compared to the better-informed Thomas Wintour, newly arrived in London, but he could still cause trouble though his 'society' connections. One such, Anthony Maria Browne, Viscount Montague, was a popular Catholic nobleman and a friend of Robert Catesby, depicted with his brothers by court artist Isaac Oliver as the embodiment of fashionable, self-confident nobility. His imprisonment for his speeches against anti-Catholic legislation became a focus of Catholic discontent both within Parliament and outside. When it emerged that he had employed Guy Fawkes, the circumstantial evidence against him seemed as strong as that against some of the other suspected lords, but he was well connected enough to escape more lightly. In cleverly written letters to his father-in-law, Lord Treasurer Thomas Sackville, earl of Dorset, Montague put pressure on him to buy him out of trouble, artfully recalling conversations with Catesby in such a way as to involve his powerful relative in his fate.

Dorset asked Montague to review and clarify his connection with 'the horrible intended treason'. Montague responded with hints of complicity, as if to say, 'I hoped to secure my absence from Parliament through you, so don't forget me', and rubbed it in by artfully reconstructing Catesby's veiled warning not to attend Parliament in a way which potentially ensnared his father-in-law:

'The Parliament I think bringeth up your Lordship now.'

'No surely but it will upon Monday next, unless my Lord Treasurer do obtain me his majesty's licence to be absent, which I am in some hopes of.'

'I think your lordship takes no great pleasure there.' Whereunto I assented.[3]

He also expressed a desire to 'speak confidently' (in confidence) to the earl, implying they might both have something to hide. The revelation of Fawkes's involvement prompted another letter from Montague to Dorset in which he put the date of his conversation with Catesby back a week, making it seem less urgent and conspiratorial, adding,

The miserable fellow that should have been the bloody executioner of that woeful tragedy was called Guy Faux. If such were his name, he should seem to have been my servant once (though I am sorry to think it) for such a one I had even for some few months, but was dismissed from me by my Lord upon some mislike he had of him.[4]

Again, this is a slightly surprising view of Fawkes, not so much that he should be in the service of one of the Catholic lords the conspirators hoped to spare, since he had that in common with Thomas Wintour and Thomas Percy, but that he should bring sufficient attention to himself to be dismissed. Perhaps that fits with the plain-speaking soldier in Flanders and the man who was shockingly unrepentant in the presence of the king, though. He was too passionate in his opinions and too convinced of their rightness to keep his opinions to himself, even in the presence of a senior member of the government he was planning to destroy.

Days later, Montague was sent to the Tower. Catesby, it seemed, did have the bravado to play a trick on a few favoured lords whom he believed bright enough to take a hint and wedded enough to him not to betray him. Unlike so many of his fellow prisoners, Montague could be confident of powerful forces working to secure his release.

7

THE TENTACLES OF TREASON

When the survivors of the siege of Holbeach reached London, the earl of Salisbury could stop reacting to events and begin to mount investigations in directions of his choosing. The picture was still chaotic, though, and his satisfaction at the success of the government's countermeasures was tinged with unease.

On 13 November 1605, Sir Richard Verney, the sheriff of Warwickshire, sent Salisbury a letter on the connection between the Digby and Vaux families and revealed his own connection to both. This was another example of the potentially embarrassing, even dangerous relationships of local law officers to the Midlands families suspected of harbouring Catholic rebels and their priests. This was not only a danger to the state's hope of suppressing current and future rebellion, but also compromising for the law officers themselves. Verney knew he could risk no delay in demonstrating to Salisbury his loyalty to the state, and sent the earl Lady Vaux's letter, which had 'come into my hands even now'. It secured the release, on family and loyalty grounds, of two young men who were later discovered to be missionary priests. This was unsurprising, since, after all, Verney's 'acquaintance with her as a gentlewoman', which he claimed was his sole connection with her, was shared by Guy Fawkes himself, who was carrying a letter from Eliza Vaux when he was apprehended. He also felt he had to explain that his connection with Sir Everard Digby came 'before we had knowledge that [he] was one of the conspirators'.[1] This was reasonable enough since Digby was such a late recruit, but it must have sounded weak. Salisbury was slow and forgetful in rewarding Verney's service, and no doubt retained his doubts about the loyalty and reliability of the sheriffs and their men in that part of the country when the Jesuit missionaries had enjoyed such success in converting the landed families to Catholicism.

Also landing on Salisbury's desk was William Tate's report of his initial unsuccessful searches of the Vaux's house, Harrowden, for the Jesuit Father John Gerard on Thursday 14 November: 'Remaining unsatisfied with my unprofitable endeavours in the former search on Thursday, towards the evening I renewed it with my servants ... approaching near to the place where this hidden serpent should seem to lurk.' After some further search and persistent interrogation of reluctant servants, Tate discovered 'the most secret place I ever saw, and so contrived that it was without all possibility to be discovered. There I found many Popish books and other things incident to their superstitious religion.'[2]

The search of Harrowden Hall failed to uncover Father Gerard, but the ongoing investigation began to reveal vestiges of rebellion and the possibility of fugitive priests fostering further attempts. Then there was the problem of bringing the suspect and his vestments together: how could you tell – aside from the fact that he was hiding in a priest hole – that the man you had discovered was a priest at all? 'These priests and Jesuits masking under other habits make me jealous of any unknown to me professing themselves Catholics,' Tate confided to Salisbury. 'Masking' does indeed describe simple disguise, but also imbues the priests and their accomplices with a certain theatricality; and for their pursuers, secure in the immunity that the unjust laws against recusants gave them, it excused them from the requirement to tell the truth about themselves.

A postscript shows Tate again wrestling with the social status of Lord Vaux and his mother, who are obviously socially superior to the searchers. This brought an odd mixture of deference and brutality to the search. Tate ensured that the other law officers did not know their destination and were all 'remote' from Harrowden. These were precautions that he took to try to ensure that the occupants of the house were not warned of the impending search by those in the search party, who might have connections to them. It was also a clear indication that he could not entirely trust their loyalty. His initial lack of success was a testament to the skill of concealment of the Vauxs, and their gentle reaction to the violence of the search was in keeping with their elevated social rank:

> Then I ransacked the coffers of linen, trunks of apparel, the young Lord's lodging and his evidence house to which he very honourably gave passage and in all things disposed himself to expedite the service, that he might stand justified from all imputation.[3]

Was even Tate himself looking beyond the imperatives of the present search to a time when being on good terms with the young Lord Vaux might be an advantage to him? Was everybody in the house free of imputation as far as the Plot and rebellion was concerned? Not for the first time, evidence was taken of a general air of preparation and gathering of provisions in Catholic households in the Midlands on and before 5 November. Statements came from the servants at Harrowden about the gathering of gunpowder. The examination of Francis Swetnam, 'baker to Mistress Vaux' at Harrowden, was taken by Tate on 14 November. It revealed that

> ... at six in the evening on 5 November at the entreaty of one Matthew a Lancashire man and servant of Lord Monteagle, they bought of James Ball a mercer dwelling in Wellingborough about 20 pounds of gunpowder to be sent to Kettering and from there by carrier to Lancashire for profit and to bestow amongst his friends.[4]

This could all be coincidence, of course, though the connection between Lord Monteagle and a possible rising in the Midlands or the North must have raised eyebrows among the investigators. It was also clear that outside London gunpowder could be acquired easily and without clear explanation of purpose. Another examination identified the mysterious 'Matthew' as Matthew Batty, confirming that he said he served Monteagle and that he intended to go back to Lancashire via the Treshams at Rushton. There was a clandestine air to the whole thing, with midnight horse rides, urgency and excitement, all suddenly evaporating as news of the failure of the Plot and rebellion spread. In later, undated evidence taken by the lesser commissioners from the plotters' servants calendared in April 1606 (but itself a digest of evidence probably taken in November) Matthew Batty appeared in person and gave his own version of what had happened to the gunpowder, some elements being underlined by the Commissioners as being of particular interest:

> Mathew Batty: Saieth that he serving the Lady Monteagle and living at Mrs Vaux's and Sir (*sic*) Francis Tresham's some few days before Allhallowtide did on Tuesday the 5 of November, <u>buy a barrel of gunpowder which he left with Francis, Mrs Vaux her man.</u>

This concatenation of evidence of the harbouring of priests and meetings between the conspirators in the Midlands suggests greater links between the core conspirators and the hunting party at Dunchurch than had come out of the evidence of the core conspirators themselves. Many people seemed to know of the rising, if not of the details of the gunpowder end of the operation itself. This prompted a sustained attempt by the authorities to establish the extent of this knowledge and preparation, 'to prove what preparation of money horse and armour they made'. It included the evidence of Richard Day, who revealed 'that Sir Everard Digby sold the whole stock of a farm for £800 and took order with this examinate a little before Allhallowtide to procure his creditors to forbear their debts full fortnight after the feast of All Saints'.

Presumably, the £800 was laid out in preparation for the hunting party at Dunchurch and the expectation that as the protector of the Princess Elizabeth he would eventually be suitably rewarded by her and her Catholic husband. The hunting party is described by several sources in this evidence as a horse race, which gives it a slightly different and unexpected character. It also gave extra first-hand detail of the extent and sophistication of the plotters' arms, including 'French pistols', at Huddington.

There was also more evidence of the core plotters, and the network of communication which allowed them to act so quickly. George Bartlett declared that on the Tuesday morning (5 November) at four o'clock he was sent 'from a house near Barnes' with a horse 'to London to Mr Thomas Wintour his inn, Robert Catesby charging him not to sleep till he came to Warwickshire to him, for that he was to use him at a hunting match, whereupon he came to him that night'.

Sir Everard Digby's servant William Handy also gave evidence of their continued confidence that

the company from Dunchurch rode to Warwick from there to John Grant's where they found his <u>tables in the hall furnished with muskets and armour. That the younger Wright</u> said openly that if they had had good luck they had made those in the parliament fly with their heels upward to the sky.[5]

Despite this continuing evidence of the uncertainty of loyalty in the Midlands, and the continued diversion of much of the state's limited resources into the investigation of the Plot, the state of semi-siege that had existed since its discovery could not continue indefinitely without damage to the government and to trade. The ports, closed since 5 November, reopened by proclamation on 15 November, 'the plot being now thoroughly discovered and the principal offenders in the hands of his Majesty'. The decision to close them had surely been a sign of the fragility of the state and the strength of its desire to apprehend conspirators. The restrictions were not relaxed until the most important survivors of Holbeach were in government hands. Clearly, the decision to close the ports had been an indication of the genuineness of the government's alarm. The interruption to normal commerce would have been considerable.

Whether or not the Plot was fully discovered was still a matter of debate. Opportunist informers continued to hint darkly at the earl of Northumberland's involvement in the Plot, though he was still too powerful to be accused directly. Instead, phantom sightings of Thomas Percy, 'the monster of the world', continued to be made, including rumours he was in the Tynemouth area five days after his death. Reports continued to arrive of Northumberland as a focus of discontent in the summer of 1605, the earl saying that 'as the state now stands it cannot hold and that will shortly appear'.[6] What store could Salisbury place on intelligence-gossip of this kind? The Attorney General, one suspects, might seize on it as evidence of Northumberland's complicity in plotting to undermine the government, perhaps in the Gunpowder Plot itself, while Salisbury himself would probably be more sceptical.

In the Midlands, too, informers' notes started to come in after the rebellion was put down. Lord Harington, who had care of the Princess Elizabeth at Coombe Abbey, and who was to have been surprised and overwhelmed by Sir Everard Digby's hunting party, reported a great store of armour being 'conveyed away by the Papists in Worcestershire'. The loyalty of the county was so doubtful that an assessment of it could not be committed to paper, so Harrington sent the bearer of his letter, Mr Milward of Alchurch, to attest to the 'state of Worcestershire where he dwells'.[7]

On 15 November 1605, Susan, dowager countess of Kent, was conspicuous, but not alone, in taking the opportunity presented by the Plot to further her own financial interests. It was a potentially dangerous business to provide the government with information about those implicated in the Plot. The authorities were always likely to ask how you knew what you knew and what your own connection was. So tempting was the possibility of cash that in her case it overcame the danger of implicating herself. In this case, the plan was to try to prise an ecclesiastical living of £200 from a poor, unsuspecting Mr Willughby, presumably a neighbour of hers at Fulwell House in Barking. She then rather gave the game away by admitting that the living of 'some other of a like estate'[8] would do just as well. The money rather the prevention of the destruction of the government seems to have been the important thing.

Perhaps her suspicions had some foundation. Undated evidence among the Cecil Papers,[9] probably from earlier in November 1605, holding information about the conspirators' meetings at The Horns in Carter Lane included the name of Sir William Willoughby, alongside Sir Edmund Baynham, Sir John Roe, Robert Catesby, Francis Tresham, Captain Winter, Lord Mordaunt, and the inevitable Percy brothers Charles and Jocelyn, so perhaps there was a genuine connection with the Plot. Susan had established her loyalty early in James's reign by giving evidence in Star Chamber in the summer of 1603, turning a case in favour of a preacher who became a royal chaplain and against the playwright George Chapman and other defendants.[10]

On 17 November 1605, Sir Richard Walsh, the sheriff of Worcestershire, reported seizing the arms of John Talbot of Grafton, then searching Huddington Court for Thomas Wintour's. He reported finding little among their papers, which was perhaps surprising, unless incriminating evidence had already been removed. He did, however, discover that the Wintours were related by marriage to the earls of Shrewsbury and that a significant portion of their goods had already been 'conveyed away'.[11] Was it by unscrupulous individuals enriching themselves while pretending to act for the authorities? Or was it friends of the powerful family keeping their goods and the evidence of the strength of their connections and sympathies beyond the grasp of the state?

On the following day, in a letter to the earl of Salisbury, Lord Clinton reflected the confusion and continued apprehension of law officers in the country 'if the Papists should grow to a head'.[12] He asked what action he should or could take if there was a concerted rising of Catholics in the area, he being the only Commissioner for miles, all the others having gone to London. With hindsight, we might consider that the rebellion had ended at Holbeach ten days earlier and there was little possibility of further trouble, but that was not necessarily the perception locally. Here, where law enforcement was thin on the ground and elements of the local population were disaffected or worse, might they be inspired by the plotters' example, as Catesby had hoped, and rise up in rebellion?

The earl of Northumberland was amicably imprisoned by his fellow privy councillor the Archbishop of Canterbury. Was he the real power behind the Plot, one of its intended victims, or, as he insisted, a man of private pursuits who had no interest in power? Surely, the fact that he had dined with Thomas Percy at Syon House on 4 November was strong circumstantial evidence of his involvement. Rumours began to circulate that law enforcement against the rebels had been reluctant in parts of Warwickshire where the Jesuit missionaries had been most successful.

News that one of those arrested was court favourite Sir Everard Digby and that Lord Monteagle was heavily implicated in a plot he had exposed was greeted with scepticism abroad, as was the official version of the Plot more generally. In some circles, the Plot's very existence was doubted. On 13 November, Dudley Carleton reported from the safety of his diplomatic posting in Paris that the Plot was considered a fable in France. He commentated with detachment on the Plot, apparently unconcerned about his own connection.

> The fire which was said to have burnt our K[ing] and counsel and hath been hot for these two days past in every man's mouth, proves but ignis fatuus or a flash of some foolish fellow's brain to abuse the world, for it is now confidently reported there was no such matter, nor anything near it more than a barrel of gunpowder found near the court.[13]

On the following day, Lord Salisbury reported to Sir Thomas Edmondes in Brussels that Fawkes, after 'standing a great while very obstinately on a vow he had made, fortified by the receiving of the Sacrament',[14] had finally made a full declaration of his role in the plot. It is perhaps striking that, mocking though his interrogators were of Fawkes's superstitious beliefs, the earl had little doubt that his faith and the taking of Holy Communion had strengthened his resolution and his vow of secrecy. Part of the state's hostility to the Jesuits was fear of the power they wielded and imparted to the faithful through communion and confession, though it was Protestant practice to deny that such power existed. Most importantly for Edmondes, as a diplomat at the Imperial Court, Fawkes had revealed that Hugh Owen was acquainted with the specifics of the Plot, not just with their general intention to do something for the Catholic cause in England, and was to have been Fawkes's principal contact to disseminate news of the Plot's success. Salisbury now felt he had sufficient grounds to exert pressure to have Owen given up to the authorities in England. The Archduke, however, was more concerned about whether any of the nobility were involved in the Plot, perhaps believing, like the investigating government, that a small group of gentlemen could not have organised such an affair on their own. Perhaps he was trying to gauge the depth of feeling against the king among the class of men who really mattered.

While Fawkes continued to suffer, Salisbury received the bill for the exhumation and quartering of the conspirators who died at Holbeach. Though they could no longer suffer, they could be exhibited. In February 1606 he would get a further expenses claim

(23s 9d) for setting Catesby and Percy's heads on iron spikes.[15] As if this were not enough to occupy him, there was the business of the core plotters still at large. On 18 November, Salisbury hastily drafted a proclamation for the apprehension of Robert Wintour and Stephen Littleton, who had both fled Holbeach. It carries on the back brief notes of their descriptions, which again shows a lack of intimate knowledge on the part of the authorities about Thomas Percy on 5 November. It also suggests that the depiction of Robert Wintour in the famous engraving at the beginning of this book was somewhat deceptive:

Robert Wintour: Of mean stature, rather low than otherwise, brown hair and beard not much beard, short hair, somewhat stooping, square made, near forty.

Stephen Littleton: A very tall man, swarthy complexion, no beard or little, brown coloured hair about thirty.[16]

It was not much to go on for a manhunt. After ten days on the run, their beards would presumably have been rather longer. Ultimately, capture relied not on general public vigilance but on local betrayal by those who knew them well. The published proclamation nonetheless tidied up these descriptions and excused itself on the grounds of the fugitives' relative obscurity: '... because the said Winter is unknown to many we have thought it convenient to publish a description of him'. A further proclamation allowed the beleaguered sheriffs to pursue the remaining rebels at large across county boundaries, the proclamation still referring to their quarry as 'Percy and his complices'.[17]

To Thomas Edmondes in Brussels fell the difficult task of disseminating news of the Plot to sceptical diplomats and securing the arrest of Hugh Owen and Father Baldwin in Flanders. 'If his majesty suffers this nest of vipers to remain unscattered, which be the chief instruments that nourish all the practices in England, and from hence all the poisoned correspondings being entertained to all other parts of Christendom, it will be an occasion to make them to hold themselves more established than ever.'[18] The vipers stayed firmly in their nest despite the efforts of the English state to dislodge them.

The earl of Northumberland continued to argue in notes to the Privy Council that he was in no position to play a part in the plotters' plans. The man who little more than two years earlier had been an obvious choice as potential lord protector argued that he was unambitious and that he had a scanty supply of arms, horses and servants. James and his council struggled to identify a nobleman sufficiently eminent to serve as protector of the realm had the Plot succeeded. The surviving plotters claimed that any decision on the protectorate had been deferred until after the explosion, but, again, their assurances failed to convince. After Thomas Percy's death, Northumberland continued to hint at Percy's double dealing and lack of accountability in the handling of his rents and in his lack of regard for his master. On 21 November, Northumberland wrote to Salisbury that he desired Percy's study at Alnwick 'sealed up, because I doubt of some bonds that are there belonging to me may be embezzled. I have also sent your Lordships a note under my auditor's hand how Percy hath dealt with me this 3 years past, whereby, though I knew it not then, yet it may appear how he was to me.'[19]

Percy is still presented by Northumberland as a family problem, as a gap in the loyalty to his household and a disruption to the affairs of his estate rather than a link to treason that could ensnare the earl himself. Whichever argument the earl made, it brought him under suspicion. If Percy was ill-affected and untrustworthy, why had Northumberland appointed him to a position of trust in the king's bodyguard? If he was close and trusted, would Percy have let his master die in the explosion? Would not dinner at Syon on the day before have been an opportunity for a warning to be given? The earl tried to argue that the trust between them was of long standing but that Percy had broken it and that he had only recently become aware of the breach. Thus, he had been too trusting but not malicious in appointing Percy a gentleman pensioner. Percy, far from being grateful, had implicated the earl in the king's failure to grant toleration to Catholics, and subsequently, though he had his own uses for the earl's money, he had too little regard for him to wish to preserve him. This was not in itself an incredible sequence of events and is quite in keeping with what emerged about Percy's character from other sources, but Northumberland's lack of judgement of that character and the peril in which it left the king remained strong evidence against him.

Four days later, Northumberland sent a reminder about the sealing up of Percy's study and the protection of the bonds inside from appropriation by his debtors. He graciously excused Salisbury and the other Lords Commissioners their forgetfulness on the grounds that they had been busy investigating the Plot, as if that business of state were somehow distinct, distant and a distraction from the really important business of his household finances. This was an even more impressive piece of self-interested insularity than it first appears, since the main plot business of the intervening days had been the questioning of the earl himself.

At this stage, the earl of Northumberland's detention was still described as a temporary precaution, but suspicion was growing. No one could quite credit that Percy would have let the earl die in the Lords. Northumberland was examined by Sir Edward Coke on his role in the Plot. His questioning again reflected Coke's twin obsessions, the earl's connections with his old friend Sir Walter Raleigh, and treasonable astrology and prophecy in 'casting of the king's nativity' (horoscope), a crime in which Dudley Carleton, then serving in the earl's household, was again implicated. After an initial period of volunteering evidence as it occurred to him or as he remembered it, Northumberland was questioned more formally against a set of prepared questions. There was still an air of deference about the whole business, but it was an unwelcome step closer to being considered a suspect rather than a well-connected witness.

Northumberland's examination over 22 and 23 November by Sir Edward Coke was so heavily revised it needed to be reproduced in fair copy to be intelligible. Northumberland's replies are reported by the clerk in the third person.

> He employed him [Thomas Percy] in divers things and trusted him with little at the first, and after he made him Constable of Alnwick but durst not let him finger any of his money in divers years, but joined Wycliffe with him and after he went with his Lordship into the Low Countries and returned with him and Percy moved his Lordship to make himself known to the King in the late Queen's time which this examinate did.[20]

There is a lot to unpick in this evidence since it is compressed in style as well as chronology. Northumberland's evidence as taken down on 23 November reads oddly next to Thomas Wintour's eloquent, level-headed narrative of the same day. By comparison, it is arcane, technical and obscure.

Unravelling the syntax and causation in this evidence is difficult enough. Deducing Percy and Northumberland's relationship and the degree of trust the earl had in him is more difficult still. He did not trust Percy with money and set a watch on him, but gave him a position of responsibility and travelled with him. Time and again, Percy emerges as a prompter of the earl's actions rather than a servant of his will. They seemed locked together in a loveless embrace like a blackmailer and his victim, suspicious but inseparable for reasons of security, the power seeming to reside with the servant rather than the master for reasons outsiders could never fully understand. Percy initiated the dinner conversation at Syon on 4 November and stayed there for two hours. Could it really be only on mundane estate business? Was Northumberland really prompted by Percy to put himself forward in negotiations with James at the end of Queen Elizabeth's reign? Was this a subtle attempt by Northumberland to involve the king and remind him of his own trust in Percy during the secret correspondence about the succession in England? Northumberland's chief fault in trusting Percy was shared, the earl seemed to suggest, by the man Percy most wanted to destroy.

Similarly, Northumberland's presumption in speaking for the Catholic party in England was placed by the earl in the context of the role James asked him to play in smoothing the path to succession. James had allowed him to give hopes to the English Catholics to reduce the possibility of their dissent. There was some coherence and justice in these arguments, but again Northumberland's political antennae seemed to let him down. An argument that his errors of judgement – which cast suspicion on him and suggested an involvement in treason – had been shared or prompted by the king himself was never going to be accepted.

There were familiar distractions too. For a man who spent so much time heaping scorn on Catholic 'superstition', Coke placed a great deal of importance on prophecy and astrology. Guy Fawkes had been identified by Coke and by the king as a 'desperate fellow' likely to have been influenced by prophecy about James's destruction. Now Northumberland was implicated in the casting of the king's nativity, perilously close to the treasonable activity of 'compassing', or predicting, the king's death. Northumberland argued that the nativity was simply a sensible precaution designed to reassure the king's potential English subjects that the new monarch would provide a sustained and lasting succession to the throne and that it had done so. Northumberland made light of the credence he and Dudley Carlton gave to the nativity, but would an unfavourable prediction have prejudiced the earl or others against James's claim to the throne? The circumstances seemed to be damning according to Sir Edward Coke, given the context in which the nativity was done and the people involved in it.

Inevitably, it seemed, Sir Walter Raleigh was implicated, and the air of rebellion clung to it, given the evidence that the nativity was cast at Essex House. Astronomer and mathematician Thomas Harriot, a link between Raleigh and Northumberland, who had the knowledge to interpret the nativity and the rumoured impiety to use it, seemed to be the originating genius. Nathaniel Torporley gave evidence that the nativity had been cast at the beginning of the king's reign out of Harriot's desire to see 'how it did agree with his happy fortune in coming to the crown'. Torporley hastily added that 'he looked upon it but did not judge upon it or make deductions about the king's life'.[21] This was the main point of the exercise, of course, but the dangerous bit. Harriot and Northumberland, Torporley said, produced only a rough-and-ready version, Harriot 'being loth to take the pains' to produce a fully methodical one. Torporley claimed he had only talked to Northumberland directly 'before Queen Elizabeth's death'. Therefore, there was no evidence as to how or whether Northumberland 'judged' the nativity to make treasonable predictions about the king's life. Harriot was imprisoned briefly on the basis of this evidence and his house at Syon was searched and all those party to making the nativity were questioned.

Sir John Popham suggested further questions to Northumberland about the involvement of Sir Walter Raleigh. He was also questioned about his attempts to buy horses at that time because of possible links to Thomas Wintour's plan to supply English cavalry for a Spanish invasion. While Coke, Popham and the other senior commissioners followed their own particular lines of enquiry, details from local law officers continued to arrive. An inquisition into Robert Catesby's lands produced evidence of the hunt for the conspirators in Middlesex on the day before Catesby and Percy made their last stand at Holbeach in Staffordshire:

> This examinate sayeth that he being the Bailey of Elthorne, having received one of His Majesty's proclamations for the apprehending of Thomas Percy, he forthwith sent to Mr Hawtrey esquire being the next Justice of the Peace for the said county, informing him of Mr Catesby's house, that it was a very likely place, for the receipt and harbouring of such persons, who immediately came, and with this examinate together with the Constables of Weybridge and Hillingdon and to the number of forty persons went and beset the said Catesby's house called Moorcrofts which was then and is now in the tenure of Sir Charles Percy. Knight, whereunto the said Justice and Constables entered, being the seventh day of November and there made diligent search for the said Percy but could not find him.[22]

During the day of 7 November, the Catesby property Moorcrofts, at Hillingdon in Middlesex, was searched by a group of about forty men including the local constables looking for Thomas Percy. Local intelligence about Catesby's house and his likely visitors was very good. John Tupper, a local bailiff, receiving the proclamation against Thomas Percy of 5 November, went to the local justice of the peace to say that they were very likely to find Percy at Catesby's house, where he had undoubtedly been many times. They had no means of knowing that Percy and Catesby were about to die together a hundred miles away, or probably even whether Catesby himself was involved. It cannot have helped Northumberland's case that Catesby had leased the house from his brother.

On 18 November, the search was renewed and Catesby's goods at Moorcrofts were confiscated. There they found Owen Midford, servant to Northumberland's brother Sir Charles Percy, who had lived at Moorcrofts rent-free for several months before taking a lease on the place in 1605. Catesby's servant Yeomans came to Richard Robinson, another local officer, on Tuesday 19 November saying he had hidden £54 in money in a cloak bag in one of the outbuildings at Moorcrofts where the saddles and bridles were, to avoid the search. When he came back, he found the bag but the money gone, adding with the suspect air of a man making an insurance claim that £34 of this money was his own and only the residue belonged to Catesby! The cook of the house was suspected of the theft, having been suddenly 'very desirous to go to London', and was there tracked down by Robinson and Yeomans, in a way that was once again efficient but slightly slapstick at the same time. Out of this document too came evidence that Catesby had used the house as a base from which to travel to Royston, where the king was hunting in the weeks before the discovery of the Plot.

In many ways, Catesby's particular personality, charismatic but desperate, shaped the Plot and made it difficult for the investigating authorities to understand. All their instincts and every precedent told the investigators that it was highly unlikely that the plotters would act without popular support, the patronage of an aristocrat or foreign aid. In fact, Catesby's ability to persuade and motivate, together with his impatience with those he could not control, made his lone, desperate attempt very characteristic. What evidence would he have given his interrogators had he not been killed in the siege at Holbeach? No doubt, he would have treated the assembled councillors as if they were his captives, rather than the other way around. Would he have regaled them with grand plans and links to 'great men' and foreign powers, which he had kept 'close', even from the other conspirators? So many of the leads followed by the investigators seemed to be based on hints from evidence about Catesby. Would he have substantiated these, or simply convinced the authorities that the plotters had indeed acted alone and that a wider rebellion was simply the product of Catesby's fevered imagination?

Perhaps fortunately, in Thomas Wintour the authorities had in their hands a historian of the Plot who was less wild, boastful and vain than Catesby or Percy, a man who had reported his role in the bloody conflict in the Low Countries with an ironic detachment that he now brought to his role in the present intrigue. Sir William Waad wrote to Salisbury of the financial concerns of his prisoners in the Tower, well-connected Rookwood deserted by his rich friends and Digby with trunks of money in London, complaining that the sheriff of Warwickshire had taken £100 from him. He also reported that Thomas Wintour was now sufficiently recovered from his injuries sustained at Holbeach to make a written confession.

Endless controversy has raged about the versions and authenticity of Thomas Wintour's confessions. The National Archives copy, Sir Edward Coke's 'corrected' version of Wintour's confession, omits some of the human element from his account, distances Monteagle and makes Jesuit involvement explicit. But it agrees substantially with the original at Hatfield House. Unjustifiable weight has been attached to the fact that the date of the National Archives version has been altered from the date the copy was made to the date of the original confession, and that the handwriting and 'signature' are quite obviously not Wintour's own. The use of fair copies of important evidence in legal cases, in the absence of the photocopier, was perfectly standard in the period and had been established as admissible in court following a precedent set by William Myll, clerk of Star Chamber, who had copied depositions taken in the High Court of Delegates for use in his own court in 1603. What is very nearly unforgeable about both the original confession and the copy is Wintour's literary style, the humorous rhythms and cadences of his prose and the naturalness of the dialogue, which historians have found so irresistible. Even after the attempts in official circles to make the plotters seem less human, something of the wit of his notes from the Low Countries remains in the style of the confession:

On Robert Catesby: 'How necessary it was not to forsake our country (for he knew then I had a resolution to go over) but to deliver her from out of the servitude where she remained or at least to assist her with our uttermost endeavours. I answered that I had often hazarded my life upon far lighter terms and now I would not refuse any good occasion wherein I might do service for the Catholic Cause, but for myself I knew no means probable to succeed. He said that he had bethought him of a way at one instant to deliver us from all our bonds and without any foreign help to replant again the Catholic Religion and withal told me in a word, it was to blow up the parliament house with gunpowder, for said he in that place have they done us all the mischief, and perchance God hath designed that place for their punishment.

I wondered at the strangeness of the conceit and told him, true it was that this strake at the root and would breed a confusion fit to beget new alterations, but if it should not take effect, as

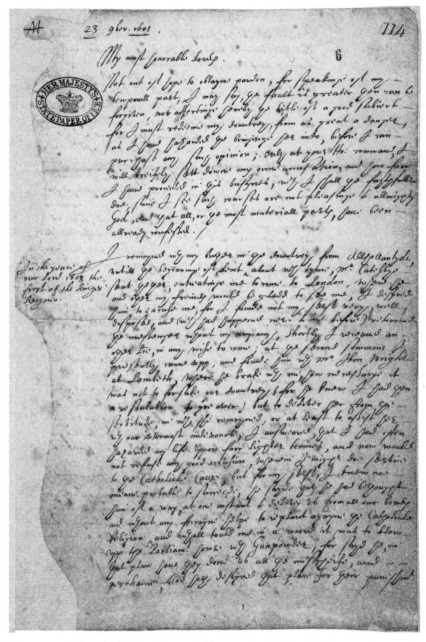

Fair copy of Thomas Wintour's confession, annotated by the king, 23 November 1605. So much of the official version of events rests on Wintour's evidence that debate has raged about its authenticity. (TNA SP 14/216/114)

most of this nature miscarried, the scandal would be so great, which the Catholic religion might hereby sustain, as not only our enemies but our friends also would with good cause condemn us.

He told me the nature of the disease required so sharp a remedy.'

On Thomas Percy: 'The first word he spake (after he came into our company) was Shall we always, gentlemen, talk and never do anything?'

There is perhaps in Thomas Percy's famous challenge to his fellow 'gentlemen' a greater meaning than there would be in any modern equivalent phrase. 'Gentlemen' is not just an antiquated polite form of 'men'. It is a reminder of their rank, and with it a reminder of two other things: their obligation to shape and organise their society in keeping with that rank, and of the punitive laws against Catholics which currently prevented them from doing so. If they were to play the role in society they were born to, rather than simply moaning about their plight, they would have to do it in defiance of the law. There was also in that defiance a sense that they could only rely on their own rank and resources and could not pin their hopes on aristocratic allies acting for them.

It is difficult to gauge the true attitude of the plotters to 'great men' or the support they might receive from them. Percy and Catesby had alternately boasted of their aristocratic connections and belittled their patrons for the ease with which they duped them. Financial contributions were expected from the rich recruits Digby, Tresham and Rookwood, and also from Thomas Percy himself, who promised 'all he could get of the earl of Northumberland's rents', with 'which was around four thousand pounds' helpfully interpolated above the line.

Thomas Wintour seemed less inclined to boast or belittle. He followed Lord Monteagle out of financial necessity, but spent little energy in protecting or implicating him. Likewise, he served Spain in order to gain pensions and military preferment from it, the gap in patronage left by the death of the earl of Essex. He seems a much more reliable narrator. Though devout and committed to the Plot, he did not react to the explosion at Holbeach as a sign of divine displeasure, rather as an accident of war, like the effect of the sea on the Siege of Ostend. His reaction was practical: fight to the last with the weapons available. Having furnished the authorities with much of what they needed to know of the plotters and their motivations, and having established his own credibility, Wintour went on to tell them rather more than they wanted to hear.

That same day, while the Attorney General sought to ensnare Northumberland and the Principal Secretary recorded the wonderfully lucid, literary but embarrassing narrative of Thomas Wintour, Lord Chief Justice Sir John Popham was on much humbler duty, albeit in the same cause. His task was the examination of Harry Watts, husbandman of Curry Rivel in Somerset, who had evidence that Sir Walter Raleigh still constituted a party against the king and was preparing an armed rising after his release from the Tower. Northumberland was said to be working for Raleigh's release, which by extension must mean he was implicated in that plot too, perhaps intended as part of the wider rising after the explosion.[23] Somehow, Raleigh was reported to be organising the gathering of provisions and arms at his Sherborne estate from the Tower. Though this all sounds very unlikely to us, it would certainly have fed the obsession of the Attorney General that Raleigh had orchestrated the Gunpowder Plot from the Tower and that powerful forces were at work to free him and place him in a position of authority when the opportunity arose.

In a note to the earl of Salisbury dated 26 November, Sir William Waad was still worrying about the conspirators' embroidered scarves and Ambrose Rookwood's 'very fair Hungarian horseman's coat, lined all with velvet, and other apparel exceeding costly, not fit for his degree'.[24] Waad enclosed Thomas Wintour's examination of the same day about his mission to Spain in 1602 and his audience with the king. There was a connection: the importance of horses. 'In all attempts upon England the greatest difficulty was ever found to be the transportation of horse.' Wintour's solution was simple: Spain must bestow pensions on him and the other angry young men who had lost patronage through the fall of the earl of Essex the year before so that they could bring 1,000 to 1,500 horses to the Spanish service once the invasion had landed. Coke's point about the Gunpowder Plot arising from the 'ashes of old plots' certainly applies to Catesby's cover for his preparations for the Midlands rebellion. He raised, quite legally, a company to serve Spain in Flanders. How could the authorities be sure that those forces would not be used at home, either now or in the future? James certainly cooled on the idea of English gentlemen gathering arms and horses to fight for Spain.

But was there also a plan to attack from the north? Sir Everard Digby's confession on the same day pointed to another possible northern rebellion and other sources of assistance. Offering his evidence in his own hand rather than responses to questions taken down by a clerk – an indication of his status, at least in his own mind – on the same day that the earl of Northumberland had been compelled to give evidence in answer to interrogatories for the first time, Digby gave insight into Catesby's plans after the 'first design', the gunpowder explosion, had taken effect. 'Which, he said, should no sooner had been done but he would have sent my Lord of Northumberland and my Lord Dacre into the North to have raised those forces there. But that they knew of this first plot or this employment is more than I know.'[25]

Catesby seemed confident that these lords would have survived the blast, so presumably they would have been warned in some way. More strikingly still, he seemed confident of getting the northern lords to do his bidding, and Digby himself does not seem surprised at Catesby's presumption that he could. The pieces of the jigsaw, linking 'Great Men' to Catesby's plot, seemed to be coming together. Four days after his lengthy examination on 23 November, Northumberland was dispatched to the Tower.

In the days that followed, Thomas Wintour's evidence about Northumberland's faith, or lack thereof – 'in the matter of religion the earl troubled not much himself'[26] – seemed designed to impress the Commissioners with the earl's lack of Catholic conviction. But like so much else about the earl, the effect was double-edged. On the face of it, this evidence was helpful to the earl because it showed a consistent lack of religious commitment to the Catholic cause when plots arose, whether in 1603 or 1605, but from a man of Wintour's deep conviction it was not a compliment. A lack of religious conviction – even worse, the suspicion of atheism – would be a source of popular rumour and engender a suspicion in official circles that such a man could not be trusted as a councillor as his opinions were not grounded in Christian faith.

Thomas Wintour went on to refer to communication with the plotters from Lord Monteagle in relation to their intrigues with Spain. Again he emphasised the importance of their rank in society, which was elevated enough to be credible to those they contacted overseas but not so prominent as to excite the suspicions of the authorities. Monteagle's name was hastily scratched out of this evidence and then shamelessly pasted over.

> In the message that was delivered me from my [Lord Monteagle], Catesby and Tresham I was wished to say that those three were of a quality most convenient, for if greater personages should have sent, the state' of England would have had them in more suspicion.

With the arrival of 'greater personages' like the Lords Northumberland and Montague in the Tower, Guy Fawkes found himself moved to more obscure lodgings. This reflected the importance of social distinction even among prisoners, but also Fawkes's declining importance. New lines of enquiry among the rich and powerful were opening up. Sir William Waad, Lieutenant of the Tower, found himself running out of comfortable accommodation for all the lords being sent there. The prisoners of the succession plots of 1603 would also have to make way.

Worse still for Fawkes, Coke had not let go of the passing reference to Sir Walter Raleigh in his early confessions. Coke planned to harangue him on the subject of Sir Walter's connections with the plots of 1603, for which Raleigh had already been tried, convicted and, after a spectacular reprieve from execution, imprisoned in the Tower: 'Fawkes to be examined whether he heard not in Spain or elsewhere of the Lord Cobham's employment or any matter concerning Sir Walter Raleigh in that behalf.'

Coke was never one to let a present treason get in the way of a two-year-old vendetta. A professed traitor became a reliable government witness in the pursuit of greater prey. It is perhaps indicative of the danger of seeing the Plot in purely ideological terms that Raleigh, the great enemy of Catholic Spain, despite lack of evidence about any actual role in the Plot, was suspected by the authorities and the plotters themselves as a likely man to support a

Further evidence of Thomas Wintour, 25 November 1605. The reference to Lord Monteagle in the opening line has been deleted. (TNA SP 14/216/117)

Catholic coup d'état in England. Raleigh's thwarted ambition and reported dislike of his Scots king were quite enough to make him the focus of discontented parties of all convictions.

In his examination on 29 November, Francis Tresham admitted his desire to save Lord Monteagle from the intended explosion by covert means, 'to deliver myself from the infamous brand of an accuser and to save his life which in all true rules I was bound to do'. His evidence, though, implicated Monteagle in the Spanish mission of Thomas Wintour; here again Monteagle's name was pasted out.

A. Denies knowledge of planned invasion by Spanish forces.
B. Advised to bethink himself better, denies knowledge of Thomas Wintour's mission in Spain.
C. Thought former questions were about James reign only, does remember Wintour's mission to Spain in 1602.
D. Catesby and [Monteagle] knew of the mission.[27]

The 30th saw the examination of Robert Keyes, who supervised the gunpowder at Catesby's house in Lambeth. As a servant like Thomas Bate, his testimony was expected to be more revealing about the cunning of Catesby and not so much influenced by the man's charm. Such men are much less careful about social niceties and less deferential. Keyes said Catesby was derisive about the capabilities of the House of Lords and had no real qualms about blowing up even the Catholic ones who did not escape his estimation as 'atheists fools and cowards'.[28] In Keyes' evidence, the rich men are clearly Catesby's dupes, with a suggestion that Digby, Rookwood and Tresham are being used for their money but are not exactly the brains of the operation.

Keyes' evidence was perhaps the closest other than Thomas Wintour's to giving us Catesby's true voice, and it has been much quoted as a result. Catesby, he revealed, would 'put a trick on' Lord Mordaunt to dissuade him from attending Parliament, manipulating him even in the act of saving his life, but would not tell him of the Plot 'for the chamber full of diamonds'.

·Ten days after he had reported the Plot as a fable from the safety of Paris, Dudley Carleton was under arrest in Westminster. The fable became a grim reality as the amused social commentator became a suspect. Northumberland wrote a letter supporting Carleton, 'formerly his secretary', but, perhaps prudently, did not send it. On 2 December, Carleton wrote to the earl of Salisbury in a very different tone, pleading for his freedom, having already been 'in restraint' for nine days:

From the bailiff's house in Westminster this 2nd December 1605

My Lord, I presume so much of your honourable favour that unless you thought I were well I would not lie by it this long and though for entreatment I have no cause to complain, yet I make so bold to write to your Lordship that I live in great misery. For there can be no greater burden to an honest mind than to be so long under suspicion of bearing part in so barbarous a villainy. Whereupon I beseech your Lordship and the rest of my most honourable lords that you will please to take some speedy course for your satisfaction in my behalf and whatsoever your justice shall assign me, I shall not complain of it. The greatest punishment shall be too little if the least fault can be proved against me and if nothing, I hope your Lordships in your favourable judgements will think sufficient of nine days restraint as close prisoner and so I rest most humbly at your Lordship's disposal DC.[29]

The note still displays the liveliness of his usual gossipy correspondence, but with an undertone of considerable strain. If the least offence really does merit the greatest punishment, he had certainly earned it by helping Thomas Percy obtain his lease, aside from the business of casting the king's nativity. It was a dangerous game to play.

Surviving letters show that Carleton was still suspected in the weeks that followed, with the prisoner using the ingenious argument on 12 December that his continued incarceration was unfair since it made him look guilty. He was still pleading to Salisbury at Christmas that he was 'a solitary prisoner at this merry time'. Eventually the Principal Secretary did authorise his release, but as late as the end of February 1606 Carleton wrote to John Chamberlain from self-imposed exile, hoping to 'take away the scent of gunpowder' in the Chilterns. There he took advice on his further advancement from

Sir Walter Cope, one of the lesser commissioners, to whom he had addressed pleading notes at Christmas. Once his gaoler, Cope had now become his host, and the narrow line between suspicion and social acceptance had been successfully crossed.

On the same day as Carleton's pleading letter, Ambrose Rookwood was examined twice. His loss of social standing preoccupied him, his confessions reflecting on the quality of his horsemanship and horses and his loss of the latter. As Sir Everard Digby had done, Rookwood suggested that Catesby was being 'close' and not telling the wealthy late arrivals the whole truth, including the possibility of the Plot's discovery. On Monday 4 November, Catesby had employed him in buying 'necessaries' while Catesby and John Wright fled London without him. Thanks to his horses, he had been able to overtake them. Six days later, Sir William Waad revealed to Salisbury that 'John and Christopher Wright were schoolfellows of Fawkes ... Tesmond the Jesuit was at that time a schoolfellow also with them, so was this crew here all brought up together.' He confirmed John Grant has four of the finest horses in the realm and that Rookwood was still preoccupied with the fate of his animals.

Rookwood's lavish riding habit and the quality of the horses, which the plotters might have been able to put at the disposal of an invading Spanish army, were perhaps sufficient worry for Sir William Waad, but on 9 December 1605 he had to report the appearance of yet more gunpowder very close to home, this batch bound for Spain.

> Great complaint is daily made to me of a ship of 60 or 70 tons which has lain these 3 weeks over against the Tower, laden with powder for Spain. And I now understand there are 100 barrels of powder in her, laden by one Barber the owner. It is much murmured that so great a quantity should at this time go forth to those parts; and the hovering and stay of the ship with so great a quantity of powder in her at this very season, when such a devilish practice was intended by powder, breed jealousy and suspicion.[30]

There is an almost comical aspect to this situation, but is a clear corrective to those who imagine the government monopoly on gunpowder in London meant tight control on its sale and movement through the capital. While Guy Fawkes was being questioned inside the Tower, nearly three times the amount of powder he needed to destroy the government was floating past him on the Thames. How secure was this cargo, and how secure were the prisoners in the Tower? Was this the ammunition for another plot against the state?

The other preoccupation of Waad's note to Salisbury was the sudden boldness and visibility of Sir Walter Raleigh. Raleigh was closely monitored in the Tower but had sufficient freedom of movement to be visible to onlookers. His renewed confidence came after an appearance before the Lords, which was taken as a sign that he was preparing to lead an anti-government party. At this distance, it is difficult to ascertain just how much this vexed Waad. Was he simply reporting a couple of disconcerting coincidences, or did it seem possible that a fresh attempt on the state was being planned, with the liberation of his most dangerous prisoners as part of the enterprise? Raleigh's wild denials of involvement with the Plot were too filled with incendiary inside information to be recorded, sadly; 'fitter to be related than written'.[31]

On 12 December, Waad also had worrying news for Lord Salisbury regarding Monteagle's debts to Thomas Percy, which he had uncovered as a further potential reason why Percy might wish to preserve him:

> Lord Monteagle has £500 of Percy's wife for which he paid £50 interest yearly; and that £25 due at Michaelmas was paid to him about the time that Percy was here, and that Thomas Percy received the same of him. You hereby see some reason why, besides the affection borne by Percy to the Lord Monteagle he and his wife had cause to warn him to be absent from that destruction intended against the rest in regard of the £500 in his hands.[32]

Given the wish to preserve Monteagle from any public connection with the plotters, there was little hope that the Commissioners would seize on this link in their investigation; nonetheless, there was continued interest from the Exchequer concerning the valuation and disposal of the plotters' estates.

Even more extraordinary evidence was about to be volunteered. From this period comes our next glimpse of Sir Everard Digby in his leading man role, acting in a way none of the other surviving plotters would have dared. We must imagine his state of mind as he wrote to Lord Salisbury with all his erstwhile confidence, offering his services as a diplomat between the king and the pope. It is one of the more remarkable and bizarre documents to come out of the Plot. The letter is undated but its social ease and assumption of bargaining power have so amazed historians that some have assumed it must come from the period before the discovery of the Plot, even before Digby had joined the conspiracy. It is quite clear from the latter half of the letter, however, that Digby is writing in full awareness that he has forfeited his life by what he calls 'our offence'. Again, the overriding sense we get from this elegant, literate letter is Digby's idea of his own social standing and importance. The letter begins recalling a conversation with Salisbury held months, if not years, before 'when his Majesty had done nothing against the Catholics' and aims to continue it as if nothing unpleasant has intervened. He has, it is true, been involved in a failed treason, but this should simply convince Salisbury that Catholic discontents are serious. Aside from this minor peccadillo he is still Sir Everard Digby, darling of the court, confidant of the most important English priests and the 'best sort' of English Catholics. He remains the ideal man to represent the government he has just tried to destroy in negotiations with the papacy, to relieve the king from the threat of excommunication and reconcile him to his discontented Catholic subjects. Only he can secure the king's safety and prevent further rebellions and assassination attempts such as the one he had helped to fund and which had just been thwarted.

The letter is in fact consistent with his confessions and perhaps not really that wrong in contending that the government should view the Plot, which had been stopped before it did much harm, as a minor infringement, despite what we now know of it. It was a bargaining chip, which could now be chanced at the table. He *was* in his own

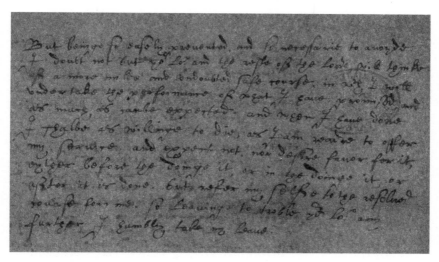

Sir Everard Digby to the earl of Salisbury, calendared December 1605. Even as a prisoner with no hope of reprieve Digby saw himself playing a major role in negotiations between the king and the pope. (TNA SP 14/17/10)

mind potentially diplomatically useful. Digby's letter is wild in places, but the report of his conversation with Salisbury on the dilemmas of Jacobean religious policy sounds genuine, and his attack on James's broken promises have been widely echoed:

> If your Lordship apprehend it to be worth the doing, I should be glad to be your instrument, from no hope to put off from myself any punishment, but only that I wish safety to the king and ease to Catholics. If your Lordship and the State think it fit to run another course and deal severely with Catholics, give me leave to tell you what I fear will happen, which in brief will be massacres, rebellions and desperate attempts against the king and state. For it is generally received reason among the Catholics that there is not that expecting and suffering course now to be run that was in the queen's time who was the last of her line and last in expectance to run violent courses against Catholics. For it was hoped that the king that now is would have been at least free from persecuting as his promise was before coming into his realm and as divers his promises

have been since his coming, saying that he would take no soul, money nor blood, which it appeared was the whole body of the Council's pleasure when they sent for divers of the best sort of Catholics (as Sir Thomas Tresham and others) and told them it was the king's pleasure to forgive the payment of Catholics so long as they should carry themselves dutifully and well. All these promises every man sees broken. And to thrust them further in despair most Catholics take note of a vehement book written by Mr Attorney whose drift (as I have heard) is to prove that only to be a Catholic is to be a traitor, which book coming forth after the breach of so many promises and before the ending of such a violent parliament can work no less effect in men's minds as a belief that every Catholic will be brought within this compass before the king and state have done with them and I know, as the Priest himself told me, that if he had not hindered, there had somewhat been attempted before our offence to give ease to Catholics. But being easily prevented and so necessary to avoid, I doubt not but your Lordship and the rest of the lords will think of more mild and undoubted safe course in which I will undertake the performance of that I have promised and as much as can be expected and when I have done I shall be as willing to die as I am ready to offer my service and expect not nor desire favour for it, either before doing it, or in the doing it, or after it is done, but refer myself to the resolved course for me. So fearing to trouble your Lordship further, I humbly take my leave, your Lordship's poor beadsman Eve: Digby.

Even at the last, there is very little humility. In offering himself as Salisbury's 'beadsman', he casts himself in role of a man of prayer whose efforts might ease Salisbury's soul. Essentially, it is an assertion of the superiority and efficacy of his own religious beliefs. Having failed to put Salisbury in heaven with gunpowder, he offers to get him there in other ways. Unsurprisingly, Salisbury rejected Digby's offer. Can he really have hoped that Salisbury would send him as an emissary to the papacy? What was the Plot hindered by priests 'before our offence'? Digby hinted he knew much more about plots against the king than his initial evidence had admitted.

Meanwhile, Digby's wife Mary was facing up to the financial consequences of her husband's treason and battling with zealous local authorities in Buckinghamshire who had stripped their house of their possessions. She, too, wrote to the earl of Salisbury, more practically and with greater success than her husband had done, for relief from the depredations of the sheriff. Again, it is an indication of the social standing of the Digbys that her claims were investigated and found support within the Exchequer and the Privy Council. Thus began the slow official process of restoring her property to her. On 3 December 1605, Mary pleaded her innocence of her husband's crime and for the restoration of her property, complaining of corruption of the law officers, who pocketed the proceeds of her Buckinghamshire estates, which had come through her inheritance rather than her marriage. She enclosed a note from an 'honest gentleman' confirming the extent of the looting:

> He has not left the worth of a penny in the grounds house or walls, not so much as great tables and standing chairs as could not be removed without sawing and cutting to pieces. He permitted base people to ransack all even unto her closet and sold cattle and grain and other things for half their worth and gave other things away. It is said the sheriff will get above £1000 underhand by this booty.

Her rank and gender were still strong cards. 'Yet these suits are far below the principal of her desires, which is the life of her husband, to obtain which no condition shall be too hard.'[33]

Sir Thomas Fleming, Chief Baron of the Exchequer, agreed with her that 'the sheriff has dealt unjustly against the law and contrary to the instructions from the Exchequer', short-changing the Crown to enrich himself, a crime more important to the government that the injustice to Mary.[34] A list of Digby goods carried away in January was properly appraised. Rights of property were still important, even in treason cases, and for practical purposes it was important that Digby should be able to continue to pay for his imprisonment.

In less salubrious accommodation than Digby, Thomas Bate, interrogated by a lesser commission of investigators, was less concerned with the loss of his property than the loss of his life. Though Bate was a yeoman rather than a gentleman, he was a servant who had servants of his own and a man of some importance in the organisation of the Gunpowder Plot. He appears rather like one of the witty servants in a Shakespeare play, with a clearer head than his masters, who are too wrapped up in their own preoccupations to take the commonsense view of the consequences of their actions. As Robert Catesby's confidential assistant, according to his own evidence, he guessed the nature of the Plot, despite the efforts of the gentlemen to keep it secret. His educated guess necessitated his admission to the conspiracy, and having thus earned the right to participate he presents himself in his evidence as a practical and determined man drawn in by his social superiors but without their recklessness or ideology, cagier than the gentlemen whose actions had forfeited his life. Unlike Catesby, Bate was not full of philosophical justifications, but proud of his role and practical nous. Had it been left to me, he implies, there would have been less risk and a greater chance of success.

By the time Bate gave his own evidence, the authorities had a good idea of his character and importance from the testimony of his wife Martha, who was examined on 8 November, while he was still on the run after leaving the gentlemen to their suicidal last stand at Holbeach. She gave evidence that her husband left her on 5 November, taking five or six pistols with him, and ordered her to convey to Lady Catesby certain trunks of armour that had lain there since the late queen's death. Bate himself gave evidence of 4 December that Catesby had sent him to look for lodgings 'near the Parliament house', a hint as to the nature of his master's business, which he soon took up. Bate was no doubt keen to show the trust Catesby reposed in him and his own acumen in deducing what was going on, but this seems a bit amateurish, a top-secret treasonable mission entrusted to a third party not yet sworn to secrecy. In fact, the whole early stage of the Plot as Bate describes it seems to be a bit like a game, buoyed by Catesby's presence and self-confidence, until the scene shifts suddenly to 6 November at Huddington, when they

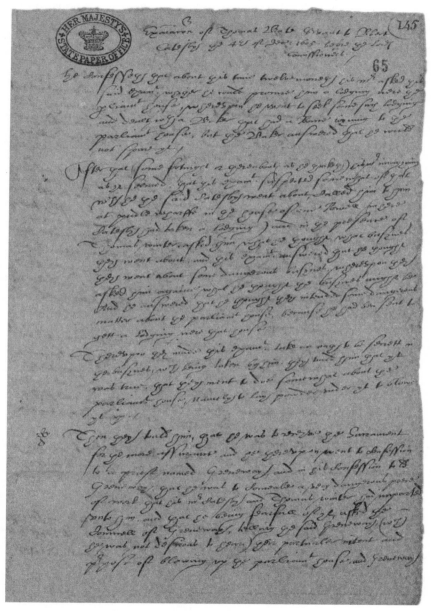

As one of the 'lesser' prisoners, Bate's confession was witnessed by investigators of lower rank but his evidence was as literate as that of any of the gentlemen and betrayed a certain ironic wit. (TNA SP 14/216/145)

are all as good as dead. Even here, there is an element of bravado, of gestures rather than actions. Nonetheless, Bate was not one to hang around when Catesby and John Wright suggested a poetic suicide pact at Holbeach using the remaining gunpowder:

> He confesseth that about this time twelvemonth his master asked this examinate, whether he could procure him a lodging near the Parliament House whereupon he went to seek some such lodging and dealt with a baker that had a room joining to the Parliament House, but the baker answered that he could not spare it. After that (some fortnight or thereabouts as he thinketh) his master imagining as it seemed that this examinate suspected somewhat of that, that he, the said Catesby, went about, called him to him at Puddle Wharf at the house of one Powell (where Catesby had taken a lodging) and in the presence of Thomas Wintour asked him 'what he thought what business they went about'. And this examinate answered that he thought they went about some dangerous business, whereupon they asked him again, 'what he thought the business might be', and he answered that he thought they intended some dangerous matter about the Parliament House because he had been sent to get a lodging near that House. Whereupon they made this examinate take an oath to be secret in the business, which being taken by him, they told him that it was true that they meant to do somewhat about the Parliament House, namely to lay powder under it to blow it up. Then they told him he was to receive the sacrament for the more assurance, and he thereupon went to confession to a priest named Greenway and in his confession told Greenway he was to conceal a very dangerous piece of work that his master Catesby and Thomas Wintour had imparted unto him, and that he, being fearful of it, asked the counsel of Greenway, telling the said Greenway (which he was not desirous to hear) the particular purpose and intent of blowing up the Parliament House; and Greenway the Priest thereto said that he would take no notice thereof, but that he, the said examinate, should be secret in that his master imparted unto him, because it was for a good cause, and that he willed this examinate to tell no other Priest of it,

saying moreover that it was not dangerous unto him, nor any offence to conceal it. And thereupon the said Priest Greenway gave this examinate absolution and he received the sacrament in the company of his master Robert Catesby and Thomas Wintour.

He sayeth moreover that they were in consultation to send to Mr Talbot of Grafton to move him to go with them and to go unto him were named and appointed Sir Everard Digby, Stephen Littleton and Thomas Wintour, but Sir Everard Digby when he was going was stayed by the company and Stephen Littleton and Thomas Wintour only went. He sayeth also that they moved Robert Wintour to go, but he answered that he would not go; desiring to be excused for refusing, because he was in hope that Mr Talbot would be good to his wife and children. Being asked whether he hath acquainted any other Priest with the conspiracy he sayeth no. But sayeth that he confessed himself to another Priest named Hammond, at Huddington, Robert Wintour's house, but that was only for his sins and not for any other particular cause.

Bate gives us another perspective on the scene at Huddington on 6 November. He is less careful than some of the 'gentlemen' of the reputation of the Jesuits, but he was also more likely to be ill-treated by the authorities to gain incriminating evidence against them. Perhaps he was also less devout than the gentlemen, who believed they might imperil their own hopes of salvation by incriminating a priest. He suggested that Tesimond knew of the Plot from him before he had it from Catesby in July.

8

DINING WITH DANGER

On 13 December, thanks to a chance conversation with a servant, Northumberland finally remembered what had happened when Percy had visited him for dinner on 4 November, the day before the projected destruction of the Lords. Unlike lesser prisoners such as Thomas Bate, who were compelled to give evidence under threat of torture, Northumberland was still in a position to volunteer his own evidence and suggest to his fellow lords what they might make of it.

He began with a lengthy preamble on the nature of memory to explain his previous forgetfulness. As he was known to be deaf, perhaps on occasion his hearing was as selective as his memory loss. As the earl describes it, Percy leads the conversation and possibly talks about him to his disadvantage below the level of the earl's hearing. If we had a mental picture of the quaking conspirator putting his head in the lion's mouth, risking a visit to his all-powerful patron in the hope of hearing some moment's conversation which might indicate that the Plot was discovered, then the earl's version of events forces us to think again. If anything, Percy is the man with the power and information and the earl trails in his wake. Here is a glimpse of the manipulator and embezzler who used the earl's position to gain access to the royal family and was apparently happy to see him die with them.

As we sat at dinner, Percy asked Sir William Lower 'What news of the Parliament?' who answered, None that he heard of; with that Percy draws out a little paper, wherein were the sum of the articles

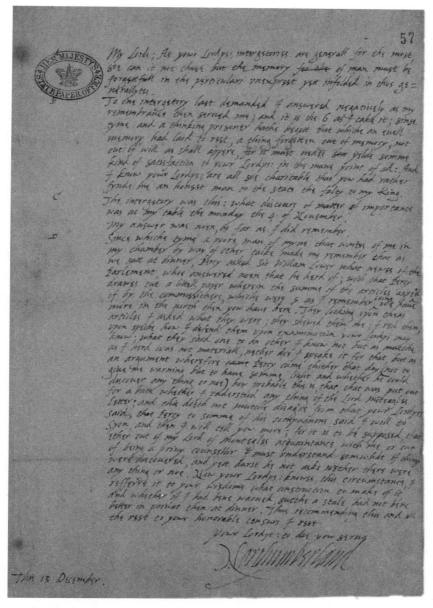

Northumberland to the Lords Commissioners, 13 December 1605. The earl's account of his dinner with Thomas Percy on the eve of the Plot's discovery confirms something of Percy's own private bragging about his ability to bamboozle his master. (TNA SP14/17/39)

agreed by the commissioners, which were nine as I remember, saying 'We have in the North more than you have here', they looking upon these articles, I asked what they were, they showed them me, I read them, upon speech how I defend them upon examination your lordships may know, what they said to one another I know not, but as much as I heard was not material, nor do I speak it for that, but as an argument wherefore Percy came thither that day (not to give me warning but to have some light and whether he could discover anything or no), how probable this is, that, that was put out for a bait, whether I understood any thing of the Lord Monteagle's letter; and this does not that muchly disagree from that your lordships said, that Percy to some of his companions said, I will to Syon, and then I will tell you more; for it is to be supposed, that either out of my Lord Monteagle's acquaintance with me, or out of being a Privy Councillor, I must understand somewhat if things were discovered and yet durst he not ask whether there were anything or no. Now your lordships knoweth this circumstance I refer it to your wisdoms what construction to make of it and whether if I had been warned, such a tale had not been better in private than at dinner. Thus recommending this and all the rest your honourable censures, I rest your lordships: to do you service, Northumberland.

Sir William Lower had already been examined on this conversation on 2 December, but had remembered even less, even whether Thomas Harriot (the astronomer and mathematician patronised by Sir Walter Raleigh as well as Northumberland and thus also briefly a suspect in the plot) was present or not, perhaps believing nothing he said could do him any good. It is clear that anti-Scots as well as anti-Protestant feeling is preying on Percy's mind on 4 November, the mischief of Parliament in trying to move towards a Union of England and Scotland as well as its anti-Catholic legislation being sufficient cause for its destruction.

The earl was questioned repeatedly about his conduct towards Thomas Percy and the trust reposed in him, and the answers sounded unconvincing and contradictory. He thought Percy had taken the oath of allegiance though he had not administered it, and he wrote to Percy only to keep track of him, as he did not entirely trust him. But if he did not trust him, why make him a gentleman pensioner and put him so close to the king? Perhaps only James and Northumberland knew how close Percy had come to the king and the murderous opportunities he might have had in the cloak-and-dagger negotiations 'in the owl light' before James's accession in 1603.

While ostensibly there had been no change in relations with Spain, the Plot began to have its effect on foreign policy. The opportunities for Catesby and other plotters to use Spanish service as a cover to amass arms at home or as an opportunity to hone military skills for use against their own government were all too apparent. Sir Francis Vere, who had faced Thomas Wintour and Guy Fawkes at Ostend, but whose authority had been undermined by the peace with Spain, had now returned to the English garrison at Brill. On 15 December, he wrote to the earl of Salisbury that the king was now less happy than before to allow English soldiers to serve with the Spanish forces in Flanders. Vere reported there was fasting and prayer among the English soldiers at Brill 'for his majesty's happy delivery from this late treason'. He had delivered letters to the States General 'that his Majesty would not suffer them to fall into utter ruin, and that to prevent further inconveniences in his own realms, he was resolved henceforth his subjects should not be so freely let pass to the Archduke's service'.[1]

As so often with James's statements, perhaps like his promises to English Catholics before his accession, this undertaking to the Dutch states held out the promise of improvement in the current situation without any definite commitment to do anything. Vere had experience of suspect Englishmen on both sides; the earl of Northumberland had objected to serving under his social inferior in the forces at Nieuwpoort and later challenged him to a duel.

While Parliament sought to limit the number of disaffected gentlemen seeking military training and opportunities with the Spanish forces in the Low Countries, it wrestled with the obstacles to bringing Plot suspects in the other direction. On 20 December, Sir Thomas Edmondes wrote to Lord Salisbury with evidence that Hugh Owen and Father William Baldwin were 'principal dealers' in the treasons of 1603 as well as the Gunpowder Plot, but there was difficulty in securing them, given the protection offered by Spain. As Thomas Wintour had found in his dealings with Spain from the other side of the argument, there were warm words but the deeds would not answer. The Archduke was astonished, said Edmondes, that Owen and Baldwin 'would so far forget themselves'. In any case 'they are not accustomed to lay hands on religious men,' especially at Christmas, 'a time of special devotion.' He would not write to Spain about Owen until it was directly demanded he do so. This delaying tactic using Catholic religiosity seemed designed to be deliberately provoking as well as potentially without limit of time.[2] Like Digby's view of the Plot as 'present mischief', Owen and Baldwin 'forgetting themselves' is presented as a piece of unintended naughtiness like taking too much wine at dinner. Other suspects Robert Persons and Edmund Baynham were reported to have been en route for England, but turned back similarly 'astonished' on news of the failure of the Plot. This supposes not only their involvement but also confidence in success, which seems unlikely.

While the alternative patronage and haven of Flanders might be subject to tighter control, there was still evidence of plotters fleeing north in the hope of sanctuary. On 18 December, Thomas Percy's servant William Talbois was examined in the North beyond the reach of the commissioners in London, before William James, Dean of the Cathedral church of Durham. This evidence provided telling insight into and dialogue from the hours after the Plot's discovery, including Thomas Percy's pessimism on 5 November. Percy and Christopher Wright rode off from the Red Lion in Gray's Inn Road on grey geldings brought, fed and watered there by Talbois and Davison. 'And this examinate holding his said master's stirrup Thomas Percy said "I am undone." "What have you done?" said this examinate "that you should say so?" who answered him again "Let it satisfy you thee I said so."'[3]

Talbois was later noted as being charged at the assizes at Newcastle for the murder of Roger Smith of Alnwick, a piece of legal business that should now continue if Talbois was not to be charged with treason in the meantime. As part of the same investigation they had apprehended an equivocating missionary priest and his clerk, now a prisoner at Hexham, 'for confessing that he gave money for the buying of powder for the late devilish attempt'.[4] How many people, how far from the supposedly close-knit secret group of core conspirators in London knew enough about the Plot, at least in outline, to support it financially?

Even in London Sir William Waad felt his authority under threat and felt compelled to link his place as Lieutenant of the Tower to the authority of the king. On 21 December 1605, he reported to the earl of Salisbury[5] that the Mayor had made a show of strength at the Tower.

This was unseasonable – if not treasonable – and certainly against the command of the Privy Council. As normal life resumed in London disputes between officers began to resurface, a reminder that national unity and rejoicing at the preservation of the Crown were only temporary.

Soon Waad had more urgent business to report. In the dark night of the Tower Francis Tresham finally succumbed to illness in a state of physical agony and moral and spiritual confusion. The main preoccupation of his keeper, Sir William Waad, apart from the disposal of the diseased corpse, was the social standing of the man and his powerful friends, who seemed confident of his acquittal had he been tried for his part in the Plot.

As I certified to your lordship there was no hope of recovery in Tresham, so it will please you to understand that he died this night, about two of the clock after midnight, with very great pain; for though his spirits were much spent, and his body dead, a-lay above two hours in departing. It may please your Honourable Lordship; I may know his Majesty's pleasure for the burying of him, both because it will not be possible to keep him, for he smelt exceedingly when I was with him yesterday in the afternoon, and I perceive means will be made to his Majesty, to have his body begged, for I find his friends were marvellous confident, if he had escaped this sickness, and have given out words in this place that they feared not the course of justice. So expecting what direction I shall fellow, I commit your lordship to God's protection, this Monday the 23rd of December 1605.

Tresham's prominence as a man of considerable landed estates bequeathed a legacy of difficulties to the authorities. He died unconvicted of any offence, the evidence against him was no more, perhaps no less, strong than that against Lord Monteagle. The official narrative could never allow him the credit for writing and sending the letter, which his brother-in-law had earned for receiving and disclosing it. The government faced a long and thorny path to having his goods and lands confiscated as a traitor because he had never been indicted. The House of Commons, for all its initial elation and desire for justice against the plotters of its destruction, was reluctant to undo the conventions on which the power of its members rested.

If Tresham, the recent head of a prominent Northamptonshire family, might forfeit his property merely on suspicion, what precedent might this set for the MPs themselves?

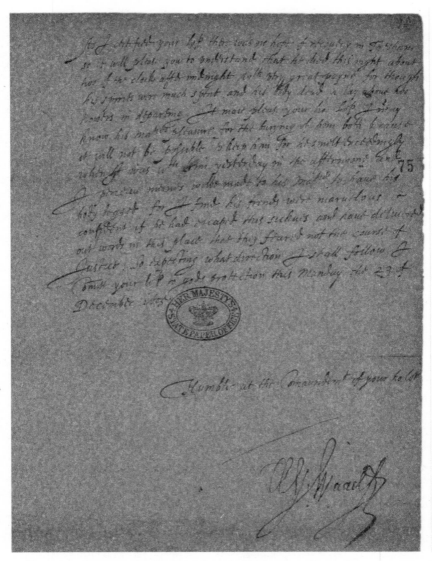

William Waad reports the death of Francis Tresham, 23 December 1605. Waad feared that someone like Tresham from a prominent county family would have sufficient 'friends' to oppose legal moves against him and his estates. (TNA SP 14/17/56)

Tresham's confessions certainly made difficult reading, not just for other landed gentlemen but also for the commissioners attempting to penetrate the layers of equivocation and establish the true role of the Jesuits in the Plot. In his voluntary confession of 13 November,[6] Tresham had explained that Catesby made him take the oath of secrecy about the Plot around 14 October and gave him a very short list of the names of the core plotters, not including Guy Fawkes. Catesby perhaps did not trust Tresham sufficiently to disclose the personnel at the London end of the operation, or perhaps he wished to present the Plot as a conspiracy of known close friends he was honour-bound to support. Catesby claimed he had not confided his scheme in any priest but that he had religious authority which showed the enterprise to be lawful – a difficult combination. In a further complication, it would later emerge that Tresham had dictated a deathbed retraction of his previous evidence, including that Father Garnet was party to Thomas Wintour's mission to Spain before 1603. It also appeared that Tresham had read and owned a Jesuit treatise on equivocation. But was the evidence or the retraction the equivocation? Tresham's deathbed declaration[7] was dated 24 December 1605. Waad had reported him dead on the previous day. The date was in another hand and the letter calendared at March 1606 when it came into the hands of the authorities after the questioning of Ann Tresham and William Vavasour. In it, Tresham denied having seen Garnet: 'I had not seen him for sixteen years before nor never had message nor letter from him.' Under pressure from his wife and the immediacy of his own likely death, Tresham intended to clear the priest of any connection to the Plot. Perhaps only one man knew; the man who became the new prime suspect for the authorities, and who, unknown to them, had written the treatise: Father Henry Garnet himself.

The authorities took a relaxed Christmas break from the investigation, giving the Jesuits the opportunity to flee the country and spare the government the political embarrassment of their martyrdom. In the New Year, final attempts began to force the plotters to confess to some international involvement, preferably on the part of the papacy rather than Spain. The state began to concentrate its efforts on emphasising the role of Father Henry Garnet in an attempt to prove loyal English Catholics had been led into treachery by theological sophistry. With the capture of Robert Wintour in January came fresh reports of the dishevelled and abandoned state of the plotters after Holbeach, which rather undermined attempts to prove any high-powered aristocratic patronage of their cause. The long-awaited trial and execution of the plotters coincided with the betrayal of Garnet's hiding place and, after more than a week of searching, his apprehension in a priest hole at Hindlip House.

The drama and tension of the search for Father Garnet at Hindlip must have been palpable to all those involved. After the discovery of Nicholas Owen and so many of the priest holes he had contrived in the house, Sir Henry Bromley gradually closed in on Garnet, aided by a small army of searchers testing the walls and floors for hollow sounds and any apertures for signs of ventilation. Standing mere yards from where Father Garnet and Father Oldcorne were hiding, Sir Henry was watched in cold defiance by the ladies of the house, Anne Vaux and Lord Monteagle's sister Mary Abington.

Garnet had hoped to meet and dissuade the plotters from treason at Coughton in the days before the discovery. They avoided him, only seeking his forgiveness after they had forfeited their lives. Instead, he gave his All Saints' Day sermon there on the text *Auferte gentum perfidam credentium de finibus*, 'Banish the Unbelieving People from the Land of Believers'. This was surely a text designed to stiffen the resolve of those determined to improve the lot of English Catholics, even those determined to blow James and his courtiers back to their Scottish mountains. Perhaps for Garnet himself it was simply something to be repeated *sotto voce* as the searchers tramped above his head. Edward Oldcorne later revealed that Cardinal Allen had procured an indulgence for all those who prayed with that verse for the reconversion of England to Catholicism.

While Father Garnet hid, Robert Wintour was finally captured. Wintour had been on the run for two months after fleeing from Holbeach early on 8 November, hiding with Stephen Littleton, the owner of Holbeach, in 'barns and poor men's houses' across Worcestershire, before being betrayed to the authorities at Hagley. We have seen that a proclamation was issued for his capture on 18 November but he remained at large until 9 January. In the weeks between his capture and his execution, Robert Wintour confided to Guy Fawkes that while he was on the run he was troubled by a recurrent dream. In it he saw the faces of those burned by the gunpowder explosion at Holbeach. It was a dream he had first had on 4 November, the day before the planned explosion in Parliament, but now it was he and his fellow plotters who were the victims, not those in Parliament. Wintour reported 'a strange dream he had in the country, that he thought he was in Cheapside, and looking towards Pauls, it was all coated black and the stones were ready to fall'. His dream and the conversation in the Tower with Guy Fawkes were recorded by eavesdroppers and re-told at their trial to show them unrepentant, Fawkes confirming Wintour 'saw the steeples of St Paul's and other churches stand awry and in one of the churches (it being now some church) he saw strange faces'. In reality Wintour's dream, like all dreams, could be interpreted in a number of ways. Was it an indication of intended revolution within the Church, or of divine displeasure at the Plot, signalled by the gunpowder explosion at Holbeach?

Despite Robert's efforts not to involve him, Sir John Talbot was ordered to London, 'setting aside all excuses' for questioning as the authorities groped for more aristocratic connections for the plotters, a noble mastermind to oversee a coup of a type they would understand. The link between Robert Wintour and the earl and countess of Shrewsbury yielded little, and as Robert had wished, the family did what it could to protect his wife and children after his death.

Robert Wintour was questioned at length. In particular, he was asked whether Monteagle had 'begged of' the conspirators, which historians have taken to mean that Monteagle may have asked for pardons for them. It seems as likely that this question arose from the discovery of Monteagle's debts to Thomas Percy. Indeed, as Thomas Wintour confirmed, Monteagle had in fact borrowed money from other plotters too. For passing on the warning, Monteagle received public praise, lands worth £200 a year, and an annual pension of £500.

In the week preceding Robert Wintour's capture, Thomas Wintour's goods at Huddington were still being embezzled and concealed before the sheriff could get to them. This seems to have been a result of local loyalty to Wintour, with people hiding his goods from the authorities, and also opportunist looting from the estate of a condemned man. The sheriff, Sir Richard Walsh, recommended that the authorities 'commit the faulty to the common gaol and bind the better sort to appear before the council'.[8] Perhaps there is a suggestion here that suspects of higher rank might be sympathisers with knowledge of the Plot who were concealing Robert Wintour's goods from the authorities, and that common people who would have no useful information were doing it for simple gain. There were still plenty of Sir Everard Digby's effects worth stealing, which, despite Mary Digby's pleas, were appraised in rough-and-ready fashion on 6 January: 'Household stuff 5 cartloads £200; 5 score sheep £45, the trunk that was my Lady's and her woman's £50; cock of hay £8. All goods are carried away, even to the very floor of the great parlour.'[9]

The job of seizing and protecting the goods of Francis Tresham and Robert Catesby in Northamptonshire fell to the sheriff of that county, Sir Arthur Throckmorton; this offers another indication that the state was reliant on law enforcement from families related to those who wanted to destroy it, albeit in this case a firmly anti-Catholic representative of one.

Putting aside the satisfaction at news of their capture, the account the earl of Salisbury received of the arrest of Robert Winter and Stephen Littleton at Hagley must have been the source of some alarm. Sir Richard Walsh had been censured and removed for his precipitate actions at Holbeach. The account of the arrest of Wintour and Stephen Littleton showed considerable confusion and disagreement locally about who had responsibility for the captured fugitives. There was dissent among the law officers about where the prisoners should be sent and in whose company. First, there was dispute between the forces of Worcestershire and Staffordshire in an alehouse. Then 'some persons began to lay hold of the prisoners and pull them, some one way and some another, inasmuch as there was likelihood of great affray amongst them'.[10] The dispute continued afterwards on the road, where William and Sir Thomas Whorwood claimed the prisoners as rightly belonging to Staffordshire rather than Worcestershire. Both counties reported having Robert Wintour and Stephen Littleton in their custody at the same time, at Worcester and Stafford respectively. Even two months after the siege at Holbeach, the process of dealing with the rebels was not smooth or without risk and there remained a reasonable chance of escape.

On 10 January 1606, the initial commission for the trial of Sir Everard Digby[11] was accompanied by Sir Edward Coke's note of the same day which revealed the elaborate legal procedure behind the commission and his own workload: 'If you knew what pains had been taken you would pity the old attorney.'[12] He was nine years older than Salisbury, and would outlive him by more than twenty. While Coke portrayed himself buried under his papers, the Principal Secretary worked on the portrayal of the fugitive priests. On 15 January, he drafted more 'Wanted!' descriptions, this time for the priests John Gerard, Henry Garnet and Oswald Tesimond. Garnet was described as

> of a middling Stature, full Faced, Fat of body, of Complexion fair: his Forehead high on each side, with a little thin Haire coming down upon the middest of the forepart of his Head: the Hair of his Head and Beard grizzled: of Age between fifty and threescore: his Beard on his Cheeks cut close, on his Chin but thin, and somewhat short: his Gate upright, and comely for a Fat man.[13]

This is an intimate and rather charming description, and as with the description of Thomas Percy issued in November, the portrait shows the close acquaintance of the government with the principal suspects of the Plot more effectively than it operates as a tool for their identification and apprehension by anyone unacquainted with them. Appearance could be disguised, of course, but perhaps his 'comely gait' would distinguish him from other fat men.

This quickly drafted verbal wanted poster of January 1606 gives a clear picture of Tesimond, not just of his features but of his fashionable Italian clothes, which the government regarded as a tool in the Jesuit's armoury, luring young men to conversion with the air of continental cultural sophistication which the Catholic world afforded:

> Of a reasonable stature, black hair, a brown beard close cut on the cheeks and left broad on the chin, somewhat long-visaged, lean in the face but of a good red complexion, his nose somewhat

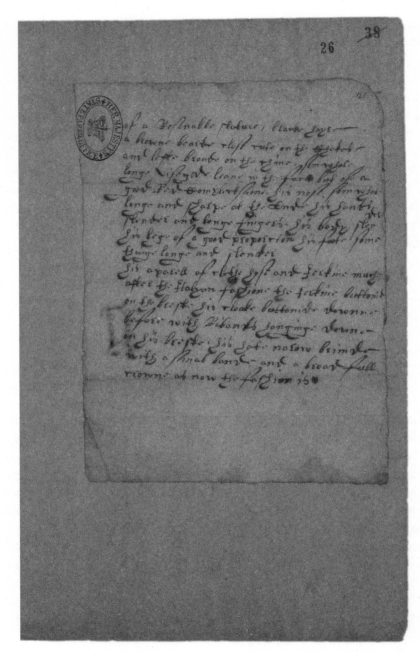

Description of Oswald Tesimond, 15 January 1606. While Thomas Wintour read Italian books, Tesimond wore Italian fashion – signs of cultural commerce with the Catholic world beyond England's shores. (TNA SP 14/18/21)

long and sharp at the end, his hands slender and long fingers, his body slender, his legs of a good proportion, his feet something long and slender. His apparel of cloth, hose and jerkin much after the Italian fashion, the jerkin buttoned on the breast, his cloak buttoned down before with ribbands hanging down on his breast, his hat narrow-brimmed with a small band and broad full crown as now the fashion is.

This was a more detailed and usable description. The published proclamation, however, was less flattering to Tesimond: 'of mean stature, somewhat gross, his hair black, his beard bushy and brown, something long, a broad forehead and a broad forehead'.[14] The published version is less descriptive and effective as a portrait of the man but was possibly revised in the light of better information or for fear of perpetuating his 'continental' allure.

Tesimond later entered the anonymity of London and saw, in the best thriller tradition, someone reading the proclamation against him and eyeing him intently. Successfully fending off an attempt by the pursuivant to arrest him, he holed up in Catholic houses in Essex and Suffolk until he was able to take a small boat to Calais with a cargo of dead pigs, of which he passed as the owner. After some time at St Omer, he moved south. In a letter to King James of 1610, Sir Edwin Rich reported Tesimond's arrival in Naples, warning James of a deadly spin-off from Tesimond's dress sense: a gift of poisoned clothing that Tesimond was supposed to be sending him. Tesimond's narrative, often cited as a corrective to the official account, is an oddity with dubious evidential value. The manuscript is in his hand, and it served his purpose in exonerating the Jesuits from involvement in the Plot, but he did not originate the account, which talks of him as 'Greenway' in the third person. It does serve as a useful corrective to Coke's obvious deliberate attempt to implicate the Jesuit order, and gives valuable context to Catholic suffering, which had no place in official explanations of the Plot's motivation. It provides pen portraits of the catholic protagonists at once intimate and rather too good to be true. The assessment of the life of Nicholas Owen, for example, is very much a hagiography, with all the familiar unverifiable moral detail of the genre.

Perhaps the most surprising of the triumvirate is John Gerard, who headed the list of priestly subjects though he had barely figured in the plotters' evidence. Salisbury had become convinced on the basis of Thomas Bate's evidence at the beginning of December that the plotters had told their confessors everything and that the desire to protect the priests was strong enough among them to withstand torture.[15] Gerard, however, seems to have been outside the progress of the Plot after being present at the taking of the original oath of secrecy.

The authorities knew Gerard well, and his portrait is perhaps more intimate than the rest. The draft description again played with detail of character and manner, which would not feature in the published version. Gerard, it was noted, was 'somewhat higher than ordinary', with 'than Sir Thomas Leighton' hastily crossed through. Perhaps Sir Thomas was notably tall and a useful comparator, at least to those people who knew how tall he was, but no doubt he would not be pleased to have his name appear in a proclamation as a guide to the appearance of wanted priests. He was, after all, a knight of the shire and commissioner of the peace in Worcestershire, whose appointment had been opposed by Sir John Talbot and others of Catholic sympathy on religious grounds. Gerard's lips and speech were a preoccupation: 'curious in speech if he do continue his custom he ... smiles much and a faltering lisping or doubling of his tongue in his speech'.[16] Assuming his pursuers engaged him in conversation and he 'continued his custom' these might be useful identifying traits, but they were understandably dropped in the published version:

> Gerard alias Brooke of stature tall and according thereto well set, his complexion swart or blackish, his face large, his cheeks sticking out and somewhat hollow underneath cheeks, the hair of his head long, if it be not cut off, his beard cut close, saving little Mustachoes and a little tuft under his lower lip, about forty years old.

Perhaps Gerard did have his hair cut to evade detection, because he was able to leave the country in the entourage of the Flemish Ambassador, whose embassy had been to congratulate the king on his preservation from the Plot.

9

HALFWAY BETWEEN
HEAVEN AND EARTH

The 'great indictment' of Guy Fawkes and others[1] came on 18 January. This key document made the Jesuits the instigators of the Plot and the core plotters their pawns. Did the government truly believe the priests were the instigators, or were they feeding – or perhaps reflecting – a popular perception of their sinister power? The earl of Salisbury was used to Sir Arthur Gorges writing to him about his reduced personal circumstances and his need for a place at court or in the household to alleviate his poverty; now the poet and translator, like so many others, found the Plot gave him new ways to demonstrate his loyalty and prove his worthiness for advancement. Writing to his cousin Lord Carew, but with Lord Salisbury in mind, he had a number of slightly surprising preoccupations. First was the possibility that secret occult practice by Catholics might be used to power a renewed attack on Parliament and end the legal proceedings against imprisoned gunpowder plotters:

> ... by wildfires and the killing of sheep in the pastures only for the fat and cauls for that purpose. It seems the fire is not yet out of their fingers and I like the worse because it is so much followed now just against the Parliament time, for certainly they hope by some wicked purpose to divert the prosecution of their former devilish purposes and the deaths of those abominable traitors.

The writer seemed in no doubt that the sacrifices were being made and that his correspondent would credit them. Tesimond's narrative estimated there were 400 missionary priests in England at the time of the Plot; could they be using their powers to free the plotters and imperil the state afresh?

Secondly, he feared the threat to security posed by the many cellars in London, including his own. It was perhaps a perilous point to make given the prevailing atmosphere of suspicion: 'I myself dwelling in the heart of London have a house and cellarage enough to shelter multitudes of such dangerous wares and traitorous people.' There were so many of these, among them the vaults of churches where a 'knave sexton' could be bribed to hide the discontents and ordnance. He feared London could harbour large numbers of undetected groups of disaffected gentlemen such as the plotters had been and from whence a new threat might come. The current system of watching and warding was not thorough enough among 'gentlemen [who] were the chief actors in these tragical determinations'.[2] Gorges felt a lack of confidence that sufficient precautions were being taken and a sense of disaffection among a class of men on whom the smooth running of society relied. In truth, the state did not have the resources to mount searches on a scale that might address these concerns. Gorges' identification of his own property and circumstances with those of potential plotters underlined a major obstacle to the investigation; he felt very differently about the status quo, but how otherwise could potential plotters be distinguished from men like him? Unlike a baronial rebellion or a lone assassin, the source of potential trouble could not easily be identified.

While Sir William Waad worried about the security of his prisoners, Mary Digby repeated her pleas for the return of her estate from the sheriff of Buckingham to pay for her husband's wants in the Tower. The postscript focussed on his release 'to incline and further his majesty's mercy towards my woeful husband, which if your lordship extend such a charitable act we and all what is ours will ever be your honour's'.[3] Was there any chance of this? Is there a hint at bribery? 'Mercy for my husband's life for which you would tie us and our posterity to you and your house forever and I hope his offence against his majesty is not so heinous in that execrable plot as is said to be contrived by some others.'[4] Would Digby really be considered a separate, less serious case? Was there really a chance that his offence would be seen in that light? Sir Edward Coke would use his trial to wish the destruction of Sir Everard Digby's posterity; Lady Mary seemed to be offering an alliance.

John Gerard's statements of innocence of the Plot both to Sir Everard Digby and to the Council contrast in their language with Mary Digby's strained but lucid, formally constructed pleas. The self-justifying narrative letters of suspects with their endless excited subclauses can make the sequence of events and the subjects identified difficult for a modern reader to reconstruct. Gerard protested to Digby that he did not know of the Plot 'till the rumour of the country brought it to the place where I was when the treason was publicly discovered'. But where was that, and when? Gerard was named as principal suspect in the government's proclamation against the Jesuits, but this appeared to be a sort of long service award for his role in previous plots, rather than proceeding from any settled conviction that he was directly involved this time. Gerard, as we have seen, had questioned Digby on 1 November about the movement of his household to Coughton and the 'great cause' which must be behind it. He asked 'whether you expected any help from foreign power', which is a strange question to ask unless the hoped-for answer was 'yes'. 'Whereof you answered holding the end of your finger that you would not adventure so much in hope thereof. Pray god you follow counsel in your doings, if there be any matter in hand doth Mr Whalley [Garnet] know of this?' Though distant from him, Gerard held a consistent line with Garnet that the plotters' actions were wicked, not simply in themselves but because they had acted without the permission and guidance of their priests. He signed himself 'your companion in tribulation though not in the cause'.[5]

Two months after Thomas Wintour's apparently definitive narrative of the course of the Plot, several major suspects were still at large. In a note marked 'Hindlip this 23 January very late', Sir Henry Bromley wrote to Lord Salisbury reporting the reception he received at the house. The letter had news important and urgent enough to be marked by him 'to my most honoured lord the earl of Salisbury with all haste for king's service'. From the occupants of the house he had found scant regard for the Council's warrant:

My especial good lord I have performed the service your Lordship and the rest of the lords have imposed on me for the search of the traitors and gave it for gone, for that I could never get from Mrs Abington nor any other in the house the least glimmering of any of these traitors or any other person to be here. Some presumptions I had (besides your commandment), to continue me here, as finding beds warm and finding parcels of apparel and books and writings that showed some scholars used. Mrs Abington was not at home when I came but was gone to Pepper Hill to Mrs Talbot's and came home on Monday night. I showed her his Majesty's proclamation and my warrant for the search, but she absolutely denieth that she knoweth or ever saw any of those parties, but Gerard in his youth some four or five and twenty years ago and never saw him since. I did never hear so impudent liars as I find here, all recusants and all resolved to confess nothing, what danger so ever they endure. I holding my resolution to keep watch longer (though I was out of all hope to find any man or thing) yet at last yesterday, being Wednesday, found a number of popish trash hid under boards, in three or four several places, the particularities I refer to the relation of this bearer. Wednesday night late I went to my house to take my rest being much wearied, leaving my brother the charge of the house within. Sundry of my servants and a sufficient guard besides, in and round about the house. So that this Thursday morning there are come forth for hunger and cold, that give themselves other names, but surely one of them I trust will prove Greenway and the other I think will be Hall. I have yet presumption there is one or two more in the house, whereof I have resolved to continue the guard yet a day or two. I could by no means persuade the Gentlewoman of the house to depart the house, without I should have carried her, which I hold so uncivil, as being so nobly born, as I have and do undergo the greater difficulties thereby.

Hindlip this 23rd of January. Very late.

I desire to know what you will have done with Mr Abington. I think good in the meantime to retain him to a magistrate's house at Worcester.[6]

Sir Henry Bromley is often represented as relishing his commission and terrorising those within the house. Certainly, the language of this letter is less guarded than William Tate's similarly frustrated notes from the search of Harrowden in November, but, as Tate did at Harrowden, he found himself in a position of some social inferiority that made his job much more difficult. After all, Mary Abington, or Habington as it is more usually spelled in modern texts, was Lord Monteagle's sister. This connection between the man credited with foiling the Plot through the divine intervention of the warning letter and the woman leading the continuing attempts, nearly three months later, to conceal the fugitive priests who had masterminded it, according to the official account, seems on the surface to be incredible. It was potentially embarrassing for the government, and, like the connection of Monteagle himself to the plotters and past plots, was passed over as silently as possible. To those who could see beneath the black-and-white distinctions of the official narrative to the web of family connections and complex loyalties behind the Plot, the connection was not surprising at all. Nor was the fact that Mary Habington was absent at Pepper Hill, where Thomas Wintour had taken his brother's letter pleading for support from his father-in-law for the Midlands rebellion. Sir John Talbot's loyalty to the Crown on that occasion, as it was reported by Thomas Wintour, had been absolute, but had that loyalty been exaggerated in the telling because Robert's hopes for his family's protection after his execution depended on his father-in-law? Family connections continued naturally after the discovery of the Plot, but who could tell when simple domestic life might involve the treasonous harbouring of priests?

Bromley also faced the difficulty of assessing the blank denials of knowledge of the suspects by those questioned in the house, and the limitations of the measures he could take to discover the truth while there. Evidently, the proclamations and other documentation identifying the suspects were not as helpful to Bromley as they might have been, or perhaps the suspects themselves were altered by starvation and confinement. He had not found Greenway (Tesimond) or Hall (Oldcorne), though Oldcorne and Garnet were still hidden in the house. The emerging men were in fact Ralph Ashley and Nicholas Owen, the man who had built the hiding places they used.

According to the 'presumptions' against Garnet and Hall listed by Bromley as proof of their lies and links to the plotters, they claimed to have been together near Evesham on the day before their discovery, Hall travelling the 12 miles to Hindlip on horseback, Garnet on foot. Bromley established that the 'apparel' whose discovery was described in the letter of 23 January belonged to them and that Thomas Habington had ridden Hall's horse (bought from a local clerk of the peace and given to Hall by Robert Wintour) from the stables at Hindlip on 25 January. Sir William Waad later doubted whether Garnet's infirmity would allow him to walk from the Guildhall prison to his execution outside St Paul's, let alone the 12 miles from Evesham to Hindlip.

On the day appointed for the trial of the principal plotters, 27 January, Sir Richard Lewkenor enclosed evidence given by Humphrey Littleton against the Jesuits to respite his own execution, confirming that Father Oldcorne alias Hall was at Hindlip.[7]

Eight plotters – Guy Fawkes, Thomas and Robert Wintour, Robert Keyes, John Grant, Thomas Bate, Ambrose Rookwood and Sir Everard Digby – were finally tried in Westminster Hall on 27 January 1606. King James, Queen Anne and Prince Henry were rumoured to be in secret attendance, which seems very likely given James's keen personal interest since the arrest of Guy Fawkes on the morning of 5 November.

The Jesuits Garnet, Tesimond and Gerard came first in the indictment, cited as the originators and movers of the Plot, the name of Robert Catesby being almost lost in the middle of a long list of their dupes. It is not a position he would have recognised or appreciated. The three priests, it was alleged, did 'maliciously, falsely and traitorously move and persuade' the hapless gentlemen to undertake the Plot when the hope of Spanish invasion faded. This interpretation certainly fit with the government's desire to show the corrupting influence of foreign-trained priests on English Catholics but it was radically at odds with the evidence presented to the Commissioners by the surviving plotters, some of it reproduced at the trial itself. This showed the priests if not as sources of restraint then, at most, as peripheral and unwilling accessories. Guy Fawkes's grounds for his not-guilty plea, that the indictment exaggerated the role of the priests, was more than a quibble. Devout though they were, Catesby and the core plotters did not represent themselves as pawns of a manipulative priesthood any more than they were tools of an aristocratic patron. Both Fawkes and Thomas Wintour in their copious evidence showed consistent detachment and scepticism about the influence of those outside their small circle, and a high degree of self-reliance. Even the prospect of certain death did not elicit an attempt to blame others for their actions.

As well as being Jesuit-inspired, the indictment presented the Plot as being simply religious in motivation. The mixture of motives – the objection to the Scottish king and his courtier compatriots and the reform of 'abuses' by the new regime – were dismissed as a front to lure the gullible to their cause or simply ignored. Reinstating the temporal power of the pope in England, 'the jurisdiction of the Bishop of Rome', was said to be their underlying aim, yet Catesby seemed only to be interested in papal opinion when it accorded with his own ambitions. Fawkes's categorical antipathy to the rule of 'any foreign prince whatsoever' seemed to rule out unfettered papal sway in England too. Yet this partial view of the plotters' offence has been very influential in traditions of the Plot and of its commemoration even to recent times. The attempted destruction of the Scottish king and his court by some of his English subjects being as big a motivation as religion, to judge by Thomas Percy and Fawkes, reported of the former and openly stated by the latter, has somehow been lost in the popular conception of the Plot. The king's preservation from their murderous designs became a source of celebration largely for the English themselves rather than the Scots.

The rhetoric of Sir Edward Philips, the king's sergeant at law, and Sir Edward Coke threatened to overstate the case even of so destructive an act of terror as the Gunpowder Plot. To modern audiences the language of the trial seems to emphasise its theatricality and the status of the trial as a display of guilt rather than a genuine legal process. The concept of the Plot was horrific, but the fact of its having been foiled always threatened to puncture the apocalyptic vision the lawyers set out. To Philips it was 'of such horrid and monstrous nature that before now the tongue of man never delivered, the ear of man never heard the heart of man never conceited nor the malice of hellish or earthly devil never practised'.[8]

There were byways for the listener here if they were not careful. Just as you had begun to scan human history for worse examples of violence actual and projected, you were confronted with different types of devil and presumably their differing varieties of malice. Philips found his feet again reminding his listeners, at least those who were not Catholic, that they were all 'excommunicated by the Pope' and therefore lawfully expendable in the eyes of the plotters. Triumphantly, he lighted on 'the damned crew' as a phrase to describe the plotters, one which stayed with them. Oddly, he cited Sir Edmund Baynham as the 'prime' member though his contribution was a memorably slow and circuitous journey to Rome to seek papal sanction for the Plot, which never came. Some new details emerged or were emphasised at the trial, one being that the thirty-six barrels of gunpowder were not covered only with 'faggots' and other timber, usually described and presumed to give the whole the appearance of a simple store of firewood; there were also iron and stones, presumably designed to act as shrapnel when the blast occurred, or, as Philips put it, 'to have made the breath greater'. Tesimond's narrative suggested that this mixture of materials was designed by the plotters to show that the vault was being used as a storeroom for heavy miscellaneous junk that would be difficult to search.

If it were possible, Sir Edward Coke's rhetoric outdid this stirring introduction. The Attorney General again would have had his listeners searching in their minds for precedents and possibly, however loyal they were, scratching their heads: 'These were the greatest treasons that ever were plotted in England and concern the greatest king that ever was of England.' Kings are used to hollow flattery, of course, and James gained a reputation for soliciting and responding to it. However, it must have been reasonably plain to Coke himself, with his acute if partial view of English history, that to judge James as the country's greatest ever monarch, if only perhaps the greatest male one, after two and a half years in the job might be premature. Coke excused himself for his departure from his usual brevity in speech, not a quality posterity usually associates with him, by explaining that future generations would not believe that such a thing as the Gunpowder Plot could be contemplated and carried out, unless he set the circumstances out in detail. Here he was on slightly dangerous ground, for if the Plot was already straining credulity even among those investigating it, there is little wonder that others at a distance would find it unbelievable. This was particularly true because Coke did not proceed with a sober recitation of the copious evidence he had from investigation. Instead, he resorted to the sonorous language we would come to associate with the Authorized Version of the Bible, then recently commissioned but still years from completion.

'For treason is like the tree whose root is full of poison and lieth secret and hid within the earth, resembling the imagination of the heart of man, which is so secret as only God knoweth it.' The tree 'planted and watered by Jesuits and English Romish Catholics' then obligingly straddled Europe in a way which allowed Coke to impose a geographical and chronological form on the Plot, which was very much his own conception. 'The first in root England in December and March, the second in Flanders in June and the third in Spain in July.' Again, Coke seemed to be disobeying his instructions, for James's new ally Spain was being carefully excluded from the official narrative of the Plot.

The presentation of the social status of the plotters fluctuated too. After so much effort had been spent in representing them as desperate men of no account, carefully editing their social connections to favoured lords like Monteagle, now, suddenly, to illustrate the malicious power of the Jesuits, they were reinstated socially in order to emphasise the ruin to which the Jesuits had brought them. They became 'gentlemen of good homes, of excellent parts, however most perniciously seduced, abused, corrupted and jesuited of very competent fortunes and states'. Catesby surely would have argued that it was the anti-Catholic legislation rather than the Society of Jesus that was robbing them of their estates, but Coke's argument again ran much more broadly than the treason at hand. He suggested the order should be extinguished as the Templars had been for their misdemeanours, a desire that arguably exceeded his brief at the trial, as well as the bounds of possibility.

Coke then returned with zeal to his main theme:

Miserable desolation; no king, no queen, no prince, no issue male, no counsellors of state, no nobility, no bishops, no judges. O barbarous and more than Scythian or Thracian cruelty. No mantle of holiness can cover it, no pretence of religion can excuse it, no shadow of good intention can extenuate it,

God and heaven condemn it, man and earth detest it, the offenders themselves were ashamed of it, wicked people exclaim against it and the souls of all true Christian subjects abhor it. Miserable but yet sudden had their ends been, who should have died in that fiery tempest and storm of gunpowder.[9]

Again, Coke's focus on religion as the prime motivation of the Plot and his desire to discredit the Jesuits drew him into a logical and theological quagmire. What, his listeners might have wondered, was the 'shadow of good intention' or the 'mantle of holiness' in relation to the Plot? Having represented it as the most heinous, inexcusable crime in the history of the world, Coke seemed to be introducing arguments in its favour; inadequate ones certainly, but ones which he expected his audience to recognise and acknowledge.

Coke dwelt on the oath of secrecy sealed by communion and the doctrine of equivocation as companion tools in the Jesuit armoury of corruption and deception. This led to a digression on the use and abuse of language, 'a very labyrinth to lead men into error and falsehood', which was an odd foundation text for a man presenting evidence in a treason trial. He was not, of course, against religious superstition, only the wrong sort. The preservation of the government was repeatedly presented as divine intervention for and through the king. The Monteagle letter and the gunpowder explosion at Holbeach clearly showed the working of divine providence.

The trouble with seeing the Plot in such terms was that it was generally possible to interpret the workings of providence in two ways. Coke could not resist the detail from the Holbeach explosion that 2½ pounds of powder in a platter drying before the fire had exploded, sending a much larger 16-pound bag underneath clean through the hole in the roof where it landed safely, unexploded, in the courtyard. Coke takes this miraculous occurrence to be a sign of divine providence acting to preserve the injured plotters to face trial. Surely, it could also be interpreted as a miraculous preservation in recognition of the virtue of their cause. Trading in providence put Coke and his rhetoric on dangerous ground. Was he more superstitious than the staunchly Catholic Thomas Wintour, who refused to interpret the ebb and flow of the war in the Low Countries as a sign of divine intervention? At times, he seemed to be confusing himself as well as bewildering the paying crowd in Westminster Hall. Referring to the plots of 1603, he accused 'Don Raleigh and Don Cobham', thus reviving the idea of a traitor in the pay of Spain. Aside from the oddity of the great anti-Spanish hero Raleigh being in their pay, Coke had allowed his own suspicions and the pattern of past treasons to undermine his clear instruction not to implicate the king's new ally Spain in fresh allegations.

Sir Edward Coke was impatient of these niceties and relished the gruesome poetic justice of the traitors' elaborate executions. Here he was more in tune with the contemporary sensibility and Jacobean theatre than with our own view of this kind of torture:

> He shall be drawn to the place of execution from his prison as being not worthy anymore to tread upon the face of the earth whereof he was made; also for that he hath been retrograde to Nature therefore is he drawn backward at a horse tail. He must be drawn with his head declining downwards and lying so near the ground as may be, being thought unfit to take benefit of the common air. For such cause also he shall be strangled being hanged up by the neck, between heaven and earth as deemed unworthy of both or either; as likewise the eyes of man may behold and their hearts contemn him. Then he is to be cut down alive and have his privy parts cut off and burnt before his face as being unworthily begotten and unfit to leave any generation after him. His bowels and inlay'd parts being taken out and burnt who inwardly conceived and harboured in his heart so horrible a treason. After to have his head cut off, which imagined the mischief. And lastly, his body to be quartered and the quarters set up in some high and eminent place. To the view and detestation of men and to become a prey for the fowls of the air.[10]

There was no defence against such grave charges. After being found guilty, Robert Wintour confined himself to a simple plea for mercy, while Thomas 'only desired that he might be hanged both for his brother and himself'. Interestingly, Robert Keyes' plea admitted his 'estate was desperate', which underlined that not all were gentlemen of comfortable estates, and perhaps there was an echo of the deterioration of Catholic estates under the penal laws of the time. He followed this with a reflection on the circumstances of his death, 'as good now as at another time and for this cause rather than for another'. This is a less gentlemanly version of Thomas Wintour's protestation that he had risked his life in worse causes before the Plot, but it is poetic in its own way. To a modern sensibility, the hopelessness of the plotters' position seems to cast doubt on the credibility of the whole enterprise. However, the determination of the plotters was not just the delusion of a small group of overconfident gentlemen or a temporary insanity brought on by the charismatic control of Robert Catesby. It grew from a culture where death was ever-present and life short and often brutal. The chance to land a decisive blow to change the lives of themselves and their families for the better – potentially forever – was sufficient motivation despite the great risks.

As if the huge crowd assembled at Westminster Hall might have forgotten, thanks to Coke's apocalyptic rhetoric, that the Plot had failed, John Grant reminded them that the offence was 'a conspiracy intended but not effected'. After the pleas came the sensational recounting of Robert Wintour's sinister but ambiguous dreams of blackened churches. That was not all. There was more prophecy, and an eye on posterity according to other remarks reported from his conversation with Guy Fawkes in the Tower, suggesting their deaths would be followed by an unending struggle: 'God will raise up seed to Abraham out of the very stones, our deaths shall be sufficient justification of it. And it is for God's cause.' This was presented as a sign of their lack of remorse and repentance, of course, but it gave them real power, the power of magic, which clung to the Catholic priesthood in the minds of many, including their enemies. It seemed to hang about the plotters even as they went to their deaths: 'Wintour told Fawkes that after Percy was buried he was taken out a good while after and his head cut off, when he bled abundantly and fresh and his quarters were set up in the country.' Even at the last there was an attempt to suggest that there was something uncanny and exceptional about them and their cause that the authorities could not contain or explain. Fawkes and Robert Wintour were reported to regret the opportunity to justify their actions to the world: 'They were sorry that none did set forth a defence or apology of their actions, but that yet they would maintain the cause at their deaths.'

Above: The Treaty of London in 1604 brought peace between England and Spain, but just over the Channel war continued between Catholic Spanish forces and Dutch Protestants. The treaty allowed Englishmen to fight for Spain, and Robert Catesby talked of commanding an English company in the conflict, but was this just a cover story for military preparations at home? (Courtesy of the Rijksmuseum)

Right: A convinced Protestant, James VI & I gave preferment to English Catholics who had defended his mother Mary, Queen of Scots before her execution. His verbal assurances of toleration towards Catholics were warmer than those he was prepared to commit to paper. (Courtesy of Yale Center for British Art)

The face of the Plot? Robert Catesby was the charismatic figure at the centre of the Plot. His many friends, including Lord Monteagle and Father Henry Garnet, were prepared to indulge and excuse him. Guy Fawkes, meanwhile, was prized by his fellow plotters for his anonymity, but is now world famous. (Philip Sidney, *A History of the Gunpowder Plot*, 1904)

Princess Elizabeth, the plotters' proposed puppet queen; she has a look of resolution and was already a convinced Protestant at nine years old. (Courtesy of the Metropolitan Museum of Art)

Some of the versions of this hastily produced image of Thomas Percy are discussed on page 68. In this version Holbeach has been identified as the scene of the siege, and the capture of Percy has become that of 'Thomas Witer' presumably Thomas Wintour who came to prominence after his confession. Throughout Percy is 'nobilis'. Overseas observers struggled to credit a rebellion of gentlemen and assumed there must be an aristocratic leader. The government searched for this 'great man' long after the discovery of the Plot, but could not be sure they had found him. (Courtesy of the Rijksmuseum)

As constable of Alnwick Castle (pictured), Thomas Percy had charge of the estate rents of his kinsman Henry Percy, ninth earl of Northumberland. He was reported to have promised to use them to fund the Plot. The relationship between the two men fascinated the investigators. Sometimes it seemed the servant led his master. (Courtesy of Matthew Hartley under Creative Commons 2.0)

Above left: Robert Wintour, whose desperate note calling on his father-in-law for support (p. 76) is a poignant record of the failed rebellion in the Midlands following the discovery of the Plot. (Sidney, 1904)

Left: Thomas Wintour, whose wit, candour and erudition made his narrative of the Plot irresistible to historians. (Sidney, 1904)

Below left: Thomas Bate, Robert Catesby's servant and man of business. Bate took a practical view of the business of the Plot and was less protective than were the gentlemen plotters of the reputations of the Jesuit priests. (Sidney, 1904)

Above: John Wright exemplified the interconnectedness of the plotters. A schoolfellow of Guy Fawkes and brother-in-law of Thomas Percy, he brought his brother into the Plot and was cousin to the Wintours. (Sidney, 1904)

Left: Father Henry Garnet, rigorously defended by one side and roundly condemned by the other. The subtleties of Garnet's character and language have rarely been explored. (Sidney, 1904)

Below: The vault beneath the Lords' Chamber. The gunpowder needed to be brought in by stealth, but faggots and lumber, which would have acted as shrapnel in the explosion, could be brought in openly by Fawkes, posing as the servant of the trusted gentleman pensioner Thomas Percy. (Sidney, 1904)

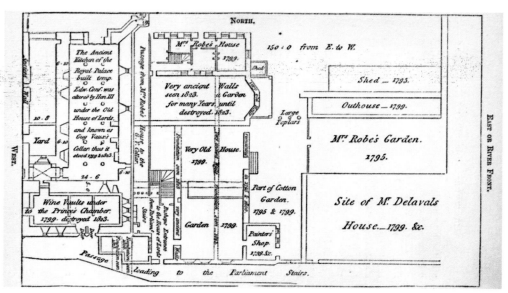

Capon's plan of the old Palace of Westminster, including 'Guy Vaux's Cellar'. The plan identifies it as 'part of the ancient kitchen of the Royal Palace', so the vault was a more impressive space than 'cellar' would usually suggest. (Samuel Gardiner, *What Gunpowder Plot Was*, 1897)

Above: A lantern held in the Ashmolean, purported to have been the one used by Guy Fawkes on the night he was discovered. (Sidney, 1904)

Left: Robert Cecil, 1st Earl of Salisbury. Often depicted as a manipulative spider at the centre of an all-seeing web of intelligence controlling the Plot, Cecil struggled to make sense of contradictory reports he received in the wake of the discovery. The Attorney General, Sir Edward Coke, failed to stick to the earl's instructions at the plotters' trial. (Sidney, 1904)

The executions following the Plot were carefully managed exemplary punishments, but they were politically sensitive. The second set of plotter executions took place at Westminster rather than St Paul's, perhaps to stress the plotters' offence was against the state rather than religion. The execution of Father Henry Garnet was moved from May Day for fear of disorder in the crowd of onlookers. (Courtesy of the Rijksmuseum)

By the 1620s, the Gunpowder Plot had become firmly established as one of England's miraculous escapes from Catholic plotting, along with the victory against the Spanish Armada. The Pope is shown directing the Plot through the central figure of Father Henry Garnet, and the core plotters have become peripheral figures. (Courtesy of the Rijksmuseum)

The tradition of lighting bonfires began on the day of the discovery of the Plot. Are we still celebrating the preservation of Parliament, or do the fireworks evoke the explosion that might have been and the excitement of the days before the 'blow' was to be delivered? (Courtesy of Aurelien Guichard under Creative Commons 2.0)

The traditional symbol of the peculiarly English Gunpowder Plot celebrations, Guido Fawkes was spurred and ready to spread the news of the destruction of King James and his government to the Imperial Court at Brussels. Now he is the face of political disaffection internationally. (Courtesy of Frédéric Bisson under Creative Commons 2.0)

Much of this evidence came from the reported conversation between them in the Tower that was overheard by eavesdroppers and set down on 25 January, only two days before their trial. The day before the trial, Robert Wintour was examined on the remarks when it became clearer whom the seed of Abraham might be: 'Touching the words of two or three little fellows that would prove themselves tall men, He sayeth that he told Fawkes that Catesby's son and this examinate's son would as he hoped prove tall men and Catholics.' Inevitably, there were elements of Fawkes and Wintour's conversation that were too embarrassing to be used at the trial. When Wintour was asked to confirm he had said that he had heard 'Lord Monteagle had begged three or four of us', Wintour confirmed it. This was duly crossed out, as the other references to Monteagle's connection to the plotters had been.

Because his treason was first committed in a different county to the others, Digby was tried upon a separate indictment at the end of the day. Alone among the eight accused, he pleaded guilty. This gave him the opportunity to make a speech with the stage to himself. He repeated the assertion made in his letter to Salisbury, that the king had reneged upon promises of toleration for Catholics, and claimed that his affection for Catesby and desire to ease the lot of Catholics had prompted his actions. His manner and bearing impressed many in the packed hall.

Coke in particular duelled verbally with Sir Everard Digby, who was as disposed as Coke himself to regard the trial as his opportunity to impress. Once Digby had pleaded guilty, he made a spirited defence of his conduct:

My Lords, my first motive was not ambition, nor malice to any in Parliament. It was friendship and the love I bore to Robert Catesby, so powerful that I was willing to hazard my life.

Next was the Cause of Religion, for which I resolved to neglect my Estate, my Life, my Name, my Memory and all earthly happiness...

Coke was in no mood to humour the nobility of these sentiments given the destruction the Plot had promised: 'Your friendship with Catesby?

Mere folly and wicked conspiracy. Your religion? Error and heresy!'
Digby then made a plea for his family and estate after his death:

> I pray for the pardon of the King and Lords for my guilt, desiring
> that my death might satisfy them for my trespass and forgive me.
> Yet given that my crime is contained within myself, surely no
> guilt can be carried over to my wife Mary my sons, my sisters.

This too was too much for Coke, who responded,

> Oh!! Now he appeals for compassion in the peril of his private
> and public estate. But before, when the King, the Queen, the
> tender princes, the nobles, the whole kingdom were designed for
> perpetual destruction, where was then this piety, this religious
> affection, this care?

Digby remained remarkably dignified in the face of Coke's rhetoric:
'Surely, I deserve the vilest death, the most severe punishment. Yet
I am a humble petitioner for mercy, some moderation of justice.' But
rhetoric was what the audience expected, and what the trial was all
about. Coke had his own grisly rejoinder to Digby's plea for his family
and posterity:

> Do not look to the King to be honoured by beheading as you
> entreat; rather, admire the great mercy that no new torture was
> devised to be inflicted upon you.
> And as for your wife and children, you shall have your desire
> as it is written in the Psalm, 'Let his wife be a widow; and his
> children vagabonds. Let his posterity be destroyed, and in the
> next generation, let his name be quite put out.'

When Coke had finished with him, the earl of Northampton took
up the attack on Digby's religious pretensions in more measured and
insidious fashion, pouring scorn on the notion that James had given
false hope to Catholics at his accession. Then the earl of Salisbury
forced him to admit he had taken his view of the king's breach of
promise second-hand from Sir Thomas Tresham. He also triumphantly
claimed that Digby had known of the powder end of the operation

long before his supposed recruitment in October and had discussed the decay of the powder with Fawkes himself during the summer.

After the verdict, only Digby of the eight accused spoke. He addressed the lords in the hope of an unlikely verbal pardon: 'If I may but hear any of your lordships say you forgive me I shall go more cheerfully to the gallows.' Again, he believed his personality might move the intended victims of the explosion to treat him differently. To some extent, he was right, for he received the gentle, ambiguous reply, 'God forgive you and we do.'[11]

On 30 January, Digby and his co-conspirators Robert Wintour, John Grant and Thomas Bate were drawn on traitors' hurdles through the streets to St Paul's Churchyard, where a gallows had been erected. All four were drawn and quartered after only a brief hanging, to ensure they were still alive as they were dissected. The first to suffer, Digby met his death bravely. John Aubrey, with his usual ear for a good story, recalled that Digby's character and sense of the dramatic survived his execution: 'When his heart was plucked out by the Executioner (who cried ... 'Here is the heart of a Traitor!') it is credibly reported, he replied, "Thou liest!"' There were also more jaundiced eyewitness accounts, which described him as 'a man of goodly personage, and a manly aspect, yet might a wary eye, in the change of his countenance, behold an inward fear of death.' Seeing the executions at first hand was no bar to religious prejudice; since he also saw 'vain and superstitious crossing of himself, [he] betook him to his Latin prayers'. The explosion at Holbeach had become a metaphor. John Grant was described as 'abominably blinded with his horrible idolatry'. Fawkes, it was noted, had to be helped up the ladder to the gallows, climbing 'high enough to break his neck'.[12]

In another bid to influence posterity, Everard Digby sent letters written in lemon juice to his son Kenelm from the Tower. They were kept secret, and only found in Kenelm's papers in 1675. They give a private view of his motivations that is remarkably consistent with his evidence to the state: 'My Dear Son, if I had thought there had been the least sin in the Plot, I would not have been in it, for all the world. I had certain belief that the Jesuits, those best able to judge its lawfulness, had been acquainted with it and given way to it. No other cause drew me to hazard my fortune, and my Life – but zeal for God's religion.'

In private, he was perhaps more honest about the role of the Jesuits in reassuring the plotters of the Plot's lawfulness. The condemned man also wrote poetry: 'Who's that which knocks? Oh stay My Lord, I come: I know that call, since first it made me know Myself, which makes me now with joy to run Lest He be gone that can my duty show. Jesu My Lord, I know thee by the Cross Thou offer'st me, but not unto my loss.'[13]

While Digby's words reflected his calm as he contemplated his end, Coke's agitated rhetoric did not, in the end, reflect the wishes of his political masters. Nor did it reflect the Exchequer's attitude to Digby's family, who enjoyed some success in restoring their estates and maintaining the prominence of Sir Everard's line. Little Kenelm witnessed his father's execution but went on to a distinguished diplomatic and literary career, and earned a knighthood of his own from the king his father had sought to destroy.

After his death, new insight into Robert Wintour's activities and dilemmas in the days before the discovery of the Plot emerged from the shadows in two sets of Exchequer depositions of 1608–9. Sir Thomas Overbury, whose murder was one of the great Jacobean court scandals, haggled with Robert Wintour's widow over Robert's rights to salt deposits in Droitwich.[14]

The cases take evidence from 'Leonard Smallpeece, 54, of Pepper Hill, Salop', Sir John Talbot's steward, to whom Wintour wrote his desperate note from Huddington on 6 November. Smallpeece and other witnesses attest to Sir John Talbot's business dealings with the Wintours and John Grant immediately before 5 November. Wintour's dealings with his father-in-law seem nervous even then, and his actions not noticeably those of a man about to risk his position and his life in 'open rebellion'.

On 24 October, he addresses a note 'Good Cousin' – probably to Smallpeece, whom he addressed as such on 6 November – about drawing up a deed to secure the rights to the salt deposits. 'I must take no denial but this deed must be ready to be sealed upon Saturday next.'[15]

On the evening of 3 November, the Sunday before the discovery of the Plot, Wintour was transacting business at Grafton, signing indentures making over his rights to the salt deposits. The indentures needed to be sealed to make the contract binding, but Wintour was willing to postpone sealing the indentures until the following Saturday, 9 November, rather than risk his father-in-law's annoyance by getting him out of bed late. If he was drawing up the indentures to secure the salt rights in his family should his personal property became forfeit through the Plot's discovery, his readiness to delay seems hard to understand. Perhaps his urgency would be impossible to explain without hinting too heavily that something major was planned. Perhaps Wintour was consistent in being more scared of his father-in-law than he was of the wildness of Robert Catesby. The result is not in doubt. The indentures were never sealed. Then his visionary dreams began.

On 29 January 1606, Sir Arthur Gorges wrote again on the subject of Catholic reaction to the trials and executions, this time warily suggesting the possible impropriety of using St Paul's as a place of execution for the conspirators. In doing so he betrayed fear of implicating himself in any criticism of the government line – 'but I willingly submit my opinion to your wisdom' – but he was also convinced of the possible political damage in feeding Catholic 'calumny' of Protestants as defilers of holy places: 'It is an ill presage to have blood and execution approach so near the capital house of God's divine service.'[16] It was also, he remembered, where Queen Elizabeth had given thanks on her knees for the defeat of the Spanish Armada. Perhaps his words had an effect, because the second set of executions on 31 January took place in the Old Palace Yard, Westminster. Parliamentary justice and poetic justice replaced divine retribution. There, to echo Catesby's words, they would have done all the mischief. Here Thomas Wintour, Ambrose Rookwood, Robert Keyes and Guy Fawkes suffered the same fate as their friends. Fawkes was the last of the eight to die.

The indictment at the plotters' trial included Father Garnet, who was 'not yet taken'. The search of Hindlip House had begun on 20 January, with Garnet and Edward Oldcorne finally being discovered on the day of the trial itself. Only on the day of the first executions did the government receive a full account of Garnet's arrest. Again, there is a nice mix of private and public interest in the man leading the search: Sir Henry Bromley, who found his duty dovetailed conveniently with an opportunity to acquire land adjoining his own.

Fawkes had been the vital if reluctant source of information in the first act, while Thomas Wintour was the better-informed source for the second. The government now had a leading man for the third act in Father Henry Garnet, whose cleverness and social standing caused them even more trouble than did the others.

ACT III

'IN HIDING AND IN THE WINGS'
FEBRUARY 1606 TO NOVEMBER 1632

Cast List

HENRY PERCY, earl of Northumberland, captain of the king's bodyguard, 'The Wizard Earl'

HENRY HOWARD, earl of Northampton, privy councillor, 'Conjuror of priests and devils'

ROBERT CECIL, earl of Salisbury, Principal Secretary of State, 'The Little Beagle'

WILLIAM PARKER, Baron Monteagle, defender of Catholics in Parliament, recipient of 'The Monteagle Letter'

ANTHONY MARIA BROWNE, Viscount Montague, nobleman, employer of Guy Fawkes

SIR EDWARD COKE, Attorney General, prosecutor and conspiracist

SIR THOMAS EDMONDES, English Ambassador in Flanders

SIR HENRY BROMLEY, landowner of Holt Castle, Worcestershire

SIR WALTER RALEIGH, prisoner in the Tower

HENRY GARNET, alias Walley, alias Farmer, alias Darcy, alias Measley, Father Superior of the English Jesuit Province

OSWALD TESIMOND, alias Greenaway, alias Greenwell, missionary priest, schoolfellow of Guido Fawkes

EDWARD OLDCORNE, alias Hall, alias Vincent, alias Parker, missionary priest, schoolfellow of Guy Fawkes

NICHOLAS OWEN, servant to Henry Garnet, carpenter and later saint

HUGH OWEN, Welsh priest, intelligencer at the Imperial court in Brussels

THOMAS PHELLIPES, correspondent of exiled Catholics, decipherer

DUDLEY CARLETON, onetime secretary to the earl of Northumberland, Gunpowder suspect, later Viscount Dorchester, Ambassador to Venice

LADY MARY DIGBY, widow of Gayhurst

ANNE VAUX, 'virtuous and zealous Catholic maiden'

IO

THE GREAT AND THE GOOD

By dramatic convention, the plotters' trial should have been the end of the action, with sentences handed out and loose ends tied up. In reality, things were not so simple. Attorney General Sir Edward Coke spent the trial hinting that the eight being tried were simply the mechanicals in the Plot. The director, the criminal mastermind, he implied, had yet to be found. Despite all the evidence that Catesby had been the prime mover, experience of previous plots made the government very reluctant to believe that there was no such hidden figure. Sir Edward Coke picked up on passing references in Fawkes's confessions and identified Sir Walter Raleigh as plotting while imprisoned in the Tower. The earl of Salisbury favoured troublesome exiles like Hugh Owen, the intelligencer at the imperial court in Brussels, or the Jesuits, and there is some evidence that part of his motivation was to absolve English Catholics of guilt of any native treason and to blame foreign influence.

Viewed as a whole, the effect of Salisbury's agenda on the investigation of the Plot and the presentation of the evidence was significant but not sinister, and its objects, though not publicly stated, are clear from the documents. Strenuous efforts began to establish a Jesuit connection and the hand of dissident Englishmen abroad, to establish if any 'great man', especially the earl of Northumberland, was involved, and to distance Lord Monteagle from the Plot. There was also some political capital to be made in blaming individuals whom the authorities had no realistic chance of catching, so that the threat remained, a constant reminder of the government's great escape.

The earl of Northampton had joined in at the plotters' trial, exercising his natural talent for long, learned speeches, scorning the social standing of the plotters and dwelling on the presumption of over-mighty subjects in daring to rebel – the implication perhaps being that only nobility like his own family, the Howards, who had been doing it for generations, should be allowed to do it. But in Henry Garnet, Father Superior of the English Jesuit Province, the government now had the perfect material to test to breaking point the hypothesis of the missing organising genius. They also had, imprisoned in the Tower since the end of November but as yet untried, the earl of Northumberland. Neither line of enquiry was particularly comfortable for the government. In Henry Garnet, Salisbury was faced with the potential embarrassment of Jesuit martyrdom and the diplomatic awkwardness of uncovering past invasion plots by King James's valuable new ally, Spain. In Northumberland there was the prospect, hardly welcome to the king, of discovering support for the Plot among the nobility he had worked so hard to rehabilitate and establish as his own network of patronage in England.

Wary of what their continuing investigations might find, Salisbury soon discovered they had taken on a momentum of their own. Sir Edward Coke had no misgivings about uncovering aristocratic conspiracy. He contrived to forget royal instructions and conspicuously failed to exonerate Lord Monteagle. If Monteagle had not received the warning letter, apparently through the happy accident of being Francis Tresham's brother-in-law, there is little doubt that there was enough evidence (in the event hastily suppressed) to implicate him heavily in past plots and in the plotters' circle, if not in the Gunpowder Plot itself. There was certainly enough to bring greater consequences than did materialise for the lords Stourton, Mordaunt and Montague, whose connections with the plotters were more distant. Instead of land and financial reward, he might have found himself in the same boat as Stourton, pleading to Salisbury for his liberty in August 1606.

Coke had also fastened on the circumstantial evidence against the earl of Northumberland: the pedigree which made him uniquely suitable as a Lord Protector sympathetic to Catholics and his appointment of

Percy to the king's bodyguard without taking the oath of supremacy. Furthermore, Northumberland had sent enquiries to the north about his estate rents on 5 November without ordering the apprehension of Thomas Percy, who was responsible for their collection. As head and patron of the family, Northumberland was answerable for his cousin. In the days after the discovery, it seemed suspicious that he had not mentioned Thomas as the then prime suspect in the Plot. The 'Wizard Earl' had a love of arcane experiment and a rumoured association with the dark arts, including an interest in using astrology to predict the king's lifespan. He also maintained a friendship with Sir Walter Raleigh, which to Coke was suspicious in itself. There were rumours that Percy had warned Northumberland at the Syon House dinner on 4 November, and that Northumberland, like Monteagle, had received a warning letter but unlike Monteagle had concealed it. In his defence against such rumours, Northumberland revealed that Percy, far from wishing to preserve him, treated him with contempt and 'railed' against him – behaviour based on an idea, however misplaced, of his social superiority. Percy 'pretended himself to be of the elder house ... which showed he thirsted after the earldom'.

The government also struggled to control what political capital there was to be made from the Plot's discovery. There were allegations as early as November 1605 that Salisbury himself had devised the Gunpowder Plot to elevate his own importance in the eyes of the king, and to facilitate a further attack on the Jesuits. There were also constant reports suggesting that stopping the Plot had not stopped plotting. Informants seeking reward or to establish their own loyalty gleefully reported suspicious behaviour and renewed boldness in the king's enemies abroad. There was unease that the resources devoted to the investigation of the Gunpowder Plot, which dominated the business of the principal officers of state for two months after the discovery and preoccupied them until the trials of Garnet and Northumberland in mid-1606, had left the state vulnerable to attack from other quarters.

The volume of papers retained by the State Paper Office increases greatly in November and December 1605, as well as in those analogous papers which Salisbury retained at home. Almost all of this is Plot business. The stock in trade of the Privy Council in deciding places and preferments and settling disputes about land

and trade was largely deferred, and with it the state lost some of its routine intelligence gathering in those areas. In investigating the failures of local law enforcement around the rebellion in the Midlands, it had, very uncomfortably, to shift its attention from the traditional areas of threat to England at its borders to its very heart. What preparations had been made in the network of Catholic families in the Midlands? What did they know about the 'great blow' planned in London, and how did they come to know of it? How loyal and effective was local enforcement, and how closely allied was it to those families? Had the rebellion failed because of deep-seated loyalty to the king, or because knowledge of the failure of the gunpowder operation had spread as quickly and mysteriously as had word of its preparation?

The Gunpowder Plot could not be viewed in isolation but was part of a series of possible plots from known malcontents. Threats to the government and death threats to Salisbury himself continued to be made and reported. The fact that the state chose to continue to devote so many resources to investigating it long after the immediate danger had passed is explained by two factors. One is that the Plot was a real threat from which the king, the royal family and principal officers of state had narrowly escaped, so they were now desperate to understand how it had been constructed and how it had almost managed to succeed. Second is the refusal of the Plot to conform to the pattern of aristocratic conspiracy familiar from past plots; this led the investigation to pursue a number of dead-ends based on hunches and the personal interest of the commissioners, which obstinately refused to yield conclusive evidence.

If we are tempted to view the Gunpowder Plot, and the investigation that followed, as unique events peculiar in their methods, a quick look at the career of Thomas Phelippes makes it clear that the gathering of secret intelligence and, indeed, manufacturing of documents was a full-time industry. It was one for which the state used a select band of spies, forgers and decipherers whose very knowledge made them dangerous. The murky world of the Gunpowder Plot is made very much murkier thanks to men like Phelippes, who spent half their time forging, deciphering and gathering intelligence for the government and the other half being suspected of complicity in the plots they were paid to uncover. Phelippes shows the limits of the trust Salisbury placed in the men who formed his intelligence networks and the pitfalls of gathering it. Heavily implicated in the Babington Plot, which led to the execution of Mary, Queen of Scots, Phelippes was never likely to prosper under the rule of her son, King James. Phelippes was neglected, and when the state did have need of him he found himself working in arrears, paying off his debt to the Crown for his part in Mary's death. When it appeared that Phelippes had corresponded with Hugh Owen and had continued to do so after Guy Fawkes had revealed that Owen was the means by which the Plot was to be justified on the continent after the explosion, his fortunes reached an even lower ebb. This is not to say that he was no longer useful, of course. Fierce controversy has raged about the documents in which he might have had a hand, from the Monteagle letter to Henry Garnet's letters to Anne Vaux.

The government suspected Phelippes of duplicity in his dealings with Hugh Owen long before the discovery of the Gunpowder Plot. In January 1605, John Chamberlain had reported to Ralph Winwood, 'I heard yesterday that Phillips the decipherer was apprehended and committed with all his papers seized.'[1] With the discovery of the Plot, the arch-forger, decipherer and intelligence gatherer found that his own letters to Hugh Owen, which were designed to draw Owen into a confession of his knowledge of the Plot, were being transcribed and sent to Salisbury's secretary Levinius Monk as evidence of his own involvement.

Thomas Barnes copied these letters from memory, and they are long and detailed. Disconcertingly for the authorities, they gave evidence of the investigation against the earl of Northumberland, which seemed to add substance to what the commissioners had discovered from his examinations. Whatever the double-dealing purpose of the letters, their content allowed the possibility that the Plot's principal apologist abroad – and the man the government most wanted and failed to extradite and question – was better informed about the investigation than many of the commissioners themselves. This included evidence from Northumberland's apothecary that the earl intended to 'take physic' on the day of the opening of Parliament, 'when that bloody tragedy was to be put in execution'.

There was also the continuing suspicion that other lords had received warnings like Monteagle but had not revealed them to the authorities, and were implicated in other plots against the king's life.

> Only the Lord Mordaunt is said to be deeper engaged than the rest, for that there was this summer, with his privity, a plot laid for the murdering of the King's person at his house, by way of a masque, which notwithstanding was countermanded and checked by a Jesuit or priest, who willed forbearance at that time, because said he there is a course in hand that will cut up the very root and remove all impediment whatsoever [that] can be alleged to hinder the cause.

It is very difficult to tell if this was anything other than a lure to coax revelations about other plots from Owen, but it does fit with the evidence from the future earl of Pembroke's wedding at Christmas 1604. Then core plotters, including Guy Fawkes, had access to the king and weapons to hand but had done nothing, as their plot offered a more lasting settlement and solution. There was a kind of exquisite irony, too, in considering using the masque, an elaborate charade of kingly power and James's favourite form of drama, as the means of his destruction. Within it is another tantalising suggestion, echoed elsewhere in the copious evidence of the investigation, that the concept of Catesby's plot if not the detail was widely known and anticipated among the Jesuit missionaries, and through them more widely among Catholics, by the summer of 1605. Through the veils of espionage and entrapment, not to mention failing memory, it is very difficult to weigh this evidence, particularly as Barnes himself added that what he had set down 'should be but the text or plain song, for I should carry the comments or descant with me when I went'.[2]

A second copied letter by Barnes is calendared at 1 December but dates from January since it reports the capture of Robert Wintour and Stephen Littleton. In it, there is more grisly detail about the death of Francis Tresham:

> Francis Tresham died of sickness and thought to save the hangman a labour belike, but notwithstanding in respect of his impertinency,

showing no remorse of the fact, but rather seeming to glory in it as a religious act, to the minister that laboured with him to set his conscience straight at his end, had his head chopped off, and sent to be set up at Northampton, his body being tumbled into a hole, without so much ceremony as the formality of a grave.[3]

Sir William's Waad's qualms about the disposal of Tresham seem to have been overcome in the end by anger at his equivocations and his lack of remorse. The scales tipped more heavily against Phelippes again in January 1606 with Guy Fawkes's admission of Hugh Owen's involvement and the revelation of Phelippes's continued correspondence with him:

It may please your Lordship though I have great cause to be grieved that your Lordship should hold any suspicion of me, yet I am content to be tried, hoping that though my enemy will not leave to calumnate, your Lordship will leave in the end to think ill of me. Sir Thomas Fowler hath surveyed all my writings, which were once under survey afore, as your Lordship knoweth, and returned back, your Lordship having still my trunk with all state causes. I leave to his own report how curiously he hath observed your Lordship's warrant, breaking up for his discharge, all my wife's cabinets, whereof the keys were not left by her being these nine months out of town. I am only in particular to satisfy your Lordship of one thing; which is that Barnes at his going over the last week prayed me he might for safety, his own lodging being a common place, leave a certain bale of apparel which he brought over from the other side, for one of the Spanish Ambassador's servants, which I never so much as looked into, but it seems there were also certain letters for the party, which Mr Fowler hath and I hope nothing of moment, for I know Barnes to be honestly devoted to your Lordship's service. And so I leave myself to your Lordship's honourable carriage, whom God preserve, your Lordship's most humble at command Tho: Phellipes.

This letter earned Phelippes a chance to explain himself to Salisbury in person, but the meeting did not go well. When Phelippes wrote

Thomas Phelippes to the earl of Salisbury, February 1606 (right-hand page). Phelippes was so deeply immersed in and knowledgeable of the affairs of state and the business of espionage that his protestations of innocence were always likely to be greeted with skepticism. (TNA SP 14/18/61)

once more on 4 February 1606, his stock had fallen still further. Unfortunately for him, all his secret undertakings with Spanish agents, some of whom could themselves have been double agents, could be interpreted in different ways. Salisbury's secretary has underlined passages in his next letter in which Phelippes recalls hearing of 'Catesby's insurrection' from a Catholic whose brother was in service with the countess of Arundel. Perhaps here was another connection between the gentlemen's plot and 'the great'. Another school of thought would suggest this correspondence between Salisbury and the forger coming between Garnet's apprehension and his arrival in London is just too neat a coincidence. Could Phelippes have been brought in by the government on a trumped-up charge, simply as a pretext, obliging him to forge Garnet's letters?

The extent to which Phelippes' work in relation to the Plot could be said to have repaid his debt to the king can be gauged by the fact that he was moved to the Tower and remained in prison for at least four and a half years. In 1609, his wife Mary appealed to Salisbury successfully for the moiety of two of her husband's suspended Crown annuities, but his final years were spent in great poverty. The government needed forgers, but it did not trust them.

By contrast, Henry Garnet and Edward Oldcorne emerged from hiding to something approaching celebrity treatment. In Garnet's later account of his capture, there is an element of relief, an end to furtiveness and an opportunity to face his persecutors. Salisbury noted that the new arrivals to the Gatehouse prison made no attempt to conceal their status, 'themselves not sticking now to acknowledge their dignities'. Garnet later recalled his room in the Tower as 'a very fine chamber, but was very sick the first two nights with ill-lodging'.

In another nice piece of etiquette, Lord Cobham, one of the chief suspects of the plots of 1603, also noted the new eminent arrivals to the Tower. He wrote to Salisbury to renew his suit for release, thinking perhaps that with Garnet's imprisonment the Gunpowder Plot crisis had subsided sufficiently to allow reconsideration of his case. Evidently, he had not wished to trouble his brother-in-law with an old treason while he was dealing with a new one.

The comfort of Garnet's situation in the Tower was deceptive. The means of torture lay close at hand, and his interrogators alternated high-flown theological debate with more direct cross-examination. Garnet began an elaborate game of cat and mouse with his captors. When Garnet was examined, initially he seemed entirely in control of the process, denying all knowledge of the Plot before receiving Sir Everard Digby's letter seeking help on 6 November, and emphasising he had refused to help 'because they acted foolishly and wickedly'. He began to deny things that the authorities already knew from other sources.

While he replied cagily to his interrogators, he found ingenious ways to communicate to his friends. He began to produce suspiciously small and inconsequential messages on suspiciously large sheets of paper. The legible part of an early letter from the Tower included a request for a pair of spectacles 'set in leather and with a leather case or let the fold be fitter for the nose', presumably designed to alert the recipient to the fact that there was another way of looking at the letter. The real message was written on the back of the sheet in orange juice, which acted as an invisible ink, becoming visible when warmed. However, John Locherson, a government agent who befriended Garnet, intercepted the Jesuit's letters. He passed them to the Lieutenant of the Tower, Sir William Waad, who had them deciphered. Once they had been warmed at the fire, they could not be passed on, so the originals survive at The National Archives and among the earl of Salisbury's papers at Hatfield House. Instead, copies were made and passed on in the hope of soliciting incriminating 'secret' replies from the recipients, which would also be intercepted. This first letter about spectacles, notionally dated to 23 February, contained Garnet's account of receiving Sir Everard Digby's letter at Coughton Court on 6 November and Mary Digby's tearful reaction to her husband's desperate plight:

> This bearer knoweth that I write but thinks it must be read with water. The paper sent with biscuit bread I was forced to burn and did not read. Pray write again. I have acknowledged that I went from Sir Everard's to Coughton and stayed 2 or 3 days after my lady went to London and then rode away alone. Also, Bates and Greenway [Tesimond] met by chance and Greenway said all Catholics were undone, not as they would have it, that Jesuits only were discredited, I read the letter [from Sir Everard

Digby seeking his blessing and forgiveness] before Bates and Greenway. My Lady Digby came in. What did she? Alas what but cry. My answer was to Bates by word of mouth. 'I am sorry they have, without advice of friends, adventured in so wicked an action, let them desist. In Wales I neither can nor will assist them if Wales were so disposed as they imagine, yet all were now too late.' I must needs acknowledge my being with the 2 sisters and that at White Webbs as is true, for they are so jealous of White Webbs I can no way else satisfy. My names I all confess but that last. Appoint some place near where this bearer may meet some trusty friend. Where is Mistress Anne?[4]

Mary Digby's great distress when hearing of her husband's destruction at the hands of Robert Catesby is often quoted, but the rest of the letter is not. Garnet's characteristic caveats and qualifications, even in this apparently secure correspondence, make it heavy going in places, but it is still revealing. It is, of course, interesting that the plotters looked to Garnet to raise assistance for rebellion in Wales, and Garnet does not sound surprised to be asked, but his refusal seems categorical. Except categorical denial was not Garnet's style either. Instead, his response reads, on closer inspection, a bit like his conversation with Monteagle and Tresham about the strength of Catholic forces in England. If the timing were different, and their strength greater, then assistance from Wales might be forthcoming and he might be the man to assist. The overall impression is not so much of indignation at their wickedness as regret at their ineptitude. Perhaps with the 'advice of friends', not least Garnet himself, the rebellion might have been better coordinated and more effective. The Jesuits seemed well informed about the strength and inclination of possible supporters. Catesby's impatience and desire to act alone potentially cut him off from this valuable intelligence. Which of his many pseudonyms Garnet felt unable to confess is not clear. He was 'Humphrey Phillips' when taken at Hindlip, a variant which had not previously appeared in the investigation.

In a later orange juice letter, Garnet commented on the concealments and equivocations of his replies under interrogation and the weakness of the case against him. On 26 February, Garnet wrote to Thomas Sayer alias Rookwood with more references to spectacles on large pieces of paper containing messages in invisible ink. In the visible body of the letter, he set out his needs to complete his prison wardrobe. In invisible ink, he gave reassurances to his friends about the limits of his confessions so far: 'I have passed this day my last examination as I suppose, for they say I am obstinate and indeed they have nothing against me but presumptions.'[5] As time passed, his comments became less sanguine; it became clear that in trials for treason presumptions were all the evidence required.

While Garnet's orange juice letters were carefully warmed, and his conversations monitored, the government was always in danger of learning more than it wanted to know. In the Tower, Henry Garnet and Edward Oldcorne were left to talk together apparently in private but with eavesdroppers stationed to listen. The earl of Northampton may have been mentioned by Garnet in relation to the Plot, but this, like other uncomfortable facts, was conveniently screened by a Parlement of Foules. There is a lingering suspicion, though, that James's 'earwig', as the earl was sometimes unkindly known, could not be as loyal as he professed. Nobody could. The eavesdroppers heard the names of the earls of Northumberland and Rutland with another whose name they could not make out.

'Well I see they will justify my Lord Monteagle of all other matter, I said nothing of him, nor will I ever confess him.' There Garnet mentioned my Lord of Northumberland my Lord of Rutland and one more who we heard not well, but to what effect they were named we could not tell by reason of a cock crowing under the window of the room and the cackling of a hen at the very same instant.

Garnet had talked with an air of incredulity about the efforts the authorities were undertaking to preserve the reputation of Lord Monteagle. Garnet implied that he could incriminate Monteagle, but that given the attitude of the government he would not waste his breath. Breath spent implicating Northampton was likely to be equally wasted.

This is an almost comical reflection on the limitations of this particular form of sly government intelligence gathering.

Informer's report on the conversations of Henry Garnet and Edward Oldcorne in the Tower, 25 February 1606 (right-hand page). Garnet did not dispute the evidence obtained by this underhand method and believed the informers were 'honest fellows'. (TNA SP 14/18/117)

Would Northampton have been warned of the coming 'blow' in Parliament? If Catesby's attitude was anything to go by, he would not be esteemed by the conspirators. If the Lords in general were godless, Northampton was worse for attending Anglican services. Northampton's Catholicism helped make him an effective interrogator. He spoke Garnet's language and could use it against him. His learned approach, which tends to bore the general reader, nettled Garnet. His connections to prominent recusant families made him dangerous to them rather than to the king.

Northampton's speech at the trial of Sir Everard Digby had strained classical parallels to show the betrayal as well as the treason of which favoured men like Digby had been guilty. The plot became 'a Trojan horse its belly stuffed with hellish gunpowder'. Northampton wrote as loyally as he spoke. He composed much of the government's main case against the plotters, *A True and Perfect Relation*. But were his private opinions masked by the crowing of a cock and the cackling of a hen?

In many ways, the figure who most closely embodies the plight of English Catholics and the besieged life of the landed Catholic families is Nicholas Owen, Jesuit lay brother, carpenter and servant to Henry Garnet, who made a career of devising priest holes. Four days before Garnet's capture, he had been taken at Hindlip in one of 'eleven secret corners and conveyances' that Owen himself had devised. Owen and a fellow lay brother companion, Ralph Ashley, were starved out of a hide in the long gallery on Thursday 23 January after four days with one apple to eat between them. Owen's lower rank left him open to harsher treatment from the authorities than was given to his master, but Garnet was confident of his courage and loyalty and that 'Little John', as Owen was known, would tell the authorities nothing. In his initial examination Owen more than confirmed this hope, denying he knew Garnet at all.

Examined again on 1 March 1606, there is evidence that Owen, despite being lame from a horse's kick and suffering from a hernia, was tortured, being suspended by his thumbs while the questions were repeated to him, though his signature on this statement was neat and firm. The witnesses to his statement include no earls or others of rank

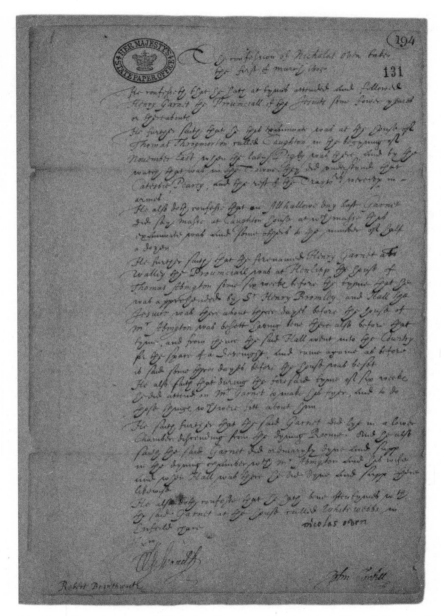

The Final Examination of Nicholas Owen, 1 March 1606. Though he would betray nothing of substance concerning the Plot, Owen gave interesting insights into the lives of the priests in safe houses as honoured guests whose stays were punctuated with terrifying raids when they cowered in cupboard-sized hiding places. (TNA SP 14/216/194)

overseeing his interrogation. As a lesser prisoner processed by the inferior commission, his interrogation could be harsher and more secret.

> The confession of Nicholas Owen, taken the first of March 1605[6]
>
> He confesseth that he hath at times attended and followed Henry Garnet the Provincial of the Jesuits for some four years or thereabouts.
>
> He further sayeth that he, this examinate, was at the house of Thomas Throgmorton, called Coughton, at the beginning of November last, when the Lady Digby was there and by the watch that was in the town, they did understand that Catesby, Percy and the rest of the Traitors were up in arms.

This time, Owen admitted serving Garnet and being at Coughton Court when the Midlands rebellion took place. Even here, though, he gave less information than Garnet had already given, not mentioning Sir Everard Digby's letter calling for aid, but rather insisting that he had heard of the rebellion by 'general report' via the 'watch', a local law officer.

Unsurprisingly, his interrogators were unimpressed with his answers and he was told that he would be racked on the next occasion. Owen contrived to free himself of his keeper by complaining of the coldness of his broth and apparently stabbed himself with a knife, which had been deliberately blunted as a precaution against suicide. Other reports after his death asserted he had died on the rack. We may think that whether his death was by torture or the threat of it makes little moral difference. He had told the authorities nothing they did not already know. The outline of the Plot in the hand of Oswald Tesimond was in no doubt that Owen would be tortured 'to give up the secrets of his many clients', presumably the myriad hiding places he had built. The process of hagiography began with Tesimond's narrative, which attributed Owen's effectiveness as a carpenter to his piety. His life was full of those little unverifiable details that mark the earthly progress of a potential saint. Owen, the narrative asserted, 'never said a swear word'. This was difficult to be sure of, given he worked alone in semi-darkness with a hammer for seventeen or eighteen years and would have had plenty of opportunities to hit his thumb without there being any witnesses to his reaction. Though his relatively low rank in society may have contributed to the manner of his death, his courage and conviction earned him sainthood. He was beatified by Pope Pius XI on 15 December 1929 and canonized by Paul VI on 25 October 1970.

The earl of Northumberland was imprisoned on rather easier terms, and on the day after Owen's death might even have been hoping for imminent release. Salisbury wrote to Monteagle's brother-in-law Lord Brouncker praying Northumberland would 'come to liberty on easy terms' because the government lacked men of 'blood and sufficiency'. Figures of noble birth and ability were at a premium, and the government could not insist on absolute loyalty and still hope to find sufficient persons of the calibre and social standing required. He suggested that the plotters' frequent references to Northumberland were a result of their basking in the reflected glory of his rank: 'Yet considering the greatness of his house, the improbability that he should be acquainted with so barbarous a plot, being a man of honour and valour, his Majesty is rather induced to believe, that whatsoever the traitors have spoken of him have rather been their vaunts, than any other good ground.' The letter emphasised that the context of the ongoing investigation was the continued fragility of the state, though the Plot had been foiled:

> Although it hath pleased God by his providence to confound the counsels of the wicked as we have had the happiness to discover and not suffer their bloody treasons. Yet must I plainly tell you as my good friend, that I must still apprehend the dangerous estate wherein we live, considering how we are forced after so long a suffering, to run a course more violent than standeth either with the ordinary rules of moral policy or with the moderation of his Majesty's mind. But necessity hath no law and the same God who blessed us in our slumbers will not forsake us when we are awake.[6]

This is a careful politician's justification of the 'more violent' course the government felt compelled to follow to secure itself in the wake of the Plot. The king, it seemed, was less inclined to pursue that course than Salisbury himself. There are some interesting parallels designed to contain some difficult and contradictory ideas. Is the state's providential delivery from the Plot a God-given licence to persecute those responsible? What safety can the king's subjects have if 'necessity hath no law'? In fact, the immediate proclamations gave plenty of opportunity for fugitive Jesuit priests to leave and for a milder course to be pursued with Catholics at home.

The man who would be accused of leading the Catholics in England, Northumberland, certainly appeared to be enjoying gentle handling. His keepers, Sir William and Lady Waad, who perhaps had a sense, even now, that his incarceration was still a temporary precaution and that he would emerge in time with his powers as a patron intact, sent him cheeses in the Tower. There seemed to be some tension in the government as to what should best be done with the suspected lords. Coke wanted the nobles to face the full severity of trial at Common Law, as the principal plotters had done. James, following the pattern of his Scottish reign, wanted them fined and grateful under the more discretionary and personal powers of the court of Star Chamber. Despite their periodic rebelliousness James relied on Catholic noblemen in England as he had in Scotland and generally found them more politically and socially acceptable than those who shared his religious views.

In a long letter, dated 'Shrove Tuesday' (4 March 1606), Henry Garnet gave Ann Vaux a full and witty account of his arrest and interrogation. Annotated 'keep all discreetly secret', it gave details of life in a priest hole, sitting immobile for seven days and nights, and implied that he and Edward Oldcorne were only forced to give themselves up by the conditions in their hiding place. They could have held out much longer if they had had a toilet – 'having a close stool we could have hidden a quarter of a year'. The searchers when they discovered them were more frightened than the priests; again, a reflection on the attitudes of local law enforcement, thinking the deadly Jesuits would be armed with pistols. The result was a vast crowd of gawping men assembled to secure two middle-aged clergymen who could barely walk. 'The fellow that found us ran away for fear, thinking we would have shot a pistol at him, but there came needless company to assist him and we bad them "be quiet and we would come forth". So they helped us out very charitably.'

Henry Garnet to Anne Vaux, 4 March 1606 (right-hand page). As so many of Garnet's letters do, this witty and self-deprecating account paints a picture of a likeable middle-aged theologian as uneasy with those who wanted to make him a martyr as he was with those who wanted him executed as a traitor. (TNA SP 14/19/11)

There is altogether more detail about toilet arrangements or the lack of them than one today might expect in a letter from a middle-aged priest to a female companion, but this simply reflects the lack of privacy and prudery which prevailed at the time. It was certainly the first thought of both men as they emerged from hiding and into custody 'We could not go, but we desired to be led to a house of office.'

Despite the seriousness of the situation, Garnet writes of the comedy of his own position and the nature of the pursuing forces, which, as at Holbeach, do not sound like the inexorable arm of a police state. Garnet and Oldcorne were carried to Worcester as prisoners, as the survivors of Holbeach had been. Sir Henry Bromley, who led the search for Garnet as an enemy of the state at Hindlip, immediately took him to dinner. Later popular calumny harped on Garnet's love of wine as if he were a drunkard, which he was not, but he does devote almost a page of a four-page letter justifying his actions to the faithful through Anne Vaux to describing the wines on offer at Sir Henry's table. Ben Jonson's *Volpone* re-told the gossip about Garnet with a characteristic black joke – 'I have heard/the rack hath cured the gout' – implying Garnet was tortured but that it did him good by curing the symptoms of his drunkenness. Neither Garnet's apologists nor his enemies would admit both parts of this rumour. Perhaps Jonson presents them as being equally untrustworthy.

The government set about confronting Garnet and Oldcorne in turn with elements of each other's contradictory testimony in the hope of extracting fuller confessions. They succeeded to some extent but also threatened to confuse themselves. Both agreed on one unacceptable fact: Lord Montagle had been heavily involved in negotiations for a Spanish invasion before 1603. Oldcorne co-operatively downgraded this from fact to opinion in his evidence by the interlineation of 'as I think' in his hand, but later confirmed he had done this only because the nature of his questioning made it clear this was what his questioners wanted.

On 9 March 1606 came Garnet's evidence endorsed by Salisbury: 'This was forbidden by the K[ing] to be given in evidence.' It promised clarity and a fuller narrative than Garnet had previously given, but 'I must needs acknowledge that I have dealt very reservedly with your Lordships in the case of the late powder treason for 2 respects'.

It was still hedged with qualifications and ambiguities. In response to a question from Catesby, Garnet gave advice as to the lawfulness of killing innocents in a just cause. Garnet answered as if it were a philosophical question from a potential captain of horse setting off for an uncertain fate in Flanders. This Garnet hastily modified to introduce an element of personal responsibility when he realised it might relate to some plan of Catesby's closer to home.

Then came the endless delicacies of the circumstances of Garnet hearing of Catesby's plot and whether he was bound by the seal of the confessional not to reveal it. Perhaps what is striking is the extent to which his interrogators were keen to trick Garnet into admitting he had heard of the Plot *outside* confession and could have divulged it to the authorities on that basis, rather than insisting he should have done so anyway. As with Fawkes's fortitude being reinforced by communion, the authorities at least half-accepted the binding power of Catholic practice. Even Sir Edward Coke, who was much more inclined to deride Catholic beliefs than were the other commissioners, fenced rather cautiously with Garnet on theological matters at his trial, despite the confidence and rhetorical flourishes of his denunciations of Garnet's supposed treason.

Garnet's evidence also contained the revelation that Lord Monteagle continued to believe decisive action might still need to be taken against King James as late as the summer of 1605. At a meeting with Monteagle and Tresham at a house in Essex, Garnet had asked about the strength of Catholic forces in England and their willingness to act, to be told by the man later pensioned and praised as the 'saver of his country' that 'if they ever were, they are able now ... The King (saith he) is so odious to all sorts.'[7]

This was starkly embarrassing given the official view of Monteagle the government was attempting to encourage, and personally infuriating for the king. Worse still, it was not a clear answer to Garnet's question – a 'conditional proposition', he called it. When pressed, Monteagle and Tresham admitted that the Catholics as it stood were not strong enough to act alone. Garnet took this as admission that that those like Catesby who blamed the Jesuits for seeking to prevent them from acting were in no position to act anyway.

The conversation then took a surprising turn. Rather than leaving the conversation at that satisfactory point, and perhaps with his suspicions of Catesby's intentions in mind, Garnet asked whether a successful plot against the king – specifically Father Watson's plot of 1603 – 'would be for the good of Catholic religion'. To Lord Salisbury and his fellow commissioners this must have sounded perilously close to an admission that Garnet was looking for a 'blow' that would alter the equation decisively in favour of the English Catholics and that he hoped Catesby might be the one to bring it about. Again, Francis Tresham was discouraging about the possibility of the success of the 1603 plot, because the nobility, namely 'Northumberland or the Howards', were 'uncertain' in their commitment. Did this in turn suggest that a plot involving the well-connected Thomas Percy might have better success in that quarter? Garnet reported that this conversation led him to write to his Jesuit superior, Claudio Aquaviva, and through him to Rome, 'that neither by strength or stratagems we would be relieved, but with patience and intercession of Princes'. Even retrospectively, and with his life in danger, there was little attempt to present this conclusion as the happy expression of relief of a man of peace who had convinced potentially 'wild heads' bent on violence of the error of their ways by reasoned argument. It sounds instead like a commander in the field reluctantly reporting to headquarters on the weakness of his army.

Though he had apparently set out his connection to the Plot at great length, on the following day Garnet was asked to expand on his earlier answers: 'His Majesty thinketh my former declaration too dry.' His answers were not short or lacking in rhetorical flourishes. I think 'dry' in this context can only mean that Garnet's endless qualifying remarks left his interrogators with more words than matter and that his evidence was considered to be very short of specific, verifiable detail.

Then Father Oldcorne shed further light on the gunpowder explosion at Holbeach. He had reassured the plotters that, in his considered theological opinion, the explosion and the failure of the Plot could not, after all, be interpreted as a sign of divine displeasure:

After Mr Catesby saw himself and others in the company burnt with powder, and the rest of the company ready to fly from him, that then he began to think he had offended God in this action, seeing so bad effects follow from the same. I answered him that an act is not to be condemned or justified upon the good or bad events that followeth it. The Christians defended Rhodes against the Turks, where the Turks prevailed and the Christians were overthrown.[8]

This was just the kind of evidence the government was looking for: that the plotters, superstitious but beaten men, who might otherwise have been recalled to their obedience by misfortune, had their resolve stiffened by the sinister hidden hand of foreign-trained priests. Lord Chief Justice Sir John Popham collated a point-by-point list of Garnet's involvement in Catholic plots which emphasised the role of the Jesuits in giving heart to plotters and casting doubt on the strength and conviction of Garnet's role as a force for restraint. In particular, he was convinced that Garnet urged restraint only because the weak position of the English Catholics would be made worse by the discovery of a plot. His curiosity about the capability and strength of feeling among them showed to Popham that he knew the plotters were best able to mobilise that potential and that the restraint might end if he were able to send the pope the happy news that the Catholics in England were strong enough to rebel with some hope of success. How close were they to that strength? Hindsight suggests there was little appetite or capability, despite the nervousness of local law enforcement long after the rebellion had failed and the piles of arms and munitions found in the houses of Catholic gentry across the Midlands. Monteagle's remark about James being 'odious to all sorts' might have suggested a Catholic revolt could carry a population generally disillusioned with their new king, just as Fawkes had believed it would, and Catesby's boasting no doubt exaggerated the possibility, but how many other would-be captains of Spanish regiments would have happily used their forces at home if the opportunity had arisen?

In the end, though, the distinction the government tried to make between the potentially loyal English Catholics and their treasonous priests was impossible to maintain, for it was impossible for them to practise their religion without priests. The life of criminality which fidelity to Catholicism involved is well illustrated by Henry Garnet's orange juice correspondent, Anne Vaux. She was well connected and wealthy, the daughter of William, 3rd Baron Vaux of Harrowden. She was eight years old when the bull of Pope Pius freed English

Catholics from their allegiance to a heretic monarch and divided English Catholics from their compatriots, ushering in legislation which implied, as Sir Everard Digby had complained in his letter to Salisbury, 'that only to be a Catholic is to be a traitor'. Anne lived her life at the centre of a recusant household, showing considerable courage and resolve in protecting priests, especially Henry Garnet.

The appraisal of Anne Vaux by Sir Thomas Tresham, father of Francis, as a 'virtuous and zealous Catholic maiden' comes from the reports of other people and her 'exterior show'. But it is in fact part of a prolonged denunciation of her conduct in slandering him and extorting money from him while he was imprisoned. It is pretty clear that the two, though related (Tresham's sister Mary was Anne's stepmother) and Catholic, disliked one another intensely. We may sometimes have a romantic idea that persecution had turned this network of Catholic families into a homogenous mass of loyalty, mutual support and devotion; in fact, they were entitled to be as divided, jealous and competitive as anyone else. Ties of blood were always considered strong circumstantial evidence of conspiracy by the authorities, but relations do not always get on. The documents connected to Anne Vaux's role in the Plot display a very human motivation couched in the language of piety.

Anne and her widowed sister Eleanor showed considerable resources and courage in sheltering missionary priests in various safe houses, including White Webbs, the house 'this side of Theobalds' that Fawkes had named as a base for the conspirators. During the summer of 1605, Anne accompanied Garnet and others, including the Rookwoods, on a pilgrimage to St Winifred's Well (Holywell) in Flintshire. Garnet himself confirmed that despite the plotters' attempts to remain 'monastical' and exclude women from the Plot, Anne was bright and observant enough to realise something was up. Several Gunpowder Plot conspirators visited White Webbs that summer and autumn, and on the way to Holywell she had noted the 'fine horses' in the Wintours' and Grant's stables. She later recalled how she had 'feared these wild heads had something in hand' and asked Garnet to dissuade Catesby from any rash attempt. On first being examined by the authorities, Anne remained conspicuously loyal to Garnet, denying he was on the pilgrimage to Holywell even though he led it.

The Holywell pilgrimage reminds us that Catholic life took place outside Thomas Wintour's carefully constructed network of close-knit gentlemen. Women may not have been invited to the party described in the classic engraving of the plotters with which this book began, but as his conspiratorial notes show, Wintour was hard-pressed to exclude them. The network of women on whom the survival and practice of faith depended required vigilance and intelligence on their part, more than enough to detect sudden changes in behaviour or whispering in corners by the men they protected. As it was later reported, the pilgrimage was overshadowed by suspicions of a 'stir' by Anne Vaux and others, and characterised by Father Garnet's unconvincing attempts to reassure them.

Anne Vaux confided in Garnet that a few of her fellow gentlewomen were asking; 'Where should we bestow ourselves until the "brut" is passed at the beginning of Parliament?' She would not tell who had heard of the intended attack or what they knew, and Garnet attempted to reassure her that the preparations they had seen were of Catesby's company preparing to fight for Spain in Flanders, and that the pope had forbidden unnecessary acts of provocation. She wanted to believe Garnet's reassurances, but was not convinced.

The degree of defiance in Anne's initial examinations clearly annoyed her interrogators. Anne's first examination of 11 March 1606 showed strength of character or impudence, depending on your point of view:

> She saieth that she went to St. Winifred's Well after Bartholomew-tide in the company of Lady Digby and others whom she refuseth to name. She will not say that Walley [Garnet] was there. But she sayeth that being at Wintour's and at Grant's and seeing the fine horses in the stable, she told Mr Garnet that she feared these wild heads had something in hand and prayed him for God's sake, to talk with Mr Catesby and to hinder any thing that possible he might, for if they should attempt any foolish thing it would rebound to his discredit. Whereupon he said he would talk to Mr Catesby and after assured her that he had nothing in the world to do, but had those horses to go into the Low Countries where he was to have a Colonel's place.[9]

Garnet gave evidence that the ladies asking where they should bestow themselves till the 'brut' had passed made him realise that Catesby's plan had been resolved upon and provided further evidence that the Plot was more widely known about than he had thought, at least in outline.

Anne Vaux concealed the fugitive Garnet after the proclamation for his arrest, and when he was arrested followed him to London. There she responded in kind to Garnet's letters in invisible ink. Her letters, like Garnet's to her, were intercepted. While maintaining the secret correspondence with Garnet, she protested in a very different tone to the authorities of Garnet's deception on the day following her evidence: 'I am most sorry to hear that Father Garnet should be an year privy to this most wicked action as he himself ever called it, for that he made me many great protestations to the contrary divers times since.'[10]

There is no loss of trust or lack of intimacy in their correspondence. Their 'secret' letters continued before, during and after the period of Anne's questioning by the authorities. An orange juice letter to Garnet tentatively dated 21 March 1606 showed that she had a better grasp of the medium than he did. It is recognisably her handwriting. He appears to be squeezing juice directly on to the paper. She does not seem to doubt him while she thinks she can communicate securely, and betrays none of the disappointment in him she expresses to the authorities:

> On Saturday at supper the Attorney said that when you were in examining, you feigned yourself sick to go your chamber and coming and coming [sic] thither you seem[ed] to take some marmalade, which even then was sent you, and burned a letter, which, your keeper seeing, did tell, and that you being examined said it was a letter a friend had sent you and fearing that there might be anything of danger to the party, you burned it and that you had acknowledged you know of the powder action, but not a practiser in it. The paper sent you with the box was concerning myself, if this come safe to you I will write and so will more friends who would be glad to have more direction from you. Who should supply you room

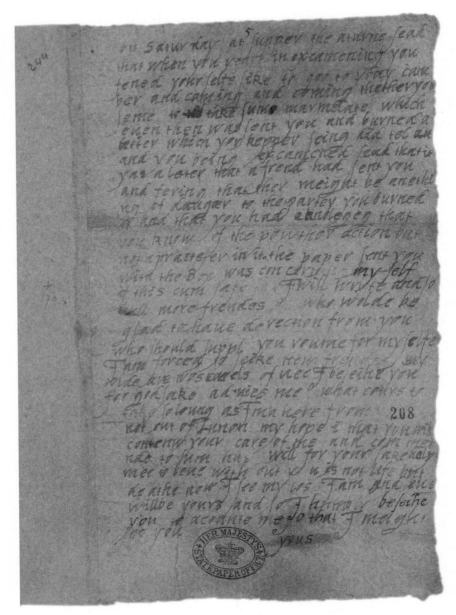

After Garnet's capture, Anne Vaux replied in kind to Garnet's letters in orange juice but their intimacy was broken by the interception of the letters. The letter formations and repetitions show the difficulty of writing in invisible ink. (TNA SP 14/216/244)

for myself? I am forced to seek new friends; my old are most careless of me. I beseech you for God sake, advise me what course to take. So long as I may hear from you, not out of London. My hope is that you will continue your care of me and commend me to some that will for your sake help me, to live without you is not life but death, now I see my loss I am and ever will be yours and so I humbly beseech you to account me. O that I might see you!

Whatever the precise nature of their love, there seems little doubt that love is what it was. The authorities occasionally suggested their love was physical, only to retract the claim in embarrassment and apology. The anti-Catholic hoi polloi were always keen on such stories and took up the suggestion eagerly.

The letter illustrates the difficulty of writing in the invisible ink, not just in forming the letters or punctuating but also remembering what you had written. The phrase 'and coming' is written twice. Oranges were an expensive commodity, whether to make ink or marmalade, but do not seem to have been in short supply in the Tower.

Garnet's reply, also in orange juice, is notionally dated 2 April but was presumably written soon after Anne Vaux's letter. It set out the arrangements for her to continue her work for the faith whether she 'goes over' to be a nun in Flanders or remains in England. 'The vow of obedience ceaseth being made to the Superiors of this mission, you may upon deliberation make it to some there. If you like to stay here, then I exempt you till a Superior be appointed.'[11]

This letter left Anne comforted by his solicitude and guidance but feeling as if Garnet were taking his leave and handing her spiritual wellbeing to others. His ongoing spiritual relationship appeared to be with Father Oldcorn, alias Hall, whose dream of 'two fair Tabernacles or seats for us' showed them beginning another spiritual journey after death, being professed of 'ten or eleven' vows more by the Father General, Claudio Aquaviva. In a characteristic final act of correction, equivocation or self-deprecation, in the last line of the letter Garnet withdrew this comforting picture of spiritual progress: 'That of the eleven vows was mistaken.' Dreams were not to be relied upon in theological matters.

Oldcorne was executed at Red Hill, Worcester, on 7 April. Presumably, this return to the Midlands was designed to avoid publicity, the executions being spread out so that there was no concentration of martyrs in London where they might attract veneration. There may have been an element of propaganda in executing missionary priests close to where their mission had taken place, though of course Garnet and Oldcorne had been taken at Hindlip together. This must have outweighed the risk of bringing Oldcorne to the Tower to confer with Garnet and then taking him back to the Midlands.

Anne Vaux's second examination, on 24 March 1606, dwelt on her meetings with Francis Tresham at White Webbs 'twice or thrice since the king's coming in and sometimes in the company of Mr Catesby and before the king's coming in he was there some few times'. Underlined in her evidence was Garnet's advice to Tresham: 'At those times Mr Garnet always gave him good counsel and persuaded him to rest contented, she remembereth he would use these words "Good gentlemen be quiet, god will do all for the best, we must get it by prayer at god's hands, in whose hands are the hearts of princes."'[12] But what would they get by prayer?

Aside from this ambiguity, Garnet's words sound a little too passive and good to be true. It was perfectly understandable for Anne not to remember when and where every meeting with Francis Tresham took place, but damning when those meetings appeared to coincide with attempts to exploit the weakness of the English state in its most perilous moments. When prompted, Anne remembered a subsequent meeting at Rushton shortly after Sir Thomas Tresham's death. This questioning was part of Sir Edward Coke's attempt to discredit Tresham, and gradually a series of meetings at a succession of safe houses – White Webbs, Fremlands and Erith – emerged.

In a nice piece of procedure on 27 March 1605, Coke asked Lord Salisbury for Anne Vaux's examination of 24 March, since he heard from Sir William Waad that Salisbury had it.[13] The note, though brief, sheds light on the system for gathering and retaining evidence and shows how the division of papers in the State Paper Office and those which eventually went to Hatfield House came about. Coke claimed he could use this evidence to expose Tresham's equivocations and ensnare Garnet.

By 22 March, impatience with Garnet's vague, half-remembered and equivocated statements, not to mention Francis Tresham's reluctant evidence and retractions on the same subject, was growing. Garnet was asked to give the titles of the papal breves which freed the English from their allegiance to a Protestant monarch who might succeed Queen Elizabeth. Waad then asked him 'to set down truly as I will answer it before God and upon my allegiance, how often I have had conference with Francis Tresham within these few years'.[14] Garnet confirmed that the most recent meeting with Tresham had been in the company of Catesby at Fremlands in Essex, presumably the occasion of Tesimond's standing confession of Catesby's plot. Earlier meetings with Tresham before the queen's death were reckoned roughly in years and 'about' saints' days, so the dates were still vague.

On the following day, Garnet expanded his evidence on his acquaintance with Francis Tresham. It must have made interesting reading to the authorities:

> I knew him 18 years ago and before but since discontinued my acquaintance, until the time between his trouble in my Lord of Essex his tumult and the Queen's death in which time he was twice or thrice with me at White Webbs in the company of Mr Catesby and conferred about the message into Spain.[15]

The trajectory of the friendship seems to have tracked moments of the English state's greatest vulnerability, when the possibility of foreign invasion or insurrection was strongest. The relationship lost purpose with the failure of the Spanish Armada, but revived with Tresham's prominent involvement in the Essex revolt and the plotting against Elizabeth and the succession that followed until the end of her reign. This suggested that, as far as the Jesuits were concerned, the period of uncertainty had not ended with King James's accession. They could indeed be a source of restraint against unsanctioned attempts against the state which had little chance of success and which would only bring their co-religionists into disrepute. But what if a more promising opportunity arose? How many Catholic 'sleepers', like Tresham, might be brought back into use?

11

DROWNING SORROW

The foiling of the Plot had not ended the feeling of uncertainty or the sense of the continuing vulnerability of the state. Quite suddenly, on 22 March 1606, their came a rumour that King James had been killed while hunting at Woking, a rumour credited widely enough to require a proclamation to refute. John Chamberlain wrote to Dudley Carleton with details of the proclamation on 27 March, and on the same day Carleton wrote to him from Oxfordshire to the effect that the report of the king's death had been generally believed. Both obviously wrote as soon as soon as it was safely confirmed that the king was unharmed without waiting to receive news from the other. The real news that Chamberlain was able to send his friend from the capital was of Henry Garnet's forthcoming trial:

> Garnet is to be arraigned this day at Guildhall with great concourse. I doubt he will deceive their expectation, for I am of opinion he will say little: once he hath been very indulgent to himself both in the gatehouse and in the Tower, and daily drunk sack so liberally as if he meant to drown sorrow.[1]

Sir William Waad was also concerned about the physical condition of his prisoner and the arrangements for getting him to Guildhall: 'The way is longer from the Tower and Garnet is no good footman.' Waad was exercised about his own place at the trial, that it should be in keeping with his rank and the importance of the services he had rendered the state. The trials following the discovery of the Plot were great theatrical and social occasions, which drew large paying crowds, sometimes too many to allow important people the prominent places they wanted. It is evident that they were theatrical in another sense, being show rather than substance. No one appears to have expected new compelling evidence, or revelations that might upset the set course of events; it was simply a chance to see the notorious defendants at first hand and comment on their behaviour before the inevitable verdict and sentence.

In the days before Henry Garnet's trial, the government was busy gathering evidence against him, but much of what they took from Anne Vaux was not what they sought. Passages in her evidence were underlined as not to be used in the trial because they showed Garnet's attempts to keep the plotters 'quiet'. So there was little evidence produced of these restraining efforts by Garnet and others, or the orders of his superiors to prevent a 'stir' by Catholic malcontents in England. Garnet's correspondence by cipher with his superiors in Rome and the anxiety not to undermine the chances of a peace between King James and Spain did not feature.

While government ministers were keen to suppress straightforward and probably accurate evidence that did not accord with the official theory, they were coming to doubt the veracity of any evidence from witnesses familiar with the doctrine of equivocation Garnet had expounded. Three months after his death it appeared that Francis Tresham had retracted on his deathbed his implication of Garnet in past plots. Sir Edward Coke, who was constructing evidence for Garnet's trial designed to show that he had been behind every Catholic plot since 1588, noted that Tresham's retraction was full of 'manifest falsehoods'. The retraction nevertheless made the authorities uneasy about any reliance placed on witnesses who were familiar with the doctrine.

Garnet contributed to government unease by continuing to implicate Lord Monteagle in attempts by the papacy to secure a Catholic succession in England in 1603. Garnet protested that he burnt papal directions about the succession and the inadmissibility of a Protestant monarch on James's succession but had shown them to Robert Catesby first, and Catesby had shown them to Monteagle. On the following day, Garnet suddenly 'did not remember' that Monteagle had seen them, an obvious indication of pressure applied.

While William Waad and the audience haggled about their places among the great crowds expected at Garnet's trial at Guildhall, Salisbury sent a note to Sir Edward Coke reminding him of his lines as the principal performer:

First that you be sure to make it appear to the world that there was an employment of some personages to Spain for a practice of invasion as soon as the queen's breath was out of her body. The reason is this for that the King doth urge it, he sayeth that some men there are that will give out and do, that only despair of the King's courses with the Catholics and his severity drove all these to such works of discontentment. Where by you it will appear that before his majesty's face was seen or that he had done anything in parliament, the King of Spain was moved, though he refused it, saying he rather expected to have peace etc.

Next, you must in any case when you speak of the letter which was the first ground of discovery, absolutely disclaim that any of these wrote it, though you leave the further judgement indefinite who else it should be.

Lastly and that you must not omit, you must deliver in commendation of my Lord Monteagle, words to show how sincerely he dealt and how fortunate it proved that he was the agent of so great a blessing as this was.

On the whole, Salisbury's instructions smack of a desire to keep Coke on message rather than a sinister attempt to subvert the evidence. He gives reasons for all his instructions. First, he wanted to counteract rumours of Monteagle's direct involvement in the Gunpowder Plot ('it is lewdly given out that he is one of this plot of powder'). Secondly, it was important to deny that one of the convicted plotters wrote the Monteagle letter, so that none of them would confuse the issue by sharing in Monteagle's glory ('though you leave the further judgment indefinite, who else it should be'). Yet, who else could it be? The government preferred to present the letter as an instrument of divine agency.

Coke continued to ignore large parts of these instructions. Salisbury, seen by many as the great manipulator of the Plot, could not even rely on the Attorney General to present the government view consistently.

Salisbury's Instructions to Sir Edward Coke, 28 March 1606 (right-hand page). This remarkable document shows the earl of Salisbury's explicit instructions to Attorney General Sir Edward Coke about how to conduct Henry Garnet's trial. More remarkable still was the extent to which Coke ignored them. (TNA SP 14/19/94)

Coke was very keen on pursuing suspect lords, men who might think themselves above the law, and would quite like to have prosecuted even Monteagle himself. He was not about to praise him. The lack of an established pattern to the Plot gave the commissioners scope to adopt their own private theories, perhaps another reason why Salisbury found a consistent government line difficult to sustain and why it seems to shift suspiciously.

Garnet's trial in the Guildhall began on 28 March. Coke blithely pursued his own agenda and retained his own rhetorical manner of proceeding, but with less assurance than he had at the plotters' trial in January. Coke set out the strength of the king's claim to the throne, which seemed a superfluous undertaking unless there were still doubts about it and the papal view of the succession was a genuine threat. After the triumphalism of the prosecution's case at the core plotters' trial, at Garnet's there seemed to be an air of doubt and nervousness about Coke's conduct. This was partly because Garnet's status and learning gave him a presence and degree of credibility that the others did not enjoy. It was also partly because Coke's thesis that Jesuit teaching and practice had given the Plot its justification and motivation lent Garnet further power and meant the arguments about the Plot had to be conducted on intellectual ground where Garnet, isolated though he was, was more comfortable than the prosecution. In particular, the doctrine of equivocation cast doubt on the whole proceeding. It was an odd preface to a show trial for the Attorney General to bring into question the nature of the evidence on which the prosecution was based. Francis Tresham, Coke said, had retracted his previous evidence and freed Garnet from any complicity in plotting only because implicating a priest would imperil his own soul.

Coke used poetic devices in language to lend weight to arguments that were by no means conclusive of guilt. Coke presented Garnet as the instigator of the Plot and showed he must be devilishly inspired – because he was guilty of so many things beginning with the letter 'D'. Garnet, said Coke,

> hath many gifts and endowments of nature, by art learned, a good linguist and, by profession, a Jesuit and a Superior as indeed he is Superior to all his predecessors in devilish treason,

a Doctor of Dissimulation, Deposing of Princes, Disposing of Kingdoms, Daunting and Deterring of subjects, and Destruction.

Salisbury then began to focus on the confession Garnet had taken from Oswald Tesimond in July and whether Catesby had offered to confirm that information outside the confessional. There followed in an exchange that was both polite and sinister: 'Why did you refuse to hear Catesby tell you all the particulars, when he would have told you if you had been desirous to prevent it'?' Garnet replied: 'My soul was so troubled with mislike of that particular that I was loath to hear any more of it.'

The torment of Father Garnet was nearly over. The earl of Salisbury took the opportunity to establish publicly that Garnet had not been maltreated as part of his questioning: 'Mr. Garnet ... since your apprehension even to this day, you have been as Christianly, as courteously and carefully used as ever man could be.'[2] This Garnet acknowledged, but was it true? Was this another equivocation, a condition of a pardon that never came? Certainly, it was suggested that Garnet and Oldcorne wrote to one another in 'sack', presumably another version of invisible ink. This Falstaffian tipple suggested a convivial confinement.

Once again, the earl of Northampton exhibited greater felicity in tackling Garnet on his own ground than Coke had done. His elaborate diction and biblical precedents lulled Garnet. His insight into the relationship of priest and plotters was more deadly for being more intimate. He nettled Garnet by using Latin precepts well known to him against his own actions. He understood that Garnet's power over the plotters was his greatest weakness and that the strongest evidence against him was not what he said, but the fact that that he could exercise his influence by barely speaking at all. 'Rookwood and Bates and others that did shrink at the horror of the project when it was first laid down, received satisfaction upon the very sound of your assent.' Based on the closeness of their relationship, Catesby was able, as the gatekeeper of Garnet's opinion to the other plotters, to use the Jesuit's status as an instrument of control. According to Northampton, 'He used your admittance as a charm or spell to keep quick spirits within the circle of combined faith, which otherwise perhaps, when hell brake loose, would have sought liberty.'[3]

The charms and incantations, oaths and vows of Catholic faith may have supported Fawkes in his fortitude under cross-examination and torture, but they also made its adherents slow to question, dissent or refuse to follow instruction. From a Protestant polemicist this could be dismissed as a fairly standard slur on the nature of Catholic faith; coming from the earl of Northampton it sounded like a genuine insight into the power of the priesthood, and more particularly into the cunning of men like Catesby who could harness it for their own ends. Rambling though Northampton's contributions to the prosecution sound to modern ears, they rattled Garnet and undermined Catholic attempts to dismiss the charges against him.

Ambrose Rookwood had claimed that he had been 'neither author nor actor but only persuaded and drawn in by Catesby'. Coke presented Garnet as the real author. But was he manipulating Catesby or was he used by him? Certainly, Garnet could not alter the plot of his trial. A treason trial was always a tragedy rather than a comedy, the charges so grave that a reprieve was almost impossible. The court found Garnet guilty as charged and sentenced him to death.

Garnet's response to his conviction was a meditation on just laws. His declaration of 1 April 1606 reasoned that

> no power on earth can forbid any action we are bound unto by the law of God, which is the true pattern of all justice. So the laws against Recusants; against receiving of priests, against Confession, against Mass and other rites of Catholic religion are to be esteemed as no laws by those who steadfastly believe these to be necessary observances of the true religion.[4]

This was an uncharacteristically clear and forthright statement, and rather at odds with the urging of restraint and quietness. To be a Catholic under the law as it stood in England was not possible, and conflict was inevitable.

There followed further clarification on the lawfulness of equivocation and the disclosure of confession. What the authorities took away from this latest evidence was more stark: 'Garnet doth affirm that if any man should undertake to kill his Majesty (whom God preserve), that he is not bound to confess it, though he be brought before a lawful magistrate, until there is proof to convince him.'⁵ John Locherson and the other witnesses then felt obliged to add that it was they who had added 'whom God preserve' rather than Garnet himself. Evidently, this was too shocking a scenario to be allowed to pass without some attempt to ward off the possibility, and too treacherous for there to be the allowance of any doubt about who had said what.

In a letter to Dudley Carleton commenting on Garnet's trial, Sir Allan Percy had noted that the earl of Northumberland's position seemed to have worsened while attention had been fixed on Garnet. The earl, his brother, had not been mentioned by the commissioners at that trial, 'yet there was a show as though they could say more than they would'. The earl was in their thoughts and the case against him was growing. Sir Allan also reported the king's insistence on parliamentary attendance after the many dubious absences in November, 'every knight and burgess to be present upon pain of fine and ransom'.⁶

On 2 April, Garnet's trial was reported to Dudley Carleton by John Chamberlain, who himself got it at second hand. Carleton was still in the country trying to scrub away the whiff of gunpowder under the supervision of Sir Walter Cope. Perhaps even Chamberlain himself felt his connection with Carleton made the trial too dangerous to be enjoyed as a spectacle at first hand. We are very fortunate to have an account written by such a keen observer of how Garnet's trial was received by those who attended. It is clear that by this time the chief interest was no longer the Plot itself and Garnet's supposed role in it but the credibility or otherwise of his evidence. 'I was not at Garnet's arraignment, but have heard it related by many that were there. It lasted from eight in the morning till seven at night. The King was there privately and held it out all day.'

Chamberlain neatly summarizes the evidence against Garnet as it was presented by Coke:

The sum of all was that Garnet coming into England in [15]86 hath had his finger in every treason since that time...

The declaration of the foresaid treasons was a long work and when all was done, he was not to be touched for them, having gotten the general pardon the first year of his reign. But touching this late hellish conspiracy he was proved to be privy to it two several ways at least; both by Catesby himself and by Tesimond or Greenway. To which he answered that from Catesby he had it only in general terms and from Tesimond *sub sigillo confessionis* and that he did not only dissuade, but pray against it. Which though it were no sufficient answer, yet it was further replied that Catesby having imparted to him the particulars of the same plot to be executed in Queen Elizabeth's time, it was not likely he would conceal them from him now and having continued intercourse with the chief actors and sending letters both by Wintour into Spain by Fawkes and Wright to the Archduke and by Edmund Baynham (captain of the damned crew) to the Pope, it would not be but that he was acquainted with all their secrets. Besides the very next day after the plot should have been performed he was at the rendezvous in Warwickshire.

As reported by John Chamberlain, part of the appeal of the trial was the intricacy and suggestiveness of the language used by Garnet and Tresham, and both sides' consciousness of the propaganda value of the theatrical spectacle the trial had now become. The earl of Salisbury wrestled with some modern-sounding preoccupations about the treatment of prisoners, the nature of the evidence produced under duress and the claims by both sides:

But to show what credit was to be given to his or any of their denials or speeches, the Earl of Salisbury delivered two notable instances: After he had first declared that by reason of their impudent slanders and reports, we are kept in such awe that we dare not proceed against them by such means as they do in other countries, to get out the truth, but are fain to flatter and pamper them. For if any of them die in prison of sickness, they say he is starved or tortured to death. If any man kill himself, he is made away by us, so we are fain to get out matters by as fair means as we can. So that this man was brought by the cunning of his keeper into a fool's paradise and had divers conferences with Hall [Oldcorne] which were overheard by Spials [spies] set of purpose, whereof being examined he utterly denied any such interlocution. But being urged further and some light given him, that they understood somewhat, he denied it still with greater assurance and protestation upon his soul. And now being asked in all this audience how he could do it, answered boldly that so long as he thought they had no proof of it, he was not bound to accuse himself, but when he saw they had proofs he stood not long in it. The other example was of Francis Tresham that his confessions having accused this man, drawing now to his end, his wife was permitted to have access to him, by whose means (as it is thought) he wrote a letter to my Lord Salisbury, not four hours before his death, with a retraction of what he had said touching this man, protesting before God to whom he was now going and upon his soul and salvation, that he had not seen him in sixteen years last past. Whereas it was proved by Garnet himself, by Mistress Vaux and others that he had been with him in three several places this last year and once not a month before the plot should have been performed. In which case Garnet's opinion of him being likewise asked, he answered he thought he meant some equivocation. It were to no end to trouble you further only I will tell you how my Lord Admiral [Nottingham] [puts] it in saying to him: 'Garnet thou hast done more good in that pulpit this day (for he stood in a pew by himself) than in all the pulpits thou ever camest in in thy life.' In conclusion he was found guilty and had judgement, but is thought he shall not die yet if at all, for they hope to win much out of him and used him with all respect and good words and he carried himself very gravely and temperately.[7]

If the words attributed to the Lord High Admiral by John Chamberlain are accurate, then they are a rare example of Garnet losing his 'mister' and being addressed as 'thou'. This might just be the result of Chamberlain rendering the dialogue in a way that better conveyed the wit and immediacy of the lines, but it is just possible that the change is an indication of a loss of respect. If Salisbury claimed respect for Garnet's priesthood and a fear of Catholic calumny at any possible maltreatment had hindered the investigation, then there may be an indication that in the end the difficulty and falsehoods of his evidence had undermined that respect. What was the 'good' which Nottingham thought Garnet had done? Had he served truth by finally admitting his true role in relation to the Plot, or had he undermined the confidence of his friends in him and in the power of the Catholic priesthood by the shifting and unreliable nature of his evidence? Francis Tresham, at least, had died with his faith in Garnet intact, happy to equivocate to preserve him and his own soul.

To a knowing commentator like John Chamberlain, at this stage it seemed like Garnet would be more useful to the authorities alive than dead, his conviction and sentence notwithstanding. He was still a source of potentially useful information, and his examinations continued. Garnet too seemed hopeful of a pardon or other intercession from his powerful connections. Chamberlain and perhaps members of the government feared his execution might provoke disorder or prove a propaganda victory for Catholics at home and abroad. The immediate effect of the trial among Catholics was disturbing and provoked some debate.

On 3 April 1606, Anne Vaux wrote Garnet a sixth letter in orange juice. It was barely legible and barely coherent in its emotional content, but it is a direct reply to his note about her spiritual welfare and disposition. She asks for direction on whether to stay or go abroad, expresses her determination to stay with him until the end, and revises Oldcorne's dream of the tabernacle to include herself: 'Mr Hall his dream would have been a great comfort if at the foot of the throne there had been a place for me. God and you know my unworthiness, I beseech you help me with your prayers.'[8] The priest's powers are still very much undiminished here, despite the gleeful popular reporting of his weakness at his trial. Condemned and imprisoned, he is still Anne Vaux's source of strength and direction.

Garnet replied the same day to Anne Vaux with advice and prayers in a long letter apparently in conventional ink, annotated 'Garnet to Mistress Vaux to be published at his death ... all of this is Garnet's own hand'. He indicates the best course for her spiritual welfare:

If you can stay in England and enjoy the use of Sacraments in such sort as heretofore, I think it absolutely the best. Secondly, if you like to go over then I do wish that you stay a while at St Omer and send for Father Baldwin and consult with him where to live, for I think St Omer be not so wholesome as Brussels...

I understand by the doctors [of Divinity] that were with me and by Mr Lieutenant [Waad] what great scandal was taken at my arraignment and 500 Catholics turned Protestants, which if it should be true, I must needs think that many other Catholics are scandalised at me also. I desire all to judge of me in charity, for I thank God most humbly in all my speeches and actions I have had a desire to do nothing against the glory of God. It may be also Catholics think [it] strange we should be acquainted with such things, but who can hinder, but he must know things sometimes which he would not. I never allowed it, I sought to hinder it, more than men can imagine, as the Pope will tell. It was not my part as I thought to disclose it. I have written this day a detestation of that action for the King to see. And I acknowledge myself not to die as a victorious martyr but as a penitent thief. Howsoever I shall die a thief yet you may assure yourself is such that I doubt not but if you die by reason of your imprisonment you shall die a martyr.[9]

That Catholics might be scandalised by the Plot and the role of priests in it, and that there might be 500 converted as result, fulfils exactly Ben Jonson's loyal prediction of his 8 November letter to the earl of Salisbury – a rare example of a prophecy coming true in a story sprinkled with them.

There was an also in it an element of the propaganda John Chamberlain had reported as a preoccupation and frustration for the earl of Salisbury at Henry Garnet's trial. Garnet did not, of course, wish Anne Vaux to die in prison, but the thought of the benefit to her soul and to the faith of her doing so had not escaped his thoughts entirely. The note ends with a Latin biblical quotation from the first book of Peter chapter four, which elides verses 7 and 17. These are rendered in King James's Authorized Version as, 'But the end of all things is at hand; be ye therefore sober and watch unto prayer' and, 'For the time is come that judgement must begin at the house of God; and if it first begin at us, what shall the end be of them that obey not the gospel of God?' In Garnet's version, the first line of the second verse is followed by the second line of the first. Perhaps Garnet had the second part of the second verse in mind as he wrote, a comfort both to Anne Vaux and himself as he faced his execution. 'And if it first begin at us, what shall the end be of them that obey not the gospel of God?' God's judgement on those who had judged them would be harsher than what they now faced.

On 4 April came Garnet's promised final declaration on the key points, a last attempt to save his reputation. But since so much doubt had been created by his characteristic use of language, what now could be gained from a further torrent of words?

I, Henry Garnet of the Society of Jesus, priest, do freely protest before God, that I hold the late intention of the powder action, to have been altogether unlawful and most horrible; as well as in respect of the injury and treason to his Majesty, the Prince and others that should have been sinfully murdered at that time (as also in respect of infinite others innocents which should have been present). I also protest that I was ever of opinion that it was unlawful to attempt any violence against the King's majesty and the estate after he was once received by the realm. Also, I acknowledge that I was bound to reveal all knowledge that I had of this or any other treason out of the Sacrament of Confession. And whereas partly under hope of prevention, partly for that I would not betray my friend, I did not reveal the general knowledge of Mr Catesby's intention which I had by him. I do acknowledge myself to be highly guilty and to have offended God, the King's majesty and estate and I humbly ask all forgiveness, exhorting all Catholics whatsoever they be in no way to build upon my example, but by prayer and otherwise to seek the peace of the realm, hoping in his Majesty's merciful disposition, that they shall enjoy their wonted quietness and not bear the burden of others' defaults or crimes. In testimony whereof I have written this with my own hand.[10]

This told the authorities little they did not know before, though it might go some way to soothing the sense of scandal among Catholics. It was a fair copy statement of the extent of his culpability with a few new assumptions built in. One was that attempts against James and the state became unlawful only when the papal breves against a Protestant succession ceased to have effect. Was Garnet distinguishing between 'innocents' and the royal family and government who were not? What form of peace in the realm could Catholics legitimately seek in their prayers? The government could argue the kingdom was already at peace. True peace, he implied, could only follow the ending of penal laws against them, or perhaps the reconversion of the realm.

After his conviction, Garnet continued to write to his various correspondents, but lacking some of the assurance and social ease that had marked his early interrogations. This was not simply the result of the seriousness of his predicament. His captors lied to him about the scandal he had caused among Catholics by admitting his knowledge of the Plot and implicating Oswald Tesimond in his absence. They lied too about the 'capture' of Oswald Tesimond and his supposed testimony, which was said to undermine Garnet's. In fact, Tesimond was still free and would live to put his name to a narrative justifying Garnet and the plotters.

On the same day as his declaration, 4 April 1606, Garnet wrote to Tesimond in a different style to his public declaration, believing him to have been captured. This letter simply reports the testimony he has given, which implicated his fellow priest.[11] There is no clear indication as to whether he represents that testimony as truthful or not, though there is an underlying suggestion that Tesimond would know his reported evidence was only half of the truth and would know how to interpret what Garnet had said and why he had said it. About Thomas Wintour's mission into Spain in 1602, he adds the observation that the gentleman conspirators did not want to involve noblemen in their conspiracy because they wanted the thanks and pensions of Spain for themselves and could provide the necessary horses from their own resources. His estimate of the number of horses (1,500) agrees with Thomas Wintour's evidence of 26 November, which suggests a degree of confidence between them and an agreement that the figure was credible. The gunpowder element of the Plot may have been a genuine source of surprise and horror for Garnet, but the business of raising horses and arms for Spain or for the Catholic cause at home seemed very familiar. Arguably, while the authorities ransacked the coffers and panelling of the houses of landed Catholic families looking for fugitive priests and evidence of proscribed religious practice, the real evidence of treason was standing in their stables.

Tesimond had some difficulty convincing his superiors he had done nothing to provoke or support the Plot in defiance of their carefully worded prohibition, not least because of the emphasis Salisbury's version of events placed on the role of the Jesuits.

The government's tactics were underhand, but they worked. Garnet became defensive and uneasy in his communications about the Plot with his co-religionists. To Anne Vaux he wrote of his mystical vision of their place in heaven but quickly followed it with justifications of his conduct, their implicit trust somewhat undermined. He then wrote a rather awkward note to the supposedly captive Tesimond, explaining his conduct in casting some of the blame on him while he believed him to be free. Sir William Waad believed there was sufficient discrepancy between Garnet's various statements 'to disclose his hypocrisy' in order to disillusion Anne Vaux. Sir Thomas Edmondes reported from Brussels that Garnet's obvious contradictions were evident even to his supporters there, though they were explained away as being proof that he had been tortured.

In fact, the unease with which Garnet dealt with his Catholic allies contrasted with his relationship with his interrogators, which was in general rather cordial. In 'a declaration for the King to see' Garnet acknowledged his fault in not revealing what he knew of Catesby's 'general intention' outside the seal of confession, which showed he was still in hope of earning a reprieve though under sentence of death. Among the Cecil papers at Hatfield House, this declaration by Garnet was designed to clear his name after all the ambiguities, rumours and calumnies that attended his trial. He felt he needed to explain his conduct to his friends as much as to his interrogators. The note itself, though, is full of contradictions and qualifications. It did little to enhance his reputation. He seemed to make definitive statements of his innocence, only to hedge them with remarks that hinted at his deeper involvement. He deplored Catesby's deception in using his name to persuade others that his scheme had been sanctioned. What were his followers, let alone the Lords Commissioners, to make of his carefully nuanced position and the way he expressed it? 'I always condemned in my own conscience absolutely this attempt; and generally I thought all insurrection against the King unlawful because there wanted the declaration of the Pope.'[12] This seemed to allow for the possibility that Garnet could support the Plot in words and deeds while condemning it in his thoughts. It transferred responsibility for ruling on the lawfulness of killing the king from him to the pope. Did this allow him to hope that Sir Edmund Baynham would bring sanction for the Plot from Rome in time for Catesby to act with his blessing? Tesimond, too, had taken Garnet's name in vain in encouraging those at Hindlip to rise in rebellion: 'It was more than I gave him commission to do.' So there was a 'commission'. What commission did Garnet give Tesimond, and by how much did he exceed it?

By contrast, Garnet treats his evidence to the Lords Commissioners and their attempts to trick him as something of a game. He says that he knew the orange juice letters were intercepted and his conversations with Oldcorne were overheard, but even the eavesdroppers he reports as 'honest fellows, though they could not hear us clearly'. Garnet's relationship with the earl of Salisbury as he records it is not exactly what you would expect between the Principal Secretary and public enemy number one:

> I never had discourteous word of the commissioners but only once, when they having taken a letter of Mrs Vaux to me subscribed 'your loving sister A.G.' my Lord Salisbury said 'What, are you married to Mrs Vaux, she calls herself Garnet? What! Senex fornicarius.' But the next time he asked me forgiveness and said he spoke in jest, and held his arm long on my shoulders; and all the rest said that I was held for exemplar in those matters.[13]

Both sides seem to have been more worried by the impropriety of the remark than actually discovering why Anne Vaux should sign a letter 'A.G.'.

Garnet's self-deprecation and disavowal of martyrdom made him an unlikely figure for veneration but a difficult man for his oppressors to hate. It was also clear that the role of conspiracist did not suit him. His final letter to Anne Vaux is that of a man overtaken by events bemoaning his own lack of guile and secrecy:

> It pleaseth God daily to multiply my crosses. I beseech him give me patience and perseverance usque in finem. I was after a week's hiding taken in a friend's house, where our confessions and secret conferences were heard, and my letters taken by some indiscretion abroad; then the taking of yourself; after my arraignment; then the taking of Mr Greenwell; then the slander

of us both abroad; then the ransacking anew of Erith and the other house; then the execution of Mr Hall and now last of all the apprehension of Richard and Robert; with a cipher, I know not of whose laid to my charge, and that which was a singular oversight, a letter in cipher, together with the ciphers; which letter may bring many into question.

Sufferentiam Job; andistis et finem Domini vidistis; quemadmodum misericors Dominus est et miserator. Sit nomen Domini benedictum. Yours in aeternum as I hope H G '

I thought verily my chamber in Thames Street had been given over therefore I used it to save Erith; but I might have done otherwise.

Garnet does not exactly present an image of wronged innocence, rather of a scholarly theologian forced by his position and anti-Catholic legislation to take on the role of a spymaster. Why did he not tell what he knew of Catesby's 'general intention' from sources other than the confessional? The government answer was that it was because he was the secret power behind the Plot, urging the plotters on, but this is scarcely borne out by his other actions. Like everybody else, Garnet evidently liked Catesby and, as Francis Tresham did, believed that there might be ways other than outright betrayal to stop the Plot. His position was that of many persecuted groups in society before and since; going to the authorities was seen as a last resort. Papal authority remained paramount. What if Edmund Baynham had brought papal blessing of Catesby's plot? Could that blessing be bestowed retrospectively if the Plot proved decisive in re-establishing the true religion? What would Garnet's conscience have told him then?

Garnet's last letter to Anne Vaux is often cited as a neat codicil recording his close but uncomfortable involvement in secret correspondence and plotting, but it was not the end of his evidence. The papal breves releasing Catholics from their loyalty to a new heretic monarch had, he said, been burnt 'at Erith or Coughton', which seemed to allow the possibility that Garnet had carried them with him until after the Plot's discovery and the beginning of the Midlands rebellion, burning them only when its failure was clear. He confirmed Fawkes's contention that a protector for the realm after the explosion had not been decided upon but would be drawn from

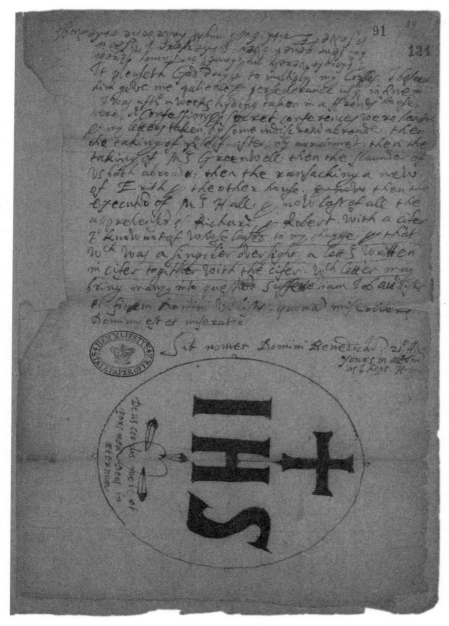

Henry Garnet's last letter to Anne Vaux, 21 April 1606. Garnet made an unlikely spymaster. Though he could outwit his captors in theological argument, he was lured by misinformation from them into revealing details of his network of safe houses. (TNA SP 14/20 no. 39)

the Lords saved from the blast. This suggested not only a shocked and unwilling disclosure of the Plot itself 'by way of confession' (though not in confession itself), but also an active involvement in the discussions about what should happen next.

Suspicion continued to envelop those close to the government too. On 29 April, Thomas Phellippes wrote from the Tower complaining to Salisbury of the 'mists and fogs of suspicion wherewith my proceedings are obscured'.[14] He was implicated in Garnet's evidence and suspected of double-dealing in his correspondence with Hugh Owen, but it was not just the professional forger and decipherer whose evidence seemed to be made suspect by its context and language.

Sir Edward Coke's proofs against Hugh Owen were largely taken from Fawkes's confession of 20 January and Thomas Wintour's declaration of 23 November but also from the rather less well-known evidence (undated) of Ralph Radcliffe. From this, it emerged that Fawkes had revealed the whole business of the Plot to Owen after he had taken the oath of secrecy. 'Owen liked the plot very well, Thomas Morgan had propounded the very same in Queen Elizabeth's time.'[15] This potentially casts new light on the apparent radical originality of Catesby's plan and perhaps further doubt on the shock, subsequently overcome by Catesby's assurances, which the surviving plotters usually expressed when first hearing of the Plot. This evidence also confirmed that Hugh Owen agreed with Fawkes's view that the restoration of Catholicism should come as an unstated consequence of the change in government, 'and willed me that by any means we should not make any mention of religion at the first'. At the same time came the familiar warning about timing. The Jesuits did not want a plot that might interfere with diplomatic efforts, and Owen sounded worried – rightly as it turned out – that the gentlemen might undermine the cause rather than further it. Success was dependent on secrecy, but could it be maintained? This was further evidence of the uneasy relationship between the plotters and their potential supporters overseas. Failure and discovery would bring ruin and disgrace to the Catholics in England, but there was genuine hope that the 'blow' could re-plant the true religion there and that papal blessing would soon be forthcoming if the Plot succeeded.

Garnet's execution was deferred to avoid the overtones of martyrdom conferred by Easter – or, as Salisbury put it, 'holy week as they call it' – and then again to avoid the possible disorder if it were held on May Day. Dudley Carleton wrote to John Chamberlain on 2 May with little fellow-feeling for a Gunpowder suspect:

> Garnet should have come a-maying to the gallows which was set up for him in Paul's Church Yard on Wednesday but upon better advice his execution is put off until tomorrow for fear of disorder amongst prentices and others upon such a day of misrule. The news of his death was sent him upon Monday last by Dr Abbott, which he could hardly be persuaded to believe, having conceived great hope of grace by some good words and promises he said were made him and by the Spanish Ambassador's mediation, who he thought would have spoken to the King for him. He hath since often been visited and examined by the Attorney, who finds him shifting and faltering in all his answers; and it is looked he will equivocate at the gallows; but he will be hanged without equivocation, though yet some think he should have favour upon a petitionary letter he hath sent to the King.

There are various social currents flowing here that might strike a modern reader as odd: that the hanging of a middle-aged clergyman was in danger of becoming a popular festival or even a scene of popular unrest; that he should, as a fugitive and then a condemned man, be on such good terms apparently with the most important ambassador at James's court; and that he furthermore appears to be on reasonable terms with Sir Edward Coke, the man prosecuting him, who scarcely needed last-minute evidence from him and had no other reason to pay so many calls on him. He even had grounds to expect mercy from the king. While official polemic singled out the Jesuits as the intellectual force behind the Plot, the reaction to Garnet as an individual priest was rather more ambiguous. His interrogators refused to recognise his priesthood, calling him 'Mister Garnet', but asked him to swear 'on his priesthood' in the hope of procuring truthful evidence and doffed their hats in cross-examining him.

Garnet's fate, however, was sealed. Like the core conspirators before him, he was hanged, drawn and quartered. As with the first set of core plotters, the place of execution was St Paul's Churchyard, so there were no reservations about the religious connotations

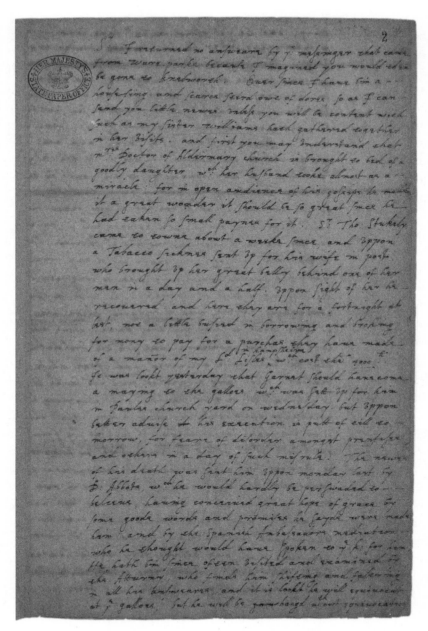

Dudley Carleton to John Chamberlain, 2 May 1606. Carleton wrote jocularly about Garnet's coming execution and his equivocations, though he had himself been under suspicion in relation to the plot. (TNA SP 14/21/4)

of his execution. Perhaps it was worth emphasising the threat he posed was to the religious convictions of the English rather than to Parliament directly. His remains were dispersed to prevent the possible creation of a shrine. English Catholics venerated Garnet as a martyr despite his own assertion that he was no martyr but 'a penitent thief'. Among the many relics associated with him was a husk of straw that bore a drop of his blood said to bear a strong resemblance to his face. The straw was eventually smuggled out of the kingdom and kept at the English Jesuit College in Liège but was lost during the French Revolution. Anne Vaux was released from prison in August 1606, and was in part responsible for publicizing 'Garnet's straw'.

Garnet was as careful of Anne Vaux's reputation as she was of his. Even at his execution, he took the opportunity in his speech to the crowd to address the scandalous rumours that had grown up around their relationship. Even *in extremis* his statement retained the characteristic careful, qualified quality of his evidence to the commissioners. Anne was 'as pure a virgin, for anything I know as she was the first day of her birth & so I desire you all to think of her'.[16] There was little else he could say, but it still seems an odd way to put it. It seemed to hint at a greater knowledge and interest in Anne's virginity than his listeners might expect a priest to have.

The man in whom Garnet placed Anne Vaux's spiritual instruction after his death, Father William Baldwin, appeared to be leading efforts to elicit the maximum propaganda value from his execution. Sir Thomas Edmondes wrote to Lord Salisbury on 29 May:

> Baldwin seemeth very much to rejoice for the death of Garnet, as of an advantage gotten for unjust proceeding against him; And he vaunteth that where it hath been sought to discredit his Society by wrongful calumnations, that they shall shortly publish a book to the world, which shall declare the colourable dealings of England and how much they have been traduced by the same. And that they will further make it appear that they are such a body that are not only able to restore any injury that shall be done them; but also to stir up the affections of the Princes of Christendom in their cause.[17]

Edmondes suspected that the main aim and purpose of Baldwin's activity was not in fact diplomatic victory abroad but some further attempt against Salisbury himself. Elsewhere, Thomas Wilson, Salisbury's secretary and occasional spy on Catholic suspects abroad, wrote in alarm that White Webbs was to be leased to Anne Vaux again after Garnet's execution: 'This I tell you because it is next neighbour to Theobalds [the earl of Salisbury's house soon to be swapped with the King for Hatfield House] and unfit it should be again a nest for such bad birds as it was before.'[18] Could Salisbury tolerate their influence so close to home?

What was Salisbury to do with the 'bad birds who might flock there'? And how many were there? Finding them was time-consuming and difficult. Would it be easier to let them go? On 9 June 1606 came a proclamation against the Jesuits, a direct result of the 'horrible treason'. It was a chance to underline the role of the Society of Jesus that the government wished to emphasise in planning and motivating the Plot, but it was also designed to reduce the chance of further embarrassing testimony from them and the creation of further martyrs. The proclamation amounted to a rather exhaustive and exhausting list of arguments against them, but allowed them to leave unpunished, according to a hastily added marginal note: 'Even those of that condition whose lifes [*sic*] are in our hands to take every hour if we were so disposed excepting only those that are guilty of the horrible treason.' These guilty men were named later as Gerard and Greenwell (Tesimond). The proclamation, it was claimed, was designed 'to avoid the effusion of blood'. There was a last-ditch attempt to stress that the proclamation targeted the actions of disaffected people rather than the beliefs of priests as such, which lent a rather philosophical, abstract air to the whole thing, as if the proclamation were a statement of principle rather than an attempt to bring anything about: 'Therefore as after times must give us trial of all men's behaviour, so must all men expect that their own deserts must be the only measure of their fortunes at our hands whether one way or other.'[19]

If this seemed to equate divine judgement of souls with the king's temporal justice, then it appeared calculated to annoy Catholics. Mind you, the idea that the king rather than the common law dispensed temporal justice might have annoyed the Attorney General.

On 16 June, Sir Thomas Edmondes in his intelligence summaries to Lord Salisbury concentrated on the intensifying war in the Low Countries, but there was also news that the plots against his life suspected by Edmondes in his letter of 29 May were already emerging, hatched by Baldwin and others in Brussels.[20]

Among the many commentators who agreed that no new evidence had come out of Garnet's trial was Sir Allan Percy, brother of the earl of Northumberland and his lieutenant of the gentlemen pensioners. With Garnet's execution, the focus of the investigation returned to the Gunpowder Percys. On 23 June, Northumberland's renewed questioning covered the old ground of letters sent to the north about his rents on 5 November and sins of omission in administering the oath to Thomas Percy. Understandably, not much new emerged, apart from a sense that the earl's failing memory and confusion under repeated questioning made his answers more faltering and uncertain. How and when was the earl to be tried and on what evidence? Unlike the core plotters and Henry Garnet, who were tried under common law in the court of King's Bench, the answer was in the court of Star Chamber. This effectively thwarted Coke's desire to try the suspect lords as the others had been, according to his jurisdiction and method. Instead, the king and privy councillors acting in their judicial capacity in Star Chamber had greater scope to dispense personal justice according to social rank. This meant a degree of discretion not only in passing sentence but also the extent to which the punishments were enforced. The wording of the earl's misdemeanours, the level of the fines, whether these would be remitted, whether imprisonment would follow and for how long, all of these depended to some extent on the level of threat the king felt Northumberland still posed. By the conventions of the court, the allegations against the earl were to be admitted before the trial began and Sir Edward Coke in his final appearance as Attorney General had simply to recite them in front of an eager public audience before the council passed judgement. As ever, Coke relished his place on the stage, exceeding and embellishing his brief, perhaps with some licence, as there was propaganda value in decorating the earl's trial with flourishes of circumstantial evidence that lent weight and coherence to, or perhaps concealed the weakness of, the substantive charges levelled.

In public, Coke explained the resort to Star Chamber as an example of the king's clemency, implying pure justice would have been better served by trial at common law. He had also to explain the slowness of the judicial process against the earl. Ostensibly the delay was, he said, to await the conclusion of the common law trials of manifest traitors including Robert Wintour and others like Garnet who had only been captured in January. Perhaps it was also true that the process of cross-examining the earl, deferential and iterative as it was, had produced such a wealth of heavily qualified and opaque evidence that it had only recently provided sufficient foundation to support a case in law.

Before, during and after his trial, Northumberland continued to add to this qualified and unconvincing evidence. On the question of whether or not he had ordered that Thomas Percy should take the oath of supremacy, his answer was vague; he 'gave order to some to give him his oath and thinketh that the order was given to the lieutenant and never asked his lieutenant whether he had given him his oath or no as he remembereth'. Northumberland later remembered that he had not ordered it at all.

There was some questioning of the timing of the trial and the judicial process generally, not least by the countess of Northumberland. Just as Robert Wintour and Fawkes had thought their trial a week away only two days before it started, the timing of Northumberland's trial seemed to come as a surprise, and there was a suggestion that it was brought forward deliberately to hinder the preparation of a defence. As late as 25 June, John Chamberlain reported to Dudley Carleton that Star Chamber had finally been decided upon as the jurisdiction following a long meeting of the council on the subject 'on Monday'.[21] On the day after this letter, the countess of Northumberland wrote to the earl of Salisbury:

Being advertised out of more than common rumour that my lord shall be called to Star Chamber, to which place I am informed none comes but for misdemeanours and are in all matters of that nature, both be made acquainted with what they shall be charged and allowed counsel to advise and plead for them. I am warranted to crave for my Lord that justice, which every ordinary subject may challenge, that he may not be surprised and locked up now when he least looks for any such strict course;

but how or to what place so ever his hard fortunes have given suspicion of cause to bring him, I beseech you that he may have that justice which is due to any that is called to that Court which for him is more needful in respect of his defect of hearing, by which he may receive disadvantage.[22]

So this powerful man is vulnerable and infirm. This chimes with Northumberland's recollection of himself at the dinner at Syon on 4 November; rather deaf and not entirely clear about what is going on. To suggest that they were unfamiliar with the proceedings in Star Chamber was disingenuous to say the least, given the number of cases brought by the earl in that court in the 1580s and 1590s.

After months of rumour but with no firm evidence beyond the circumstantial, the earl was charged and on 27 June 1606 and tried in Star Chamber. The demand for seats was so great that 'there was a great scaffold erected for the courtiers and other men of great account'.[23] This time, unlike for the core conspirators, no shadow of the executioner's scaffold fell across proceedings; James did not care to shed the blood of aristocrats. Northumberland was found guilty of three offences, for which he was effectively fined £10,000 each.

The first was pretending to lead the Catholic party in England (this was an offence against rank assuming royal power in leading men not bound to him in service). It also rested, according to Coke, on Northumberland presenting himself as the principal means of easing the penal laws against Catholics and of suggesting that the king had agreed to this only to go back on his word. He was also implicated as the leader in the supply of horses for a Spanish invasion after the death of Queen Elizabeth: 'The Earl increased his stable so much he told his Majesty his revenue was scarce able to maintain the charge.' Why the earl would bring his horse buying to the king's attention if he was preparing for a Spanish invasion was not explained. Garnet and Thomas Wintour appeared to agree about the number of horses required but he suggested the gentlemen could supply them themselves without needing to share the glory and rewards of a Spanish invasion with an aristocratic patron. However, there was further damning circumstantial evidence. The invasion was to be through Milford Haven, a port nominated by Sir Walter Raleigh at a time when he and the earl were 'very inward and secret friends' and while 'the Earl had the command of Castle Carew, the only strength of the said haven'.[24]

Secondly, as we have seen, he was guilty of employing Thomas Percy in the king's personal bodyguard, a 'Jesuited recusant' being made a gentleman pensioner in the summer of 1604 soon after the May meeting where Percy and Catesby had agreed on the Plot. This offence was compounded by failing to ensure Percy had taken the oath of allegiance. Somewhat unnecessarily, it added that Percy had deserted his post rather than protecting the king at the time of discovery, which in the circumstances was hardly surprising: 'The Earl made Percy a pensioner to attend on the King daily with a poll-axe; but he was never sworn. Percy fled.'

Thirdly, he had failed to order Thomas Percy's apprehension as the prime suspect when sending to the north about his rents on 5 November, without the consent of the rest of the Privy Council. This was interpreted by Coke as a means of warning Percy rather than pursuing him: 'A councillor restrained ought not to write to any without leave, but Northumberland wrote that his treasure should be in safety, which was a watchword to Percy that the plot had been discovered, not no word to apprehend Percy.'

Outside the scope of the main offences, Coke also threw in among the earl's misdemeanours and misfortunes the casting of the king's nativity in 1603, which he implied could only proceed from unwarranted malicious intent: 'Northumberland had neither discontent, want nor disgrace, but he must calc[u]late the King's nativity.' Biblical suspicion was heaped on the associates of Northumberland and Raleigh who had forwarded the enterprise. Poor Thomas Harriot was ill-omened simpy on account of his name: 'Herriot is a funeral beast.' New nuggets were seized upon to increase the circumstantial evidence around the Percy connection. 'Wright's sister nursed the Lady Mary', the royal baby who had been born on 8 April 1605. To be relevant to the Percy connection, this meant Martha Wright. Thomas Percy's wife had acted in this capacity to the youngest royal child. Once again, the group of fanatical outsiders bent on the destruction of the government seemed remarkably close to it in the months leading up to the discovery.

Perhaps it was not after all unlikely that the wife of a gentleman pensioner would be used in this way. It is typical of the age that this evidence of a female role in the Percy's connection to the royal family in a position of trust should appear almost as a footnote, a tiny piece of trivial additional detail. It is striking to think of her cradling the youngest royal child while her husband plotted the destruction of her father and siblings. Another example perhaps of the curiously well-qualified plotters and their network, few in number but well placed, being able to care for the surviving royals as part of a wider plan to establish a Catholic dynasty.

Northumberland's defence of his actions was reasoned but muted. His representation of the king's intentions in religion was designed, he said, like so much else at that time, to ease the path to succession. As for Percy, he was a kinsman, and as the head of the family Northumberland was nominally responsible for him, but all extended households had their bad eggs. There remained the suspicion that Northumberland, like Monteagle, must have received a warning to absent himself from the opening of Parliament, but that unlike Monteagle he had concealed it. Sir Allan Percy had attempted to help his brother by insisting that he as lieutenant had administered the loyal oath to Thomas Percy, only for it be proved that he could not have done so when he said. Unsurprisingly, Sir Allan in turn lost the lieutenancy of the gentlemen pensioners.

Northumberland was condemned to imprisonment during the king's pleasure and remained in the Tower until June 1621. As a man of 'blood and sufficiency', there was always hope of reprieve in this period, but none came. The earl occupied his time in the Tower quietly and profitably in reading and experiment, those quiet recreations he had claimed were his only ambition. On his release, he withdrew from the affairs of state. He attracted little sympathy in any quarter; his behaviour was too suspect and his manner too abrasive. Some commentators did, however, suggest that he had suffered more than he might have done because of the rebellious reputation of the 'Gunpowder Percys'.

Sir Allan Percy wrote to Dudley Carleton about Northumberland's trial on 16 July 1606 when he was back at Essex House after his own release from the Tower. He was given 'full liberty to go where it shall please you only the court excepted from which place you shall abstain until you know the King's farther pleasure'. The air of suspicion still clung to the family. The countess of Northumberland also met a rebuff from the king and the earl of Salisbury when suing for her husband's release after his trial and fine:

> My lady was at court on Sunday and spake to the King to be favourable to my lord, who had long endured prisonment by reason of this misfortune. Now that his majesty had brought all things to an end, she hoped he would be so gracious to give him liberty and be favourable otherwise, who said all the Star Chamber was witness to what had been done and so went his way. After she spake to my lord of Salisbury to be a mediator to the King for my lord, who after he had taken some deliberation and set on a grave countenance, told her she had no reason to expect such a favour from him, who was neither his brother nor kinsman and therefore would not undertake that which he knew would not be pleasing to his majesty. In the end she fell to chiding and did until they were friends again and so parted.[25]

There is a sense here that Salisbury was not being sincere in his deliberation and had no intention of mediating with the king, a strong indication early from both king and Principal Secretary that they did not regard the trial and fine as the end of Northumberland's punishment.

On 16 July, in a letter to Dudley Carleton, John Chamberlain also recorded this encounter with the hopeful postscript, 'She was noted to part cheerfully from them.' The earl's trial and fate was already old news, and Chamberlain regaled his friend with news of fresh treasons with much greater enthusiasm. To the Percy family, and perhaps to Dudley Carleton too given his close connection to the earl's household, the earl's fate remained a pressing preoccupation. Other routes to the king proved equally fruitless, and the reasons given were consistent. The objection to Northumberland's release came not from a conspiracy of counsellors but from the king himself. On 31 July, Sir Allan Percy reported to Dudley Carleton:

> My lady is a daily suitor for my lord, but hath every day less and less hope, for those that were supposed to be his enemies now in a manner say as much, and my Lord Chamberlain, to confirm

the opinion we had of his love, showed it in the sending back of the new year's gift which my brother sent to the King.

The earl of Suffolk, who as Lord Chamberlain had led the search of the vault beneath the House of Lords that discovered Guy Fawkes, now had command of the gentlemen pensioners which Sir Allan had lost. His reason for not passing on the gift was the same as Salisbury's reason for not pressing Northumberland's case: the king would not like it.

It is reported that the Queen hath begged my lord's fine towards the paying of her debts and my lady is now in hand to compound with her, conditionally he may have his liberty, but my opinion is such that he must lie there and nothing we can do can set him free.[26]

While the court haggled about what to do with Northumberland's money, Hugh Owen had his pension increased by Spain. The English responded with a bungled assassination attempt in 1608, presumably motivated now by revenge and the desire to prevent further plotting. No wonder Spain refused to let him go. Father Baldwin was allowed to return in 1610 and languished in an English prison for eight years; no charge of treason was brought against him.

Father Baldwin's fellow prisoner the earl of Northumberland's continued incarceration kept the Plot alive and relevant in official circles. The investigation remained a going concern in the sense that suspicions could still deepen or new evidence could still make his release more or less likely. By 1611, Dudley Carleton was much more comfortably situated as ambassador in Venice but was still in correspondence with Sir Walter Cope, his minder in Oxfordshire when he was under suspicion in 1605–06. Cope now addressed him in more deferential terms on 20 August 1611:

The embers of the powder treason being raked up again by one Elks, servant as you know of my Lord Northumberland who by private conference and other presumptions seeks to bring his master within the compass of a prescience, your name inter alia being like to come upon the stage, although the part be small you have to play, so small as perchance it may rather pass over in silence than once come to question, yet because I know that fame ever jumps her wings in flight and may multiply by this in so far a carriage. That you shall hardly know what to believe I have endeavoured by all the good means I may to inform myself truly of all the particulars which may seem to concern you whereof you shall not need to make narrower or larger confirmation than they deserve. For since by your place you were interested in all motions or letters passing to or from his lordship. Whether you moved it or not moved it (which I rather believe because you so constantly denied it when it was more fresh in your memory) yet in the general opinion of all and of the best men, I hear you are acquitted and freed of all suspicion in the point of your duty and loyalty.

The postscript is reassuring if carefully worded 'from him who interpreteth favourably your actions there and will defend your innocency here'.[27] Rather disconcertingly, this allowed for the possibility that other interpretations of Carleton's conduct were all too possible.

In fact, the business of the Westminster lease to Percy put Dudley Carleton in the firing line again. Northumberland's half-remembered evidence was reported to have changed, implicating Carleton and another member of Northumberland's household, John Hippesley: 'Percy did ask Mr Carleton whether it were done or no, who answered it was done.' Going from Whitehall to Essex House on the morning of the gunpowder treason, the earl asked him whether Percy had any house in Westminster, 'unto which [Hippesley] answered that he had spoken to Whynniard for a house for him'.[28]

John Chamberlain reassured Carleton that the fresh scandal had blown over and began writing cheerfully of other matters, but it remained threatening for some time, and rumours continued, including one that the Northumberland had been executed in the Tower.

The evidence presented by Timothy Elks related to the complicity of the earl in matters very familiar from his trial: Thomas Percy's oath as a gentleman pensioner, the hire of the vault under the Lords' Chamber and Northumberland's actions on 5 November. As a former servant of Northumberland now free of his allegiance, his allegations offered new detail and carried some weight. He also suggested renewed lines of enquiry, centred on figures in whom the earl's true conduct, he claimed, had been confided, before and after the discovery of the Plot.

Elks was so fearful of the earl's revenge that he pointedly did not reveal his location in his letters and did not send them direct to the king or Privy Council, but directed them via 'my good friend Thomas Lumsden gentleman of his majesty's privy chamber'. Elks knew 'that the Earl of Northumberland was to have been absent from the Parliament that day that the house [of Lords] was to be blown up and upon what pretence'.[29] His own informant, Captain Whitelocke, was now inconveniently dead. He had been bribed into silence by the earl, it was hinted, and worse still had died in suspicious circumstances soon after a visit to the earl's physician. The list of those in whom Whitelocke was said to have confided was long and illustrious, including the earl of Westmorland, Sir Jocelyn Percy and perhaps less predictably 'Henego Jhones'. They would be reluctant to give evidence, Elks warned. 'All these men will be very nice to speak of so great a man whom they affect well', but they might be persuaded to do so on oath.

Some of Whitelocke's claims, such as 'that he held the earl's life in his hands', sounded like the idle boasting of a blackmailer or the repeat of gossip about the earl's absence from Parliament. Other elements suggested new information for the investigation and a deeper relationship. He knew 'the earl was to meet that day one that should be his heir and where' and that Whitelocke 'dare not take a company of the earl's in the Low Countries which the earl promised him a little before his death, lest the earl put a trick upon to make him away there', that is to say, have him killed.[30] This all sounds a bit like the murky world of Catesby's company for the Low Countries, if not a chimera then at least a device to satisfy personal ambitions closer to home. We have seen that Catesby talked of leading a company of English soldiers to fight for Spain in the Low Countries. It was never quite clear if this was genuine or a cover story for gathering resources at home for the Plot. Similarly, the earl of Northumberland's company (to fight for the Netherlands against Spain there) might be genuine military patronage or just a way of getting inconvenient people out of the way abroad or – better still – killed in action.

The questions to be put to those in whom Whitelocke had confided were very specific. Inigo Jones, for example, was to be asked in relation to his dealings with Whitelocke,

Whether he [Whitelocke] spake to him for poison and when. Whether that he said not that he had the earl's life in his power and whether he told him not of a man, that day of the Parliament sitting, that would make the earl his heir and whom the earl with Percy the traitor should have gone to meet that day. And whether my Lord had provided a company for him in the Low Countries but he durst not go for fear of treachery.[31]

The evidence rehearsed all the earl's oversights and indulgences in relation to Percy in a way designed to show a dangerous pattern of favour. This is all very difficult to evaluate, of course. Had Thomas Percy 'put a trick' on the earl as Catesby had suggested, with the intention of luring him to Highgate to meet a man about a legacy? Was Inigo Jones, at that time collaborating uneasily with Ben Jonson on court masques, part of the same murky world we noted Jonson inhabiting at the time of the discovery of the Plot – a confidant of blackmailers and a purveyor of poison? Farfetched though it all seems, the fear both Whitelocke and Elks felt of the earl's power and its ability to reach them even overseas seems very real.

As late as November 1611 there was continued uncertainty about whether Dudley Carleton or the earl himself had directed Thomas Percy to John Whynniard about obtaining the lease in Westminster and whether this had been done in writing or by word of mouth. On 27 November, John Chamberlain felt secure enough to pursue further evidence from the earl's connections still in London on Carleton's behalf, including the mathematician Thomas Harriot:

Finding master Heriot at great leisure in Paul's I accosted him to see what I could learn of his great lord. He told me he had some inlargement and that any of his servants or friends might have access to him, that this last tempest was already blown over and that Elks and his accusations began to vanish. Only there was some doubt that his fine of £30000 would be called on for the matter wherein you were mentioned. Only it fell out thus that the

Lord being urged about a letter that should have been written for Percy's lodging, firmly denied it: but his man Roliffe debating the matter with him wisht him not to stand too stiffly in it, because he remembered Percy going up and down the house inquiring after you and told him it was for such a purpose. Whereupon the Lord at his next examination (though this point were no more in question) of his own motion told them, that he could not call to mind any such letter, but if there were, it were without any ill intent and it was likely you had written it. This was taken hold of and *pro concesso* whereas he spoke it doubtfully and by way of caution, But Epsley [John Hippesley Carleton's fellow officer in Northumberland's household] utterly denied all this and said his Lordship had forgotten and wronged himself, for that there was no letter written, but himself was employed to Whynniard in his Lord's name by word of mouth.[32]

Even now, the interpretation the authorities might make of the earl's faltering evidence was crucial, not only to his own fate but also that of his former servants. As Whitelocke had been, Elks was worried that Northumberland was working to have him killed before he could reveal his evidence against the earl, 'that great man who heretofore hath sought my life', as Elks described him in a petition for protection from the Crown.[33] Having failed to secure this protection and then having fled the country, Elks explained his absence as necessary to avoid his persecutors, rather than 'despairing of his majesty's favour'.[34]

One might think that a shadowy figure like Elks would lack credibility and have no great influence on the fate of the earl, but his evidence seems to have chimed with the king's own suspicions. On 12 July 1611, the earl of Northampton reported to Viscount Rochester renewed questioning of the aristocratic suspect and a deterioration in his physical condition, apparently worn down by the repeated interrogation and fading memory.

For whether by the distemper of his diet or the disorder of his hours or the disquiet of his mind, god knows but I never found so great a change in so short a time his conceit being exceedingly blunted and his spirits weakened. We found him more ready to answer with less forwardness than we looked for. But with so great caution and consideration intermixed with doubts and distractions as might express a great fear and very great uncertainty. He took notice very quickly of the fountain whence the ground of his examination was drawn, ascribing all to one Elks whom he marked out as a man deeply discontented towards him.

Northumberland obviously resisted the rehearsal of so much old matter, so they broke down the questioning into 'little pills fit for a queasy stomach and a narrow throat'. Eventually the tactic worked and there was a real, new confession about Thomas Percy's oath as a gentleman pensioner: 'He plainly confessed that he advised his brother to spare him and that he did this at Thomas Percy's own request which was denied so stoutly, renounced at the Star Chamber.'[35]

This showed the specific discomfort of Northumberland's position, particularly the open-endedness of the process. Royal justice as dispensed through Star Chamber was merciful compared to the strictures of the Common Law, but it was discretionary and elongated; the trial was not the end. Revelations of this kind would prompt further questioning and deepen suspicions. The prospect of release or remission of fines receded. The Lords Mourdant and Stourton had been released, so Northumberland must have felt a sense of isolation and persecution. Northampton also reported a 'bout' that the Commissioners had had with Sir Walter Raleigh, full of his predictable 'boldness, pride and passion'. Raleigh had been imprisoned since 1603, so perhaps Northumberland was not alone. There was a growing sense that Northumberland had never been entirely frank in his evidence, a conviction strengthened by the opacity and qualifications of his language. His prose style. with its hints and allusions, was well suited to the secret correspondence leading to James's succession but was not a good medium in which to clear his name.

After his own trial in Star Chamber, Edward, Lord Stourton, one of the lords suspected of having been warned not to attend Parliament by Catesby, had been committed to the Tower. From there he wrote a plea for release to Salisbury: 'I crave my speedy enlargement, in pity of my health and my decaying estate, unable to support so great charges and supply the wants of so many children.' This prompted only a transfer to the Fleet prison, which indicated his offence was being regarded less seriously, without necessarily improving the prospects for his health. Moved with him was Henry, Lord Mordaunt. Both were released in 1608; the fines against them were not enforced. Mordaunt died in 1609 and used his will, written despite 'languishing sickness' after long imprisonment, to protest his innocence of the Plot with a dramatic dying breath:

> And for the clearing of my conscience before God and man and to give a public satisfaction to the world concerning such and those imputations which lately have been laid upon me, and for which I have in an high degree been censured, I mean the late Gunpowder Treason, which fact for the heinousness thereof in the offenders therein, I do loathe to remember and now sorrow to repeat: Therefore at this time when all hope or desire of long life hath forsaken me and now Almighty God (into whose hands I am instantly yielding my soul) is my immediate judge to witness with me that I lie not, I do solemnly protest before God and his Angels and without all Equivocation or duplicity whatsoever that I am innocent of that fact and guiltless of all foreknowledge thereof.[36]

The government had heard protestations of this sort before. Familiarity with the doctrine of equivocation was grounds for suspicion in itself, even in a denial, and Mordaunt admitted that his past censure for his conduct in relation to the Plot could only be mitigated by the king's mercy. Perhaps unwisely he called the indenture designed to dispose of his lands 'my plot and project', just as the Gunpowder Plot had been 'the project of the powder'. Those named in the indenture were suspected Catholic lords, the earls of Rutland and Worcester.

At the time that the lords Mordaunt and Stourton were moved to the Fleet, Antony Maria Browne, Lord Montague, was released. In 1611, he made a £6,000 payment of lieu of recusancy fines and tendering the oath of allegiance. If you were rich enough, it seemed, you need not face the inconvenience of choosing between your loyalty to king or pope. Most people were not in this position.

The lands of the plotters, forfeited by attainder, were theoretically in government hands in their entirety but were still being picked over and the rights to their goods disputed. Sir William Waad's suspicions of Lord Monteagle's debts to Thomas Percy prompted extensive further investigation by the Exchequer. Were there further sources of Percy income that might be due to the Crown? It was said that Lord Monteagle had granted an annuity of £50 in trust for the use of Thomas Percy, his wife Martha and their daughter Ellen in return for £500. To tangle the web further, it is possible, of course, that the Percy family's £500 had come from Northumberland's estate rents.

Evidence in the case was taken at York in the Easter term of 1609. By that time, it was hardly likely that anyone would testify against Lord Monteagle and cement the connection of the 'saver of his nation' with the principal suspect of 5 November. So it proved among the witnesses. One Marmaduke Machell dutifully reported that he 'thinketh that Thomas Percy should not have any benefit thereby'. Others including Allan Percy of Beverley believed no payments were made to Thomas Percy 'in his lifetime'.[37] This did not preclude them being made to his wife and child, however. It was in no one's interest to rake over the embers of that relationship.

Sir William Waad had a more direct interest in the Middlesex county inquisition as to the attainted goods of Sir Everard Digby, since they included 'a bedstead, curtains, bolster and valance' claimed by Waad in lieu of 'necessaries' supplied to Digby in the Tower.[38] The inquisition as to the possessions of Ambrose Rookwood poignantly revealed the hidden religious life of English Catholics through its inventory: 'Item certain things found in a hole near the clock house with boxes of needlework one box with 3 French hoods and certain mass books. Item in the same hole, one box with a cope and other ornaments for a mass.'[39]

Perhaps the most revealing inquisition involved Sir Thomas Overbury and John Talbot in relation to the property of Robert Wintour of Huddington, lately of high treason attainted. This centred on the questioning of Leonard Smallpeece, Sir John Talbot's steward, to whom Robert Wintour had written his unwilling note on 6 November. It investigated whether Robert had secured rights for his family in the days before the discovery.

This document,[40] which showed Robert Wintour's fear of his father-in-law to be greater than his fear of death in the days before the discovery of the Plot, pitted the Talbot family attempts to secure his property, as Robert Wintour had wished, against the claims of a young, rising court favourite. Unsurprisingly, the law found for the the favourite and Overbury gained the rights to the salt workings at Droitwich. Wintour in his last days in the Tower imagined his descendants avenging him, and perhaps he was right; Sir Thomas Overbury's death in the Tower in 1613, possibly by poisoning, finally eclipsed the Plot as the most shocking and notorious event of James's reign.

Elsewhere in the Tower, Northumberland entertained notions of conspiracy against him centred on the political jealousy of the earl of Salisbury, but Salisbury's death in 1612 made little difference. In 1613, the Star Chamber fine of £30,000 was remitted upon a present payment of £11,000, but this was probably more of a reflection of James's need for ready money following Salisbury's death than intransigence on the part of the Principal Secretary.

Raleigh's execution in 1618 broke the spell of a sinister alternative power bloc opposed to James's reign, and the death of Northumberland's wife Dorothy in the following year seems to mark the end of the earl's political and personal ambition. Raleigh had lived in the shadow of the scaffold since his theatrical reprieve from execution for his involvement in the plots of 1603. At his beheading, he famously jested with the sheriff that death would be 'sharp Medicine … a Physician for all Disease', a remark generally taken to illustrate his courage and wit. But were there echoes of Robert Catesby's famous justification to Thomas Wintour of his plan to destroy James and his government – that 'the nature of the disease required so sharp a remedy'? This, in turn, was echoed in Fawkes's justification of his actions when he said that 'a dangerous disease required a desperate remedy', part of the evidence that prompted further investigation of Raleigh's own possible involvement in the Plot. James had been a torment to Raleigh since 1603. Was he agreeing with the plotters about the solution to the problem of the Scottish king? If you could not kill him, you could at least rid yourself of him by dying yourself. Was there a hint in this echo of Catesby at the very end of his life that Raleigh's role in the Gunpowder Plot or the rebellions that would follow was not just a fantasy of Sir Edward Coke's invention and was not as incredible as it now might seem to us?

It is ironic that Northumberland was finally released through the agency of a Scottish favourite of the king, James Hay, earl of Carlisle. Hay had married Northumberland's daughter and presumably found having a father-in-law locked up in the Tower something of a social embarrassment. Whatever his private feelings about his son-in-law, Northumberland had his own reasons to accept his mediation since it freed his own son from the taint of an old conspiracy and the whiff of gunpowder. Meanwhile, in 1628, Lord Algernon Percy married Ann Cecil, Salisbury's granddaughter.

The other advocate for Northumberland was George Villiers, by then duke of Buckingham, the second son of a Leicestershire knight. The duke was only thirteen in 1605. How long ago it must have seemed that Northumberland himself was a power in the land and a potential protector of the kingdom. From his private seclusion at Petworth House, he maintained his correspondence with Dudley Carleton, now Viscount Dorchester, whom the earl addressed as 'my Lord' at court, his former servant now the more powerful man, adviser to Buckingham and then Principal Secretary of State after Buckingham's assassination. In 1629, responding gratefully to news of Carleton's dealings in the Low Countries, where Northumberland had indulged his intellectual and military interests in the period of his own growing influence, Northumberland could not resist contrasting the current constraints of his retirement with the headier days when he had been the master and Carleton the aspiring courtier in his household. Back then, at the time of the Plot, the air at Syon House had seemed full of possibility.

> If your Lordship will send your letters at any time to Taylor his house my steward upon Tower Hill they will be conveyed safely to me. Your Lordship if you remember walking under the vine wall at Syon said that you were drunk with eating of grapes. I pray you be drunk again for I give your Lordship full possession to take what you will of any fruits there, not only now, but ever hereafter when you like best.[41]

The politics of the Low Countries and the endless war between the states of Holland and Spain prompted a further letter to Carleton, 'his majesty's principal secretary', as Salisbury had been to James. This time Northumberland sought advice on the best course for his son Henry in travelling in and through those countries with a limited entourage and with little protection. 'He travels a younger brother and not in pomp.'[42] As always with Northumberland, there were the same statements and retractions which made him such an engaging and self-deprecating correspondent but which had made his meaning and intent so difficult to establish and which had got him into so much trouble. On 18 April 1630, he offered Carelton his opinion of the current state of politics in France but with the uneasy and unanswerable rider: 'But what do I discourse of these things to you that know all those corners better than I do? I will leave therefore further prattle and ceremonies towards your Lordship I will use none. God send your Lordship a good wife, I hear you are towards one.'[43] Carleton did marry again, but died of a fever on diplomatic service only two years later.

Our last glimpse of Northumberland comes in a letter to his son-in-law the earl of Carlisle, who had sent him George Heylin's book on St George: 'I shall pass some of my night watches to drive away a time to peruse him.'[44] What had previously occupied the earl's night watches? What do great men who have tasted power and lost it dream of in old age? Northumberland died, perhaps appropriately, on 5 November 1632.

12

'SOONER DEAD
THAN CHANGED'

John Donne
The complexity of Catholic loyalty and the difficulty of the choices
they were compelled to make is illustrated by the poet John Donne,
an exact contemporary of Robert Catesby whose Catholic childhood
had been filled with the same scare stories of murderous decrees from
the Privy Council. Donne's family and connections were Catholic
and long-suffering; he had Jesuit uncles, and at the age of twelve
had visited William Weston in the Tower, Garnet's predecessor as
Superior of the English Jesuit Province. His brother Henry was
arrested for harbouring a priest in Lincoln's Inn and died of plague in
Newgate before he could come to trial. For John, a short life ending
in martyrdom beckoned, perhaps he was even a plotter in the making.
As a young man, he travelled in Catholic countries including Spain
and like Thomas Wintour, he picked up cultural influences closed
to most of his fellow Englishmen. He appears in an engraving by
William Marshall dated 1591 as a fashionable young man marked
by the experience and sophistication of his travels, wearing earrings
in the shape of crosses and holding an ornate sword. The portrait
carries the Spanish motto 'antes muerto que mudado', 'sooner dead
than changed'. Here it seemed was a man like 'Guido' Fawkes, ready
to die rather than adopt the orthodoxies of the English. His early
poems seem to bear out some of this; he lives the backstairs life of a

loner, on the fringe of society, difficult, cultured and superior, quite unlike the materialistic, beer-swilling, self-satisfied place-hunters he mocks in his love poems. But Donne did change. He took the path away from martyrdom, studied the religious controversy between Catholicism and the established church and convinced himself that his spiritual and material interests were the same thing.

By 1610 he had written in favour of the oath of allegiance that James enforced on Catholics after the Plot, a work called 'Pseudo-Martyr', which criticised those who preferred to die rather than change, though his private opinions about the oath of allegiance were very much more ambiguous. As Dean of St Paul's, one of the senior and most conspicuous figures of the established church, Donne gave the sermon on 'Gunpowder Day' 1622 'intended for Paul's Cross but by reason of the weather preached in the church'. In the sermon, he tells how the plotters would have turned Parliament from a hive producing the honey of benign legislation into a giant gun designed to shoot God (King James as God's representative) back at God in heaven. As with the oath of allegiance, it is doubtful whether Donne's private opinions about parliament mirrored his public utterances, but from a poet's point of view, the genuine element was the irresistible vividness of the image of king, nobles commons and people being shot out of an enormous artillery piece into the air. The imaginative possibilities of the poet's sermon allowed him to fantasise the destruction of a society or state that had compelled him to abandon his faith; but from the comfortable position of a favoured royal preacher.

Shakespeare and the Midlands Rebellion

If Donne's place in the established church gave him a clear role in relation to the Plot, albeit one he chose to exploit in characteristically ambiguous fashion, what, if anything, does the Plot tell us about the life of Shakespeare? As we noted in the Prologue there are plenty of allusions to the Plot and its cross-currents evident in the plays, which suggest there was more in them to concern the playwright than a topical theme to raise a laugh or a shudder of horror in a knowing audience. Shakespeare is seen in glimpses at the edge of the Plot, alluding to its trials and evidence in *Macbeth*. He is not quite in Warwickshire when the rebellion happens or the right area of London when the Plot is hatched, but he is very close at times. There but for the grace of God. We cannot know Shakespeare's private faith or deduce it from his work despite the endless popular and scholarly attempts to do so. It is just possible, however, that the Plot sheds some chink of light on an issue which has interested (and to some extent disappointed) me about Shakespeare's life for many years and which can be summed up briefly and anachronistically in the question 'Why didn't Shakespeare go to Belgium?'

Of course, Shakespeare and his contemporaries spoke of Flanders, though not with any degree of precision, not least because they often meant Antwerp and its surroundings and therefore Brabant. To Guy Fawkes and Thomas Wintour, no less than to Ben Jonson, George Chapman and Christopher Marlowe, Flanders meant opportunity. This included the diplomatic patronage of the Imperial court at Brussels. It meant the financial lure of Antwerp, 'the Metropolis' on which the English wool trade and city of London depended and which produced more English books than London. It offered the military opportunities denied to Catesby and others at home in the armies of Spain and the Holy Roman Empire. There were opportunities for non-Catholic Englishmen to fight against and to spy on the great Hapsburg machine just over the water. But the principal lure and rewards were for Catholics and Catholic sympathisers. As far as we know, Shakespeare was never lured. Our traditional view has him coming to the parlous world of London theatre, enjoying royal patronage as a king's man and overcoming a number of legal challenges to establish at the Globe an operation that gave his company increased financial as well as artistic control. This eventually allowed Shakespeare to retire comfortably to his native Warwickshire and present that final balding, alderman image of himself, which we all find so difficult to reconcile with our idea of a sublime genius.

Looked at again in the context of the Jesuit Edmund Campion's successful mission there and the rebellion planned by Robert Catesby of Lapworth, Warwickshire begins to look a slightly less comfortable and insular place. Perhaps Shakespeare did not need to travel. The tensions, rivalries, risks and rewards in the Low Countries that were shaping Europe on a grand scale were also being to be found in day-to-day life on his doorstep, between the besieged Catholic gentry and the searchers, the sheriffs and the missionary priests. The drama of the overnight loss of fortune and the betrayal of neighbour by neighbour were all too common and real. His place, more pressingly than in normal circumstances, was to secure his family and interests closer to home. The generally held view, particularly by foreign observers but also by the investigating councillors themselves, that the Plot could not have come from a small group of gentlemen and been carried through with their own connections and resources is an assumption not dissimilar to the one made about Shakespeare's inferior rank and his success as a playwright. For both, aristocratic patronage was a possibility but not something to be relied on. In both cases, the gentlemen did it.

'Who chooseth me must give and hazard all he hath'

One of the reasons why the Gunpowder Plot attracts such controversy and so many conspiracy theories is that Catesby's choice of scheme and justification of it seem so inadequate to a modern reader. Why risk so much for so little? Why go to the trouble and hazard of blowing up the king and nobility in order to replace them with James's younger son or elder daughter and those lords who survived the blast? The planners had considered all the younger siblings of the uncongenial Prince Henry as a puppet Catholic monarch. They 'knew not how to take the Duke Charles' as Percy's reconnaissance of his lodgings had found them altered to be more secure and easy to defend. Could Catesby have dreamed that Duke Charles would become king, one as sympathetic to Catholics as his countrymen suspected him to be? Instead, they concentrated their efforts on Princess Elizabeth who would make an impeccably Protestant marriage at the age of sixteen.

Catesby's reported contempt for the majority of the lords sounded genuine but he was hardly planning social revolution. Were the plotters so desperate that they really risk death for even a slim chance of interrupting an unending Protestant succession and an ever more hostile England? There is some evidence for this. Many of the plotters had already risked their lives in rebellion or fighting in the Low Countries; in the Plot at least, they were in command of their own forces, however small. Did they even deliberately court martyrdom?

They certainly appeared dressed for it, in their finest clothes with their engraved swords and religiously embroidered scarves. Since the church taught that the consequences of apostasy were worse than death, perhaps they really were sooner dead than changed.

On the other hand, many of the plotters were not from settled Catholic backgrounds, but were converts who had lived in outward conformity for long periods. Thomas Wintour had apparently fought on both sides in the Low Countries; Catesby lived a life of quiet conformity until the death of his wife. Fawkes adopted the religion of his stepfather and John Wright was imprisoned as a precaution during Queen Elizabeth's illness in 1596 but only converted to Catholicism in 1601. They were a group for whom religion was a badge of disaffection as well as its cause. They were hardly models of simple religious loyalty. Catesby, tired of Garnet's religious diplomacy, decided to take decisive action while the Jesuit was away on pilgrimage.

Though their own loyalties were complex and shifting, they decided and perhaps really believed that the mass of people was a much simpler proposition. Given a decisive blow and strong leadership the people would throw off the new religion with a shrug and hail their saviours, elegantly dressed gentlemen of the old faith to whom they had temporarily closed their hearts, but who would now appear as model Englishmen at the head rather than on the fringes of their society.

The pursuit of self-interest was perhaps more deeply ingrained than the plotters would have liked to believe, not least in themselves. As we have seen, there were few players behind the Plot whose loyalties were not questionable. The society which was so hostile to the plotters was unsure of its own loyalties. James had invented and re-instated a whole layer of aristocracy and gentility to give him networks of patronage in his new kingdom, where he was widely accepted but had little deeply rooted support. Beneath them, suitors followed their patrons not out of ancient loyalty but for what they could get. Though they regarded the place-hunting materialistic court with contempt, the plotters were part of this culture. Thomas Wintour took Lord Monteagle as his patron when he needed him but was ready to throw him off when he was rich enough to be 'his own man'. Northumberland suggested Thomas Percy was simply biding his time with the earl in the hope of supplanting him, as perhaps Northumberland was biding his with the king. Loyalty to any principle or idea is very often difficult to detect. The plotters had looked to Spain partly because it promised to fill the gap in patronage left when the earl of Essex fell in 1601. No matter that Essex had been head of the anti-Spanish faction at court and that one of his main objections to Cecil was that he was pro-Spanish and that he and most of the Privy Council were 'Spanish pensioners'. Waad wrote to Salisbury 8 November 1605 informing him of Francis Tresham as a Spanish pensioner worth watching, knowing that Salisbury had been the best-paid Spanish pensioner in the country. Despite the plotters' despairing of help from Spain after 1604, it seems Catesby still saw himself leading English soldiers in a Spanish army and exercising petty patronage of his own, like a nobleman, promising to take Humphrey Littleton's 'base boy' as a page.

Against this background, had Catesby really believed that the Catholics would act uniformly, believing religious loyalty and self-interest were the same thing? Was he in this sense living in the past? At the same time as he reported that the king and Salisbury were dead, Catesby reported that the Privy Council had ordered that the throats of all the English Catholics should be cut, a scare story taken from Catesby's childhood in the years before the defeat of the Armada. Would they stick together as a group as they must do in those circumstances, or had their motivations become more difficult to harness?

Parliament and democracy

It is striking to a modern audience just how little attention was paid by the plotters or the government to the probable destruction of the House of Commons in the gunpowder explosion. We are accustomed to seeing the period around the Gunpowder Plot as the time of the great rise of the Commons in power and influence, from haggles over taxation late in Elizabeth's reign intensifying under the early Stuarts and ending inevitably in civil war. The documents of the Plot show little sign of this. The 'principal commons' are an afterthought on the list of possible casualties. Sir William Waad as Lieutenant of the

Tower reported the occasional spat between his office and that of the mayor and the city of London, perhaps showing underlying hostility to ancient court privileges from a clear opposition group, which drew Waad's curse – 'a pox on all offices and officers'. However, the possible loss of popular representation in parliamentary government was barely an issue. This is not just striking in a modern context, but also given the fact of the English Civil War less than forty years after the Plot. Then Catholics, including the descendants of the plotters, had little option than to side with the king. Both plotters and king believed government was about a few 'great men' and democracy was an equally alien concept to both.

Perhaps the most telling moment of the Midlands rebellion was the plotters' reception at Lord Windsor's house, Hewell Grange, where they plundered weapons. As recounted by Robert Wintour's servant Thomas Maunder, they looked for support among the country people, announcing they were for 'God and the Country'.

> Whereupon one of the countrymen set his back to the wall and set his staff before him saying he was for King James for whom he would live and die and would not go against him, whereupon some of the company cried out, 'Kill him, kill him.'[1]

Given the fluctuating loyalty of many of the players behind the Plot and the 'cavalier' (in the modern sense) attitude of both the plotters and the government to popular opinion, this overt demonstration of loyalty appears almost as inexplicable as it is touching. Guy Fawkes had reported to the Spanish court that popular opinion in England was so against their new foreign king that the country was ripe for rebellion. Later, he was equally confident that if the plotters proclaimed themselves to have acted out of a desire to prevent union with Scotland the popular acclamation would be such that a carefully introduced Catholic government would be welcomed as part of the deal. Both the plotters and the government believed that the success or failure of rebellion depended on great leadership and the people being borne along in its wake on an unstoppable historical tide. Not so. The people, like so many others behind the Plot, had their own motivations.

EPILOGUE

In the light of the voluminous evidence of the investigation of the Plot and the hints and nuances of its language, we, like an audience reflecting on a play, can cast our minds back to the Prologue and judge whether our expectations have been met since we first took our seats. We can pick up themes of the Prologue in the light of all that has emerged.

The Gunpowder Percys

On the face of it, The earl of Northumberland's passage through the tumultuous events of the Gunpowder Plot looks like it has followed the standard cycle of a Percy in Shakespeare's plays; or even the more recent history of the family that was too close to Shakespeare's own day to be written about safely for the stage. There he is, following the Percy path: a rehabilitated outsider turned trusted councillor, flirting with the possibility of real personal power against the monarchy when the opportunity arose, suspected, tried in Star Chamber with his reputation under a cloud and then fined heavily. But his is a much subtler, more veiled rebellion and because of the depth and length of his examinations, an oddly intimate and vulnerable portrait of a great nobleman emerges. Northumberland's misplaced then waning confidence, his devices and evasions, his political blind spots, his selective deafness and failing memory, all are fleetingly visible as the circumstantial evidence against him grew. At the same time, the carefully worded but unconvincing, heavily qualified denials mounted on the desk beside him, crossed through, interpolated in his own distinctive hand and then in the standard script of the overworked, exasperated clerks tasked with preserving his meaning, so it could be pored over and endlessly revisited by the investigating commissioners. He allows different views of himself to be presented. What was his attitude to power and his level of personal ambition? In the end, he was brought to what the authorities believed was the truth of his role in the Plot by the circumstantial evidence against him being broken down into 'little pills', so that he could admit to things gradually under pressure. He could be worn down and led by a strong personality, as it seemed he had been by Thomas Percy.

Looked at with the perspective of the expectations of historical drama and the cycle of the loyalty and treachery of the earls of Northumberland towards the English crown, the ambitions and vicissitudes of the ninth earl, Henry Percy, take on an almost comical, predictable aspect. In Shakespeare's *Henry IV* plays, Harry Hotspur is trapped in time, always impatient, rushing forward to his own doom. Prince Hal and Falstaff seem memorably to step outside it and take on the cyclical time of comedy plays and renewed performance. Falstaff even in death goes to Arthur's bosom rather than Abraham's, the once and future fat man guaranteed to entertain us again next time. In the case of the ninth earl, the cycle of rise and fall seemed almost predetermined, scenes of outward loyalty followed by soliloquies of hidden treachery when the opportunity arose. In the flesh, Northumberland seemed to lack the political smoothness, however, to conceal his mixed loyalties in his language. His letters are full of tensions, dangerous plays of words and parallelisms and hasty revisions when it occurs to him that he has said too much or said it in a way which might be misinterpreted. The blackmail sub plot of Timothy Elks, the reminiscences with Dudley Carleton, his strange relationship with Thomas Percy where trust and power seemed to shift in unexpected ways – all suggested a love of influence and a reluctance to turn down any opportunity to gain it.

At the same time, there was also a tendency to be manipulated by ambitious men around him who sought his power for themselves.

Was Northumberland the power behind the Plot or was the earl being used by his poor relation Thomas Percy? Had the earl been flattered by his cousin to assume a role in acting as Protector to James's daughter, as others had planned to use his mother? Though it seemed to fly in the face of all the commissioners knew and revered about superior social rank, it seems possible that Thomas Percy was the *primum mobile* and not his illustrious cousin.

Henry Garnet and Catholic Rebellion

Henry Garnet's carefully qualified statements were consistent in maintaining his confidence in papal authority and the clarity of his own conscience. As in the case of Northumberland, it was not characteristic of Garnet to make outright denials. His evidence is often quoted in small snippets suggestive of innocence. Context tends to give a much more uncomfortable view. His remarkably clear, characteristic voice is audible across the centuries, for all the pressure exerted during questioning it remains authentically his. Even when writing in orange juice, which might have encouraged brevity and cramped the style in a lesser man, Garnet maintained the rampant flow of sub clauses, which puzzled his friends as well as his interrogators. Was he just too clever and reflective to be blindly obedient to his faith or to the state? Did he deceive his persecutors or simply confuse himself? What would he have done if Catesby's blow had created an opportunity to restore the true religion in England? What is striking to me looking at the evidence of both Northumberland and Garnet is the contingency of their language; so many responses were conditional on what might happen.

How real were the possibilities of help from other sources? Sir Edmund Baynham's mission to Rome to seek papal blessing for the Plot seemed absurdly slow and irrelevant in the light of the discovery of the Plot, but what blessing might it have received if it had achieved its purpose? If the Plot could really be a catalyst to the reconversion of England, it can hardly have failed to gain that approbation. The language used by Henry Garnet seemed to qualify his disapproval. If the wickedness of the plotters had been to act without the 'advice of friends', what would that advice have been? The Jesuits were well placed to advise on the disposition of potential allies and the timing of the 'blow'. Did Catesby's impatience with Garnet's advice and his decision to exclude him from his confidence cut him off from that advice?

The view historians have taken of the role of the Jesuits in the Plot has generally taken one of two forms. One concedes the government's case that the Gunpowder Plot was just the latest in a string of Jesuit-inspired plots, which seemed to them to be the principal function of the English mission. This version seems to fly in the face of much of the evidence collected by the government's own exhaustive investigation, which revealed the reluctance of the plotters to submit to or confide in their confessors and the genuine attempts made by Garnet and others to dissuade and deflect them. The second version accepts the contention of Tesimond's narrative that there was no role for the Jesuits in the Plot other than as a source of restraint. The carefully hedged language of Garnet and others is clearly suggestive of a third possibility. There was a consistent sense in the Jesuits' evidence that the plotters had brought ruin on their fellow Catholics by acting precipitately. There was an underlying suggestion that the priests expected to be involved in the planning, timing and coordination of plots to restore the true faith and had been disappointed not to be. The grounds of their disavowal of the Plot were contingent, it did not have papal blessing or military support overseas, or in the country. With their advice and support, they implied it might have had all those things. The state was very worried about the binding power of Catholic ritual and the use that could be made of popular superstition.

Robert Catesby and Banquo's Ghost

The witches' prophecies of Macbeth's rise and circumstances of his fall and Banquo's royal posterity are part of a mysterious background to the 'Scottish play', which conventionally is said to show the ancient barbarity of that kingdom to a sophisticated London playgoing audience. It is striking to modern readers how much the king and investigating commissioners were still swayed by prophecy and used the power of ambiguous, 'oraculous' language. The Monteagle letter was itself a kind of prophecy – 'they shall not see what hurts them' – part of a chain of events which showed the operation of divine providence in the discovery of the Plot. We tend to think of the witches and their vatic statements as a piece of period colour, showing a primitive, misty, alien culture where the old gods still lurk under the veneer of recent Christianity. In fact, prophecy was of pressing importance to the king and the Attorney General in the investigation of the Plot. The Lords Commissioners took Catholic credulity and the secret Vaux prophecy about Tottenham turning French very seriously. Catesby, Tesimond, Robert Wintour and Guy Fawkes were all looking to posterity and the power of prophecy to fuel unending struggle and revenge.

It is tempting coming to the Plot in isolation to see it as a one-off work of Catesby's genius, rather as students of literature are tempted to see Shakespeare's plays as miraculous acts of lonely literary originality. We are led to overlook or at least downplay the importance of the copious sources he drew on. Contemporary audiences expected writers to be craftsmen, working their sources into new forms. They also expected plays and their 'plots' to be a group activity. Playwrights regularly found themselves, as the earl of Northumberland did, in the court of Star Chamber. Conspiracy was one of the charges in which the court specialised and if a production caused offence, it could readily be tried there, as theatre was by its nature considered to be a work of many hands. The plots of plays and the planning of plots were not seen, as we would later come to see them, through the prism of Romanticism as the work of solitary geniuses conjuring originality from their fevered brains in a lonely garret.

In some ways, the authorities came to the investigation of the Gunpowder plot with similar expectations. They expected to see a wider conspiracy and influences more powerful than just Catesby. The depth of suspicion against Northumberland despite the lack of direct evidence is at least partly explained by the conviction of the authorities that there had to be an aristocratic connection, a 'great man' behind the Plot, they could not easily conceive of a plot without one. The Gunpowder plot refused to conform to an established pattern. The length of the investigation reflected not only the seriousness of the shock that the government had suffered but also its refusal to yield to the facts as discovered. It can be argued that the Plot was different in some important and interesting ways and that

Catesby had no clear sources for his plan, which the authorities could use to contextualise and explain it. Though even here, there was the tantalising suggestion that a similar proposal had been made to Hugh Owen in the reign of Queen Elizabeth. He had been abandoned by Spain after the Treaty of London, but the cover of a Spanish company in the Low Countries was still attractive. Fawkes became the image of the lone assassin, the unknown face becoming the enduring image of the political killer. The process began early with his aspect and accoutrements reused for the assassin of Henry IV of France only five years later. As a lone figure, he could scarcely be less credible. His strength and determination under questioning came not only from the faith which bound him to the oath he had taken, but also from the knowledge that he was only part of the plan and more powerful forces were at work. They might bring about the change he sought if he could only buy them time.

Jacobean society had a small circle of movers and shakers who expected to know each other well. The oddly intimate verbal portraits of the government proclamations against many of the traitors and suspects showed this social circle included those intent on its destruction. The shock of Guy Fawkes as the unknown face carries down to our own day. The king's exclamation 'I can meet with no man that knows him' was so unlikely that it needed repeating

James and the lessons of the Gunpowder Plot

As reported by the Venetian ambassador, King James was initially terrified and melancholy in the wake of the discovery of the Plot. The duration, scale and thoroughness of the official investigation, the resources devoted to it, and the urgency and confusion with which it was conducted in its early stages are compelling evidence to me that the Plot was a genuine attack on the government and that those involved believed they had had a lucky escape. What lessons did he and the government take from it and what should a modern audience make of it at this distance? Sir Arthur Gorges feared that every London cellar, including his own, could hide cabals of disaffected gentlemen. How many did he think there might be and what could the state do about it? The earl of Salisbury's much vaunted intelligence networks were not able to undertake the kind of intensive investigation and searches Gorges advocated and there were not the resources available to strengthen them. Parliament remained vulnerable, the Palace of Westminster and its surroundings remained a central part of the overcrowded life of the city and could not be meaningfully secured or cordoned off without the use of disproportionate resources and the risk of major disruption to the business of government and the courts. The government's solution was to treat the symptoms, to banish the Jesuit priests of the English mission and to attempt to secure others like Owen and Baldwin who threatened agitation abroad and further plots at home. There was no hope of cure until the investigation produced a proper diagnosis. What was the disease?

Sir Edward Coke's summing up in the great trials following the discovery made the answer seem relatively simple. A small group of disaffected gentlemen had been corrupted by their priests to make an attempt on the government and their path had been smoothed by a group of sympathetic lords, Northumberland chief among them, who would be spared the blast and reap its rewards, but whose direct part in the plan could not now be proved. That was not the end of the investigation, however.

Long after the trials had finished, evidence continued to be taken and sifted as the authorities tried to make sense of what had happened beyond this simple summary. The evidence of the investigation refused to yield neatly to Coke's interpretation and constantly suggested new avenues of enquiry. Convenient though the explanation was, this continued activity suggested the government itself did not believe its own line about Jesuit manipulation and that the plotters themselves had indeed devised the Plot and had sought to manipulate the sympathetic Catholic lords rather than being controlled by them. Though they were few in number, the plotters appeared well connected and well equipped. Fawkes had the appropriate knowledge of military mining and explosives and diplomatic introductions to the court at Brussels. Thomas Wintour had credit with Spain, Thomas Percy with the earl of Northumberland. Sir Everard Digby was the exemplary courtier who could soothe the captive Princess Elizabeth. They had some of the best horses and horsemen in England, the missing link in past attempts to coax a Spanish invasion. Catesby seemed at least retrospectively to have the power to charm anyone he chose to his cause. Yet they were to become famous as a small group of gentlemen plotting from their own resources with no need and apparently no desire for help from outside.

The authorities were used to certain types of threat; firstly, disaffected noblemen leading rebellions against the Crown, often out of the North; secondly and more recently Catholic intrigues against the state led by idealistic young men and their shadowy priests, possibly paving the way for a Spanish invasion. Then there was the perennial possibility of an assassination attempt by a disillusioned individual. By 1605 the threat of Northern rebellions had apparently diminished with the union of the crowns in 1603 and the possibility of invasion and Catholic intrigue had apparently receded through peace with Spain and a softening of the attitude of the papacy to the new king. Would any lone assassin want to kill the king after such a smooth transition of power and the prospect of stability in the succession for the first time in so long? Even that possibility seemed to have shrunk. In the end of course, even James's famous caution could not protect him from the possibility of the lone assassin. Indeed, there is some suggestion his death would eventually come from poisoning by his favourite, the duke of Buckingham. His son Charles I could not protect the duke himself from assassination three years later, or himself from the executioner.

Was the Gunpowder Plot just another failed assassination attempt, a Catholic intrigue designed to pave the way for a Spanish invasion or a shadowy northern rebellion led at one remove by the Gunpowder Percys? There were certainly elements of all three. Was it in truth something entirely different in character? Perhaps Catesby used all three possibilities to gain allies and resources. Which scenario did he see taking shape after the blow and what role did he see for himself? With the benefit of hindsight, we tend to think that only Catesby and his companions took the Plot seriously, that its discovery was inevitable and that hope of wider support was a pipe dream only considered when their own scheme failed them. Perhaps we even like to think that only Catesby knew his true longer-term plans and that no one outside their circle had invested hope in it. Any sense of a wider conspiracy evaporated in the narrow failure of the explosion. But what would have been the reaction and the attitude of those parties to Catesby had the 'blow' succeeded in its intended full effect? Would Spain, would the earl of Northumberland, would Sir Walter Raleigh or Henry Garnet have failed to take advantage of the opportunity which destruction of the government, lords and principal commons might bring?

Looking again at the evidence there are traces I did not detect my earlier examination, which suggest the despair and fatalism which followed the failure of the Plot was not felt in the days leading up to the blow, not just in the plotters' letters among themselves but more widely. Obviously, it was in everyone's interest after the discovery to pretend they knew nothing of the Plot, that it was doomed from the beginning and implicated no one beyond those caught in the act of rebellion or of planning the explosion. However, there is an excitement and anticipation in the air in the days leading up to the discovery that even fear of implicating oneself could not hide entirely in the words of those giving evidence. It is evident in Garnet's questioning of domestic Catholic military strength and his apparent acceptance of his role in raising rebellion in Wales if the timing and conditions had been right. Then there was the stock-piling of arms and provisions in the Catholic houses in the Midlands, Northumberland's willingness to have his actions guided by Thomas Percy, and the plotters' confidence in their own links with established diplomatic contacts in Brussels and beyond. All these point to readiness to exploit the situation Catesby's blow might create on the part of a number of parties who professed their unwavering loyalty to the Crown once the window of opportunity closed. Was Catesby exploiting these possibilities to gain the resources he needed for this own coup or would he have been conveniently disposed of by Spain or by Northumberland once he had served his purpose? Perhaps the Plot in some way forms a stepping-stone between the familiar plots of the reign of Elizabeth and the execution of King Charles I. The gentlemen after all felt they could raise a wider rebellion and dispose of king and lords in a blow and that they could retain popular support. Garnet's exhortations to prayer and patience would have to wait until the 1830s for the removal of the penal laws against Catholics in England.

What if the Plot Had Succeeded?

Perhaps it is time to half close our eyes and imagine an alternative history in which the celebrations of 5 November are an annual remembrance of the restoration of the true faith in England, the prevention of a union with Scotland and the destruction of a hated Scottish monarch and his followers. No doubt, the victors could have written this chapter into English history. Elizabeth's reign would be consigned to history as a black period of persecution and isolation from Catholic civilisation, a relationship triumphantly reinstated after Catesby's daring plan had brought to pass what the prophecies had foretold, 'Tottenham turned French' and 'the tyrannous heretic confounded in his cruel pleasures'. In the light of the smooth succession of James VI & I to his throne in England, it is easy to forget the depth of anti-Scots feeling in England in 1603. Very few bonfire night revellers would nowadays cite that feeling as a major motivation and justification for the Plot. Even at the plotters' trial very little was made of the anti-Scots rhetoric of Thomas Percy or the consistently xenophobic evidence of Guy Fawkes himself. Presumably, this was because the popular appeal of this stance was such that the government could not highlight it without the risk of fostering sympathy for the plotters. It was agreed among themselves and with Hugh Owen that the prevention of the political union of the two countries and the ending of 'abuses' (presumably the bestowal of land and offices on the king's Scottish followers) rather than the restoration of Catholicism, was to be proclaimed as the principal reason for the 'blow' and the rebellion which followed.

Was it, after all, inevitable that the Catholics would lose the civil war that followed the blast and then be subject to still greater retribution and persecution? Could the state rely on the local militias? There were doubts, even in the aftermath of the brief and abortive Midlands rebellion about the loyalty of the sheriffs themselves, not to mention of their men. How might they have reacted in the chaos following the blow? What about the continually rebellious Northern earls? Francis Tresham had reportedly ascribed the failure of Father Watson's plot in 1603 to the reluctance of the Catholic noble families to lend material support, but the opportunity presented by the destruction of the government in London would surely be too great to resist. Garnet reported tumults in Wales that came to nothing. Where, except among those to be destroyed in the blast, did deep-seated loyalty to the king lie?

The rumour of the king having been killed at Woking in March 1606 seems in retrospect to be a comical episode of misinformation, but the wording of the proclamation designed to suppress the rumour was deadly serious. 'Tumultuous spirits' it said had taken the opportunity to raise people in arms without warrant. Was the government fragile enough that an accident of this kind could spark a rebellion and were the discontents numerous, prepared and bold enough to take their chance? Perhaps the 'tumultuous spirits' were loyal subjects taking arms in defence of the government, raising the militia themselves fearing the local law officers would not do so because of their Catholic connections. Both scenarios were potentially dangerous and indicated a lack of underlying political stability and confidence in authority. Though the core plotters had been tried in January perhaps a March insurrection might free Raleigh, Northumberland and the other suspected lords to form part of a new government. Catesby in his desperate rallying of the hunting party at Dunchurch had proclaimed that the king and Cecil were dead (it did not seem to matter how) and that the change they sought could still come about in the confusion, even though the blow had not been struck. Beyond the king himself and the Principal Secretary, the loyalty of the government seemed to be a matter of persuasion and negotiation.

The plotters naturally enough gave no thought to the government of Scotland, but presumably the famous calmness which would enable James to rule that historically turbulent kingdom 'with his pen' from London after 1603 would not have survived his assassination. Would a puppet monarch under a strongly Protestant regent provoke further bloodshed, or forestall the tensions which would lead to the Civil Wars? Regardless of the immediate outcome, what precedent might a successful Gunpowder Plot set for subsequent unpopular regimes and the course of British history? Despite the shock and horror of the execution of Charles I and the 'revolution' which exiled James VII & II, Britain seemed to follow a relatively moderate course that allowed a coherent line of land-holding and record-keeping free from the revolutionary blood-letting and radical re-writing of history which beset so much of Europe. Catesby's scheme was always presented in the light of its failure as a shocking aberration, an almost incomprehensibly bloodthirsty idea that evoked instinctive horror and revulsion even in the minds of the plotters when it was first revealed, only to be made palatable by Catesby's sense of poetic justice and his personal charm. Its failure and the exemplary punishments of those found guilty of planning it bred an instinctive horror of plots of that kind and by and large left domestic political killing to the lone assassin. If successful, the Plot might instead have formed a precedent, a proven way for a persecuted minority to bring about radical change or at least confusion and an interruption of the hated status quo.

Had the Plot succeeded, the suppressed desire to celebrate the explosion itself, evident in the imaginative flights of John Donne's Gunpowder day sermon and in our own firework displays, would then have legitimate expression. Celebrating the prevention of an explosion with lots of explosions somehow seems psychologically unsatisfactory. There seems to me to be a strong element of fantasy celebration of the destruction of the political class in our own commemorations and the celebration of the preservation of James VI & I's government. The ostensible purpose of the celebration from the beginning is at best a rather half-hearted afterthought in most people's minds. In our own era of widespread, bored online disillusionment with the political establishment does Bonfire Night, half-remembered in its detail and blurred in its significance, still act as a kind of safety valve, reminding us annually that, as bad as things may be, the consequences of sweeping all away could be worse? Perhaps all sides have reason to be glad the Plot did not succeed.

According to Ben Jonson (and the ambiguities of his feelings about the Plot have already been noted) the Plot had become an established money-making opportunity by 1614. Leatherhead in Jonson's play *Bartholomew Fair* notes that of all his puppet shows *The Gunpowder Plot* was the best get-penny. 'I have presented that to an eighteen or twenty pence audience nine times in an afternoon.' Domestic subjects were simplest for an audience to understand and not too much 'learning' was required to enjoy the story. But was the plot of the

Plot really straightforward and purely domestic, or had the process of simplification and half remembering begun less than ten years after the events themselves?

Steps to begin official commemoration of the king's preservation began quickly and an act for public thanksgiving on 5 November was passed in January 1606, an annual service in every parish in England and in the prayer book until 1859. The commemoration was kept going for varying political reasons at various times, the preservation of parliament rather than the king by the Parliamentarians in the Civil Wars, back to providential preservation of the crown at the Restoration. There was a tradition that the fires burnt with greater intensity in response to any moves by the government towards toleration. With hindsight we can see the Protestant succession as an inevitable consequence – and the prolonged delay to the toleration of Catholics in England – worse than even Catesby could imagine.

Legacy

There is a long-standing Bonfire Night tradition of Guy Fawkes masks and an equally long-standing tolerance of them by the authorities, who might be expected to take a dim view of collective attempts to disguise identity. However, there was a consensus around the celebration, that this annual group concealmentw as a social rather than anti-social activity. Consensus is perhaps rather unfashionable at present, the plot of the loner and the various conspiracy theories around him are easier to focus on and harder to dismiss. The modern Guido Fawkes is very much of our own making. Gone is the well-travelled gentleman soldier whose languages, learning and general bearing made the monarch he was trying to kill mistake him, on first acquaintance, for a priest; a man whose lasting physical distinction was a body so broken by torture he had to be helped to the scaffold. In his place, we have a nightmare trickster, a well-groomed inscrutable clown offering virtual terror. Fawkes the social being at the heart of the plotter engraving with which we began, who became a loner in the popular imagination by virtue of his role and capture, has become a symbol of isolated disaffection. The modern wearers of the Guido Fawkes mask may have common cause in individual demonstrations but are just as likely to face each other as disaffected individuals on opposite sides of the same issue. Fawkes' enduring power as a symbol for all of us comes not from our view of his causes. but from the guilty shadow in the corner of our celebrations and underlying John Donne's sermon: that we are not celebrating the preservation of the existing order but fantasising about its destruction.

Recent attempts to turn Bonfire Night displays into a simple ahistorical night of communal autumn celebration tend to prove unsatisfactory. A few years ago my local display played pop music at us while the fireworks were on, in an attempt presumably to render it just like any other modern fair or festival. I felt oddly uncomfortable, as if there was a conspiracy to stop us reflecting on the Plot and what, if anything, it might still mean for us. Then I dismissed my own discomfort as an eccentric reaction unlikely to affect the parents and children I saw around me. Perhaps there was a more general negative reaction though, as the experiment has not been repeated. There is still, after all, a prize for the best guy and perhaps imposing the norms of an anodyne adult music festival on Bonfire Night distracted attention from the efforts of the children, who have greater and gorier imaginations.

Language

My work as historical consultant saw many iterations of *Gunpowder 5/11 The Greatest Terror Plot* including extended versions of pure drama, which did not make it to the screen. These dramatic treatments gave visual immediacy, urgency and a sense of possibility to the story. They took me back to the sources to look through the layers of fatalism and doom to the flashes of enthusiasm and excited dialogue in the weeks leading up to the discovery of the Plot revealed in the evidence of the plotters' family connections and their servants. The closeness of the landed Catholic families of the Midlands, their besieged lifestyle, having at short notice to pull up the drawbridge and hide the evidence of their faith from the pursuivants, can make them appear insular to an outsider. In fact, they were well connected and well educated, perhaps better connected than many of their countrymen to the learning and networks of continental Europe. Lord Vaux of Harrowden explained his absence from services at his local parish church on the grounds that his house was a parish unto itself.

He had his own chapel and his own priests, his own extended family and connections, not to mention his servants many, of whom had servants of their own. Their voices reach us from the documents of the investigation, intelligible to a modern audience with a little glossing, but not plain in their meaning, rather poetic, dark, allusive and suggestive. Their official disavowals of involvement after the event were especially artfully worded. The excitement and defiance of their servants' depositions were often less well disguised. Under official interrogation, in fear of their reputations and sometimes of their lives, still the language tumbles out barely punctuated by the clerks, sub clause after clause layering and qualifying what has gone before, but always articulate and often knowing and literary, full of the rhetorical arts on which their schooling insisted.

This is difficult material for historians to interpret and certainly to cite briefing as evidence to prove a point and it is always tempting to omit the swathes of rhetoric and layers of meaning in pursuit of clarity and brevity. The trouble with using selective quotation as evidence of fact is intensified in this period by the possibility that words may not mean to a contemporary audience what they appear to mean to us. Worse still, phrases may not be used to convey 'matter' at all, being euphuistic exercises. Whole letters give a much clearer idea of the working of the mind and a clearer view of what to make of their evidence.

It is doubly difficult for television drama to do justice to the language of the sources, since it is quite difficult to portray the ambiguities and nuances of character that are presented in the evidence of the investigation and present a coherent and recognisable character over the course of the programme. History is not always about the battle between good and evil. It is difficult for television to resist our craving for heroes and villains. Sometimes the drama comes from human beings presented with choices and opportunities; sometimes they make decisions that seem at odds with our sense of their role.

The prolonged questioning of Northumberland and Garnet and their revisions and retractions have left a vast body of evidence, deep and obscure, but ultimately revealing of character and motivation. Others, like John Grant, left us little impression of themselves at all.

Very often, there is among the investigating lords and lawyers as well as the suspects who gave evidence, just enough of their characteristic style and language for us to hear hints and nuances that tell us more than perhaps they intended.

Sir Edward Coke's flamboyant rhetoric as Attorney General lends itself to the easy interpretation that the government's case was weak and could only be carried off with bluster and theatricality. There was a strong cumulative persuasive effect in all that repetition. There was an element of theatre in trials in any case (there still is). Coke as always seemed to have a personal agenda, one which evaded even the supposedly all-powerful earl of Salisbury's attempts to control it. His brief was embellished with additional detail and damning sonorous biblical prose. This could disconcert his victims but also take him down paths that the king and Principal Secretary would not tread. His ambivalent attitude to the king's 'merciful' prerogative justice and his championing of the Common Law only worsened his relationship with James as time passed. He was eventually removed as Lord Chief Justice. He would live to be a scourge of the prerogative powers of the monarch through his writings, beyond the reign of James I and beyond his own death and into the Civil War.

The earl of Northampton's copious flowing language, which the king had called his 'ample, Asiatic and endless volumes', is not to the modern taste and it is easy to assume that he bored his fellow privy councillors and trial audiences in the same way he may bore us. In fact, he was highly effective in unsettling those he cross-examined, bringing their own language and learning to bear on Catholic suspects, particularly the priests. He cited their texts, knowing he had them to hand whereas they had often been deprived of them in custody. Worse, he was a living example of the principle that 'outward observance' to the law could lead to advancement, as the king had promised. He confounded those who claimed that the king had made loyalty to him incompatible with their faith. He also had an advanced notion of his own status, which made him sceptical of the evidence of his inferiors. For all his apparent rambling, it was he and not Coke, Waad or even Salisbury himself who dissected Sir Everard Digby's evidence and pinpointed his inconsistencies and evasions. He was not one to give credit to a fallen favourite because of his social graces.

After the death of Lord Salisbury in 1612, Northampton briefly gained the prominence in political life he felt his rank entitled him to. He wasted no time in consigning his former colleague to hell along with Queen Elizabeth, imagining 'the little lord where he kneels before his old mistress by an extreme hot fire's side'.[2] When he himself died in 1614, where would his fellow Catholics consign his soul on the basis of his own compromises of faith and his actions towards them?

In the case of Ben Jonson, how different is the literary style of his poetry from the language of his letter to Salisbury of 8 November? The letter lacks a certain amount of the verbal polish, Latin tags and self-confidence of *Volpone* or *The Alchemist*, but the habits of language are not so easily cast off and they reassert themselves under pressure. Was the recusant who imagined how he would behave in the wake of the Plot if he were he a Catholic priest equivocating about his loyalty? Certainly, his repeated summonses to the Consistory Court to settle his 'doubts' and explain his absence from parish services in the wake of the Plot, suggested he had not changed his allegiance after the its discovery, though 500 others may have done.

Francis Bacon came to the Plot as an opportunist full of political ambition rather than from the murky world of a recusant in government service. For a man who defined prose style and wrote so much about language, his evidence relating to the Plot is slightly disappointing. As an investigator rather than a witness, he seems to give much less of himself away in his letter to Salisbury of 8 November than Ben Jonson does on the same day. His personal ambition and increasing role in legal affairs led him to develop a distinct style as a man of business, which hid his true feelings very effectively. In his essay 'Of Simulation and Dissimulation', he defines three ways of hiding the self. Secrecy: the virtue of a confessor', Dissimulation, which includes 'equivocations or oraculous speeches', and Simulation 'false speeches'. This essay written in 1625 sounds rooted in his experience of the evidence of priests twenty years earlier.

Oswald Tesimond's narrative of the Plot is a curious, many-layered document. It is in his hand but not originated by him, since he appears in it in the third person as Father Greenaway. It is in Italian, but written by someone close to the plotters' circle. As edited and translated by Father Francis Edwards, the agenda of the narrative is pretty clear, but what about the nuances of his language? He justifies the actions of the plotters in the context of the continuing persecution of English Catholics and paints a vivid picture of what this meant on a daily basis. The narrative distances other Catholics and the Jesuits from the Plot but does not deny the genuineness of the conspiracy, its intent or the fundamentals of its progress as narrated by Thomas Wintour and others. It is a counterbalance to the official account in sympathy but not in substantial matters of fact. It is repeatedly admitted that the account has been edited to protect those still living, so it is not clear how much weight can be attached to the specifics. Henry Garnet is said to have 'prevented serious trouble on four occasions'. How did he know about all this trouble and what was his role? Did these troubles include the murderous masque at Lord Mordaunt's house? Presumably they did not, since the unknown priest intervening to prevent trouble on that occasion was a less conspicuous figure than the Father Superior. How many priests were engaged in suppressing what Tesimond called 'private treasons'? Just how many of these abortive plots were there? Again, the 'private treasons' sound like those concealed from the priests and then discovered and prevented by them as being likely to fail and bring discredit on the faithful. This posits another class of 'public' treasons planned with Jesuit support and approbation. Tesimond believed that if the conditions worsened, 'all the Catholics may be forced to take arms,' which in turn suggests that they had them and might be prepared to use them. Garnet had written to Claudio Aquaviva on 24 July 1605 of the 'recent disturbance in Wales which came to nothing'. Might they have come to something if properly managed and supported? Did they want them to? Tesimond's narrative further suggested that the discovery and the loss of his safe houses in London had prompted Garnet's pilgrimage to Holywell while a replacement was secured. Was part of the object of the journey to Wales to gauge the appetite for rebellion their after the recent failed tumult? Little wonder the plotters thought he might raise rebellion there. Tesimond notes that the explosion would have destroyed the archives and records of the courts, a possible source of regret not expressed in the official account.

For many years the polarised language of Coke and Tesimond clouded our view of the Plot. The words of the characters themselves copiously recorded in that unprecedented and dangerously resource-sapping bureaucratic effort of the investigation remain our best guide to their true feelings and the true nature of the Plot. Whichever bits we choose to discount as unreliable or produced under duress, we have a body of evidence broad and weighty enough to undermine airy and convenient theories. They include the government's concoction of a Jesuit conspiracy carried out by their superstitious pawns and the conspiracy theories of those who see the whole desperate and lovingly documented exercise as a sleight of hand by the government for its own political advantage. What seems much clearer to me now than when I first looked at the evidence is the number and variety of people who, if they did not know the detail of the intended plot, knew a major blow was planned in 1605 and seemed prepared and willing to act when it came. The resource devoted to the investigation months and years after the discovery surely reflected a continued nervousness on the part of the authorities. They could not publish, but dared not ignore, the evidence of so many whose disloyalty could not be proved retrospectively, but who might still take advantage should a renewed 'blow' against the state prove more successful.

Had Catesby survived the siege of Holbeach, what account would he have given of the leadership of the Plot and the political settlement that would follow it? Would he have soured even erstwhile supporters with his bluster and self-aggrandisement or would the famous Catesby charm have wooed the lords as Digby attempted to at his trial? On balance, Catesby was unlikely to have taken defeat and trial with good grace or have confided in those he despised. By comparison, Thomas Wintour's prose style is extraordinary for its wit and clarity. Perhaps it is after all his measured and literate narrative which has given the plotters such an attractive human face and made an appeal to posterity that attracted so many apologists.

The state papers of the investigation at The National Archives and the earl of Salisbury's related papers retained at Hatfield House are perhaps together the greatest body of early modern letters devoted to a single subject. They allow us to trace the circumstances of the Plot itself, but also have the power of great literature to move us with their narrative of personal tragedy. The Plot coincided with a flowering of the English language, not just among Shakespeare and his contemporaries the poets and dramatists of the period we still celebrate, but among all those officials, courtiers and gentry who had rhetoric at the heart of their education. The result of this coincidence is a body of prose of supreme depth and quality. Tesimond's narrative noted that the plotted explosion would have destroyed many official records if it had succeeded. Its failure and the investigation that followed created some of the most precious. Whatever our view of the events themselves and whatever we secretly hope for our political masters and ourselves as the fireworks explode, we have genuine cause for celebration in the continued preservation of that unique evidence.

CHRONOLOGY

1586

Henry Garnet arrives in England. Discovery of Babbington Plot. Arrest of William Weston, Father Superior of the English Jesuit Province. Garnet appointed Superior, begins to build on the network of Catholic safe houses established by Anne Vaux and others

1588

Spanish Armada sails to attack England; defeated

1596

Dangerous illness of Queen Elizabeth. Known malcontents, including John Wright, imprisoned as a precaution

1601

Rebellion and execution of the earl of Essex. Francis Tresham, Robert Catesby, Lord Monteagle and the Wrights all involved in the plot

1603

Death of Elizabeth. Accession of James VI of Scotland to the English throne Main and Bye Plots combine priestly assassination of the king and the possibility of Spanish invasion

1604

Treaty of London ends war with Spain

1605

June Henry Garnet leads several of conspirators and their families on pilgrimage to Wales

July Garnet hears of the Plot in 'walking confession' from Oswald Tesimond, confessor to Robert Catesby

26 October; Saturday Lord Monteagle receives an anonymous letter warning him to avoid attendance at Parliament. He reports this to the king and the Privy Council

Sir Thomas Edmondes, English ambassador in Flanders, reports from Brussels English Catholic confidence and reported conversions in letters to Lord Salisbury

27 October; Sunday Plotters learn of the 'Monteagle letter' thanks to Thomas Wintour's connections with the Monteagle household. Catesby, Fawkes and Thomas Wintour staying at White Webbs, a house rented by Anne Vaux near Theobalds, Salisbury's house in Hertfordshire

30 October; Wednesday Fawkes ventures out, unaware of discovery although other conspirators knew of the letter, and finds the powder undisturbed

31 October; Thursday The king returns to London from hunting. Thomas Wintour comes to London

1 November; Friday Thomas Wintour and Catesby accuse Tresham of having revealed the Plot; his denials only half convince

Tresham urges abandonment or at least postponement; believes the letter has achieved this. Tresham plans to be out of the country and urges Catesby to leave too

2 November; Saturday Another letter about a plot to assassinate King James is 'found on the street'

Passport for Francis Tresham to travel for two years

3 November; Sunday Percy stiffens the resolution of the conspirators and resolves to gauge official knowledge of the Plot through his master, the earl of Northumberland

4 November; Monday Percy dines with Northumberland at Syon House

Initial search and the midnight raid on the vault. Fawkes arrested, gunpowder discovered

Percy and Catesby leave London

5 November; Tuesday Thomas Wintour goes to Parliament on Tuesday morning to confirm the rumours of discovery, then rides north

Initial examination of 'John Johnson', Fawkes's alias

Proclamation issued for the apprehension of Thomas Percy. Percy reported escaping from London in all directions

Sir John Popham's investigations lead immediately to the core plotters

Rendezvous at Dunchurch, Catesby Percy and the Wrights bring news of the arrest of Fawkes and the failure of the Plot. Catesby begins to tell wild lies of the king's death and suggests open rebellion; the majority melt away

Raid on Warwick Castle

6 November; Wednesday morning 'Johnson' examined on the Percy connection

James writes letter authorizing the torture of 'Johnson'

Afternoon 'Johnson' answers on Percy connection, yielding little

Sir John Popham revises his list of suspects, additions and omissions based on 'Johnson's' confession

First reports of the Midlands rebellion

The king's daughter, the Lady Elizabeth, removed to Coventry

Robert Wintour writes urgent letter, found later at Holbeach House

Digby writes to Henry Garnet at Coughton for pardon and support; receives neither. Mary Digby, also at Coughton, overhears her husband's fate discussed

7 November; Thursday Thos Wintour absolved with Catesby at Huddington, picks up armour from Lord Windsor's and goes to Holbeach House

Gunpowder explosion at Holbeach stirs fears of divine disapproval; further desertions of rebel supporters

Proclamation against the rebels issued, countering rumours of the involvement of a foreign power

Salisbury's narrative of the Plot is read alongside Fawkes' confession in Parliament

Chamberlain writes to Carleton with news of the first 'Bonfire Night', and encloses copy of the 'Monteagle letter'

Catesby's Hillingdon house 'Moorcrofts' searched. Thomas Percy unsuccessfully sought there

8 November; Friday Siege of Holbeach

Gentlemanly arrests and suspicious deaths of vital witnesses including Percy, Catesby and John and Christopher Wright, all mortally wounded. Rookwood and Thomas Wintour captured

Third proclamation aims to set rebel against rebel by singling out Percy on the day he is mortally wounded at Holbeach. Percy is taken prisoner but dies on 9 November

Percy 'seen' riding towards Rochester

Sir William Waad notes Francis Tresham and other 'Spanish pensioners' in London as being worth watching. Tresham is not formally connected by the authorities with the Plot until implicated by Fawkes on 9 November

Fawkes's next confession names conspirators and details the development of the plot – but is rendered superfluous by the information flooding in from Holbeach

Digby rides away from Holbeach before the siege on the pretext of getting reinforcements; he is cornered by a posse while trying to find someone of rank to accept his surrender

Lord Montague begins a conspiratorial correspondence with his father-in-law the earl of Dorset, Lord Treasurer

Fawkes makes declaration to Salisbury with failing signature

11 November; Monday The use of White Webbs, Enfield, a safe house for priests including Henry Garnet, Father Superior of the Jesuit Province in England, is revealed

King James sends an account of the Plot to his brother-in-law Christian IV of Denmark

12 November; Tuesday Warwickshire prisons overflowing with recusants in the wake of the Midlands rebellion; reports of patchy law enforcement, local loyalties and alliances

Catesby household at Ashby searched

Search of the Vaux home at Harrowden begins and lasts nine days

Survivors of Holbeach House siege brought to London

13–30 November Declaration of Francis Tresham

Plot reported as a fable in France

Further reports emerge of siege of Holbeach, 'the multitude beat the grievously wounded traitors, Catesby, Percy and the two Wrights beyond hope of recovery'

Lords Mordaunt and Montague sent to the Tower

Reports of earl of Northumberland being a focus for discontent in the summer

Ports (closed since 5 November) re-opened by order of the Privy Council – 'The plot being now thoroughly discovered and the principal offenders in the hands of his Majesty'

Fawkes's further declaration strongly suggests Tresham as author of Monteagle letter as he was 'exceeding earnest' to warn him; backs nobles' stories regarding absence from Parliament

Exhumation and quartering of the conspirators who died at Holbeach

Second search at Catesby's Hillingdon house; his goods confiscated

Sir Richard Walsh reports seizing the arms of John Talbot of Grafton, searching Huddington Court and seizing Thomas Wintour's papers

Proclamation issued for the apprehension of Robert Wintour and Stephen Littleton

Permission granted to sheriffs enabling them to pursue rebels into neighbouring counties – rather after the event

Official chronology of the meetings and proceedings of the plotters compiled

Circumstantial evidence links the plotters with the Jesuits

Attempt made to establish a link between Robert Wintour and the Countess of Shrewsbury

Sir Edward Coke examines the earl of Northumberland

Thomas Wintour makes a confession, annotated by the king

Comfortable accommodation at the Tower is over-subscribed, causing problem for Sir William Waad. Northumberland joins the other lords in the Tower, exacerbating problems with appropriate accommodation

Examination of Francis Tresham, Monteagle's name pasted out again

Examination of Robert Keyes reveals Catesby's contempt for the Lords

Garnett writes from hiding at Hindlip House to protest his innocence to the Privy Council

December Further enquiry made about the possibility of a northern rebellion and a Spanish regiment led by Catesby

Examinations of Sir Everard Digby, and Ambrose Rookwood

Mary Digby's plea of innocence and for her property; complaints made of
corruption of the law officers who pocket the proceeds

Examination of Thomas Bate

Anonymous warning letter of assassination attempts against Salisbury

Discovery of the priests' hole at Huddington Court

More information on Fawkes's background supplied by Sir William Waad

Sir Walter Raleigh closely monitored in the Tower; his renewed boldness taken
as a sign that he is preparing to lead an anti-government party. Raleigh's wild
denials of involvement with inside information 'fitter to be related than written'

Circumstantial evidence emerges from Salisbury's spies about papal backing
for the plot

Examination of Francis Tresham. Monteagle's debt to Percy uncovered –
offers a further reason why Percy might wish to preserve him

Reference to Percy's two wives – suspected of bigamy

Northumberland recalls his conversation with Percy on 4 November

Waad reports Tresham's death in the Tower

1606

January Sir Thomas Edmondes reports to Salisbury that after initial sympathy
for a fellow monarch, the Spanish court now fears reprisals against English
Catholics

Further examination of Guy Fawkes; negotiations with Rome

Arrest of Robert Wintour and Stephen Littleton at Hagley in Worcestershire

Humphrey Littleton, brother of Stephen, reveals that Henry Garnet is hiding
at Hindlip House

Proclamation issued for the detention of Gerard, Garnet and Tesimond

Examination of Robert Wintour

Examination of Stephen Littleton, who had 'laid hid in barns and poor men's
houses'

Hindlip House searched; Nicholas Owen and Ralph Ashley discovered

Guy Fawkes, Thomas and Robert Wintour, Robert Keyes, John Grant,
Thomas Bate, Ambrose Rookwood and Sir Everard Digby are tried in
Westminster Hall on the 27th

Fawkes and Robert Wintour reported to regret the opportunity to justify
their actions to the world

Sentence against Sir Everard Digby; pleads guilty. Sentence against Thomas
Wintour, Fawkes, Keyes, Robert Wintour, Grant, Rookwood and Bate,
they plead not guilty

Fawkes complains that the indictment. can be denied due to untruth of Jesuit
involvement

Summary execution of the aiders and abetters of Littleton and Robert
Wintour; those who might provide further information are spared

Garnet and Oldcorne emerge from Hindlip House after eight days in the
priest's hole

Digby, Robert Wintour, Grant and Bate executed at the west end of St Paul's in London on 30 January

Thomas Wintour, Rookwood, Keyes and Fawkes executed outside Westminster Hall on the 31st

February Examination of Lords Stourton and Mordaunt for their non-attendance in Parliament

Thomas Phelippes protests his innocence to Salisbury. Unclear whether he was brought in by the government on a trumped up charge to forge Garnet's letters

Garnet brought to London from Worcestershire – slowly because of his physical weakness

Oldcorne and Garnet committed to the Gatehouse prison in London

Mary Digby sues to be allowed to buy her unsold goods back and for copies of the inventory of goods sent to the Exchequer

Interrogatories put to Garnet and Oldcorne; their conversations reported, but their testimony is contradictory

Garnet moved from the Gatehouse prison to the Tower

Lord Cobham in the Tower thinks the Gunpowder Plot crisis has subsided sufficiently to renew his suit to Salisbury (his brother-in-law) for release from imprisonment on another charge

First of Garnet's letters written in orange juice, 'invisible' ink, intercepted and deciphered

Garnet writes on the lawfulness of blowing up Parliament

Garnet admits telling less than the truth about White Webbs and his connection to the plotters

'Confession' of Nicholas Owen: he admits nothing

Submission of expenses claim of 23s 9d for setting Catesby and Percy's heads on iron spikes

March Final examination and death of Nicholas Owen

Further 'orange juice' letters from Garnet to Anne Vaux intercepted

Oldcorne contradicts Garnet again about the use of White Webbs

Oldcorne implicates Monteagle; subsequently made to qualify his statement

Sir Thomas Edmondes writes to Salisbury of Catesby's plans to be lieutenant colonel of a Spanish regiment

Salisbury writes to Edmondes that Garnet guilty 'ex ore proprio' of concealing treason

Garnet's holograph declaration of his proceedings in the Plot, endorsed by Salisbury; 'Forbidden by the K[ing] to be given in evidence'

Lords Mordaunt, Stourton and Montagu tried in court of Star Chamber, not at common law

Examination of Anne Vaux

Garnet testifies he knew of the Plot in July 1605 'under the seal of the confessional'

Northumberland writes to Salisbury, still exercising patronage and administering his estates

Intense questioning of Garnet and Oldcorne; Popham displays accumulated evidence of Garnet's guilt

Initial commission issued for the trial of Henry Garnet

Persistent rumours of other planned plots

'Orange juice' letter from Anne Vaux to Henry Garnet declares that life without him 'is not life but death'

Rumour that James has been killed hunting at Woking becomes serious enough to need a proclamation to refute

Indictment of Henry Garnet

Francis Tresham's retraction (examined posthumously) of his implication of Garnet

Garnet gives evidence of papal directions on the inadmissibility of a Protestant monarch

Chamberlain reports that Garnet will be arraigned at Guildhall; claims that he will be too drunk to give evidence

James I gives instructions to Coke via Salisbury on the conduct of Garnet's trial

Garnet pleads not guilty, but is sentenced to death

April Theological questioning of Garnet in Latin

Garnet writes in the fifth 'orange juice' letter to Anne Vaux of his dreams of the heavenly tabernacle

Official reports of Garnet's trial issued. Chamberlain describes it in letters

Garnet writes to Anne Vaux again with a view to posterity, describing her place with the Jesuits

Garnet writes declaration to the king – very different to his thoughts expressed to Anne Vaux

Garnet induced to write to the 'captive' Tesimond

Contradictory declarations of Garnet drawn from him 'to disclose his hypocrisy'

Garnet's obvious contradictions excused as evidence of torture by apologists in Flanders Rumours begin that Nicholas Owen died of torture, not suicide

Examination of Warwickshire recusants reveals they have 'not been to church these forty years, brought up in the old law'

Edward Oldcorne, John Wintour and Humphrey Littleton executed at Worcester

Garnet's last letter to Anne Vaux reports Oldcorne's execution

Salisbury recommends to Edmondes that Garnet's execution should be deferred to avoid 'holy week, as they call it'

Garnet continues equivocation discrediting his own evidence

May Garnet's execution deferred from May Day for fear of disturbance

Garnet executed in St Paul's churchyard on 3 May. His 'portrait' on the 'miraculous straw' becomes an object of veneration among English Catholics

Reports from Brussels of Catholic propaganda after Garnet's execution

June–August Proclamation issued that all Jesuits should leave the country

Fresh plots are hatched by Baldwin and others in Brussels; plots made against Salisbury's life

Secular clergy and lay Catholics dissociate from the Jesuits who are blamed for the treason

Declaration that proofs of James's pre-succession promises of toleration towards English Catholics are to be published

Interrogatories to the earl of Northumberland focus upon his conduct towards Thomas Percy and the trust reposed in him

Countess of Northumberland writes to Salisbury about her husband's coming trial

Trial of Northumberland begins in Star Chamber. Northumberland is imprisoned for life for misprision of Treason (released sixteen years later)

Lord Stourton writes unsuccessful plea for liberty to Salisbury from the Tower. (Lord Montague will be released from the Tower in 1611 after a payment of £6000)

1608–1609
Inquisitions into the plotters' lands
Will and death of Lord Mordaunt

1611
Investigation of the claims against the earl of Northumberland by Timothy Elks

1618–1619
Execution of Sir Walter Raleigh
Death of Dorothy, Countess of Northumberland

1621–1622
Earl of Northumberland released from the Tower
John Donne's Gunpowder Day sermon

1632
5 November Death of the earl of Northumberland

NOTES

Prologue
1. 'I will neither persecute' Cecil Papers 135.100 printed by Akrigg pp.206-207
2. 'Secure him from his allegiance' TNA SP 12/241/112
3. 'Being discontented they were not advanced' TNA SP 12/243/11
4. TNA SP 38/4 10 Dec 1594
5. 'It were pity' Nicholls p.102 citing Bruce Camden OS 78 p.56
6. 'What should I do here?' Cecil Papers 92.42

1 Guy Fawkes and the Great Blow
1. 'Ask of 3' Cecil Papers 134.72

2 Plans and Preparations
1. 'Jack, certain friends of mine' TNA SP 14/15/44
2. 'Though all you malefactors' British Library Cotton MS Titus ii 290

3 'They shall not see who hurts them'
1. 'The tyrannous heretic' TNA SP14/16/4
2. 'On Tuesday at night' TNA SP 14/16/23
3. 'He having desired' Cecil Papers 112.162

4 'This letter only were enough to hang me'
1. Proclamation TNA SP 14/16/20a printed in Larkin & Hughes no 58
2. 'Mr Catesby and my cousin' TNA SP 14/216/176
3. 'Good cousin' TNA SP 14/16/19

5 *The Eye of the Storm*
1. 'Nearness of name' TNA SP 14/16/23
2. 'May it please your lordship' TNA SP 14/16/30
3. 'As they knew not how' TNA SP 14/216/49
4. 'Make his chamber more private' TNA SP 14/16/35
5. Proclamation TNA SP 14/16/35a printed in Larkin & Hughes no 59

6 *Hoist by their own petard*
1. Confession TNA SP 14/216/114
2. 'Interrogatories administered' TNA E134/4JASI/TRIN6
3. 'The Parliament I think bringeth up your Lordship now.' TNA SP 14/216/74
4. 'The miserable fellow' TNA SP 14/216/86

7 *The Tentacles of Treason*
1. 'Into my hands even now' Cecil Papers 112.173
2. 'Remaining unsatisfied' Cecil Papers 191.71
3. 'Then I ransacked' TNA SP 14/216/92
4. The examination of Francis Swetnam TNA SP 14/216/93
5. The examination of Matthew Batty and others TNA SP 14/216/240
6. 'As it stands' Cecil Papers 113.9
7. Informers' notes Cecil Papers 113.7 and 8
8. 'Some other of the like estate' Cecil Papers 113.11
9. A genuine connection with the plot Cecil Papers 112.60
10. Attorney General v. Joanes TNA STAC 8/8/2
11. 'Conveyed away' Cecil Papers 191.74
12. 'If the Papists should grow to a head' Cecil Papers 113.18
13. 'The fire which was said' TNA SP 14/16/69
14. 'Standing a great while' Cecil Papers 227.129
15. An expenses claim Cecil Papers 190.47
16. 'Of mean stature'. TNA SP 14/16/85
17. 'Percy and his complices' TNA SP 14/16/90
18. Nest of vipers TNA SP 77/7 [f.287]
19. 'It may appear how he was to me' TNA SP 14/16/97
20. 'He employed him' The original and fair copy TNA SP 14/16/100 and 101
21. Deductions about the king's life TNA SP 14/216/122
22. 'The examinate sayeth' TNA E 178/4162
23. A wider rising after the gunpowder explosion. Cecil Papers 113.33
24. 'Very fair Hungarian horseman's coat' Cecil papers 113.44
25. 'Sent my lord of Northumberland and my lord Dacre' TNA SP 14/16/104
26. 'Troubled not much himself' TNA SP 14/216/116

27. Monteagle's name in brackets again. TNA SP 14/216/124
28. 'Atheists fools and cowards' TNA SP 14/216/126
29. 'Most humbly at your lordship's disposal'. TNA SP 14/17/4
30. 'Great complaint is daily made to me' Cecil Papers 113.88
31. 'Fitter to be related than written' Cecil Papers 113.94
32. 'Lord Monteagle has £500 of Percy's wife' Cecil Papers 113.91
33. 'No condition shall be too hard' Cecil Papers 113.71
34. 'The sheriff has dealt unjustly' Cecil Papers 113.73

8 Dining with danger

1. 'His Majesty's happy delivery from the late treason' Cecil Papers 191.94
2. 'Would so far forget themselves' TNA SP 77/7 f.312
3. 'Let it satisfy you I said so' TNA SP 14/216/158
4. 'The late devilish attempt' TNA SP 14/18/66
5. A show of strength Cecil Papers 113.103
6. Tresham's confession of 13 November 1605 TNA SP 14/16/63
7. Tresham's retraction TNA SP 14/216/211
8. Thomas Wintour's goods Cecil Papers 190.20
9. 'The very floor of the great parlour' Cecil Papers 191. 145
10. 'Great affray amongst them' Cecil Papers 109.108
11. Commission for the trial of Sir Everard Digby TNA KB 8/60 m.14
12. 'If you knew what pains' Cecil Papers 109.111
13. Published in Larkin & Hughes no. 62
14. Ibid. Cited in Childs p.322
15. To withstand torture Cecil Papers 113.77
16. 'Doubling of his tongue' TNA SP 14/18/20

9 Halfway Between Heaven and Earth

1. The great indictment TNA KB 8/59 m.16-17
2. 'These tragical determinations' Cecil 109. 130
3. 'My woeful husband' TNA SP 14/18/37
4. 'Tie us and our posterity to you and your house forever' TNA SP 14/18/36
5. 'Your companion in tribulation' TNA SP 14/18 35ii
6. 'Hindlip this 23rd of January very late' TNA SP 14/18/38
7. Confirming that Father Oldcorne alias Hall was at Hindlip Cecil Papers 109.149
8. 'Hellish or earthly devils' Howells 'State Trials' ii p.164
9. 'What a tempest and storm' Ibid p,177
10. 'Fowls of the air' Ibid p.184
11. 'God forgive you' Ibid p.194
12. 'Break his neck' Ibid p.218

13. 'Who's that which knocks' Digby papers cited by Fraser p231
14. Exchequer depositions TNA E 134/7JAS1/EAST30
15. 'Ready to be sealed' Cecil Papers 112.134
16. 'The capital house of God's divine service' Cecil Papers 190.34

10 *The Great and the Good*

1. 'Phillips the decipherer' McClure I p.202
2. 'Should carry the comments or descant with me' TNA SP 14/17/61
3. 'Without so much ceremony as the formality of a grave' TNA SP 14/17/62
4. 'Let the fold be fitter for the nose' TNA SP 14/216/241
5. 'Nothing against me but presumptions' Cecil Papers 110.16
6. 'Yet considering the greatness of his house' TNA SP 63/218/21
7. 'If ever they were, they are able now' Cecil Papers 110.30
8. 'The Christians were overthrown' TNA SP 14/216/202
9. 'Where he was to have a Colonel's place' TNA SP 14/216/200
10. 'Many great protestations' TNA SP 14/216/201
11. 'The vow of obedience ceaseth' TNA SP 14/216/245
12. 'In whose hands are the hearts of princes' TNA SP 14/216/212
13. Coke to Salisbury 27 March 1606 TNA SP 14/216/215
14. 'To set down truly as I will answer before God' TNA SP 14/216/205
15. 'Conferred about the message into Spain' TNA SP 14/216/206

11 *Drowning Sorrow*

1. 'As if he meant to drown sorrow' TNA SP 14/19/89
2. 'As ever man could be' Howells State Trials ii 242-243
3. 'When hell brake loose' Ibid p.251
4. 'No power on earth' TNA SP 14/20/2
5. 'Until there is proof to convince him' TNA SP 14/20/3
6. 'They could say more than they would' TNA SP 14/20/4
7. 'Very gravely and temperately' TNA SP 14/20/5
8. 'Help me with your prayers' TNA SP 14/216/246
9. 'You shall die a martyr' TNA SP 14/20/11
10. 'I have written this with my own hand' TNA SP 14/20/12
11. Garnet to Tesimond 4 Apr 1606 Cecil Papers 115.154
12. 'There wanted the declaration of the Pope' Cecil Papers 115.13
13. 'I never had a discourteous word' Ibid
14. 'Mists and fogs of suspicion' TNA SP 14/20/50
15. 'Owen liked the plot very well' TNA SP 14/20/52
16. 'So I desire you all to think of her' Childs p.350 citing Bodleian MS Eng. Th. B 2 p.134
17. 'The affections of the Princes of Christendom' TNA SP 77/8 f.107

18. 'A nest for such bad birds as it was before' Cecil Papers 193.57
19. A proclamation against the Jesuits TNA SP 14/22/13
20. Plots were already emerging TNA SP 77/8 f.115
21. A long meeting of the Council TNA SP 14/22/20
22. 'He may receive disadvantage' Cecil Papers 116.117
23. 'A great scaffold' Hawarde p.292
24. HMC 6ᵗʰ Report Appendix p.232a Northumberland Syon Papers N 1 19
25. 'You shall abstain until you know the king's farther pleasure' TNA SP 14/22/53
26. 'Nothing we can do can set him free' TNA SP 14/22/67
27. 'Will defend your innocency here' TNA SP 14/65/83
28. 'He had spoken to Whynniard for a house for him' TNA SP 14/65/83i
29. 'That day the house was to be blown up and on what pretence' TNA SP 14/66/28
30. 'Lest the earl put a trick upon him to make him away there' TNA SP 14/66/28i
31. 'Durst not go for fear of treachery' TNA SP 14/66/28ii
32. 'In his lord's name by word of mouth' TNA SP 14/67/67
33. The great man who heretofore hath sought my life' TNA SP 14/66/93
34. 'Despairing of his majesty's favour' TNA SP 14/72/16
35. 'So stoutly renounced at the Star Chamber' TNA SP 14/65/26
36. 'Guiltless of all foreknowledge thereof' TNA PROB 11/114 quire 84
37. Exchequer deposition Lord Monteagle's annuity TNA E 134/Jas1/East39
38. 'A bedstead, curtains, bolster and valance' TNA E 178/4179
39. 'Ornaments for a mass' TNA E 178/4006
40. Property of Robert Wintour TNA E 134/7JAS1/EAST30
41. 'Ever hereafter when you like best' TNA SP 16/149/53
42. 'A younger brother and not in pomp' TNA SP 16/150/90
43. 'I hear you are towards one.' TNA SP 16/163/73
44. 'Some of my night watches' TNA SP 16/184/86

Epilogue
1. 'Kill him, kill him' TNA SP 14/216/119
2. 'By an extreme hot fire's side' TNA SP 14/71/3

A note on sources
The Domestic State Papers for the reign of James I [SP 14] contain an enormous amount of material including the 'Gunpowder Plot Book' [SP 14/216], a collection of over two hundred documents including the Monteagle Letter and many of the confessions and examinations taken after the discovery of the Plot. I have also made use of less well known sources such as Exchequer: King's

Remembrancer: Depositions taken by Commission [E 134], and Exchequer: King's Remembrancer: Special Commissions of Inquiry [E 178] now well described in the National Archives online catalogue Discovery. This incorporates the descriptions of records relating to British history, which continue to be collected by the National Register Archives.

There are of course many relevant sources in other archives, the most important being the earl of Salisbury's own papers at Hatfield House, some very similar in character to the state papers preserved at The National Archives. They are available in published form in the Historical Manuscripts Commission's [HMC] *Calendar of Salisbury (Cecil) MSS (1870-1976)*. Both these sources are now available online in various forms via subscription

The papers of the Percy family, Dukes of Northumberland at Alnwick Castle, as described in the Appendix to HMC's Third Report (1872) and the Syon House papers described in the Appendix to the Sixth Report (1877) include private papers of Henry Percy, earl of Northumberland from the time of the Plot. The Star Chamber case paper remains at Syon.

The Tresham family papers now at British Library [Additional Manuscripts 39828-38] also published by HMC, *Various Collections III (1904)*, include Sir Thomas Tresham's less than flattering assessment of Anne Vaux in the summer of 1599 and Francis Tresham's bleak appraisal of the worth Robert Catesby's promises in early 1604.

Other relevant collections include the papers of the Digby family of Gayhurst held by the Centre for Buckinghamshire Studies, which highlights Mary Digby's attempts to obtain the restoration of her estates after the death of Sir Everard Digby; and the Catesby documents among the Ashley family papers at Northamptonshire Record Office, which include a copy of the marriage settlement of Robert Catesby on Katherine Leigh in 1592 and other deeds associated with the marriage.

BIBLIOGRAPHY

The Gunpowder Plot has spawned an enormous number of books, many controversial and polemical. Together with the primary sources given, here is a short list of publications that make those sources most accessible.

Acts of the Privy Council of England, New Series, eds. J R Dasent and others (46 vols.) London (1890–1964)

GPV Akrigg (ed.) *Letters of James VI & I* (Berkeley 1983)

J Bruce, 'Correspondence of James VI of Scotland with Sir Robert Cecil and others in England' (Camden Society Old Series volume 78 (London 1861)

Calendar of State Papers Domestic Series, ed. M A E Green (London 1857–1867)

J Childs, *God's Traitors: Terror and Faith in Elizabethan England* (Bodley Head 2014). Despite its title, contains a major section on the Gunpowder Plot and the Vaux connection

A Fraser, *The Gunpowder Plot, Terror and Faith in 1605* (London 1997)

Gardiner, S R (ed.), 'Two Declarations of Garnet Relating to the Gunpowder Plot', *The English Historical Review* III 1888 pp. 510–519

J Hawarde, *Les Reportes del Cases in Camera Stellata 1593-1609*, ed. W P Baildon (London 1894)

HMC Reports and Calendars Marquis of Salisbury (24 vols.) (London 1883–1976)

A Hogge, *God's Secret Agents: Queen Elizabeth's Forbidden Priests and the Hatching of the Gunpowder Plot* (2005).

T. B. Howell, *A complete collection of state trials and proceedings for high treason and other crimes and misdemeanors: from the earliest period to the year 1783, with notes and other illustrations, compiled by T. B. Howell and continued from the year 1783 to the present time by Thomas Jones Howell* (London 1816-26)

D Jardine, *Criminal trials: supplying copious illustrations of the important periods of English History during the reigns of Queen Elizabeth and James I.; to which is added a narrative of the Gunpowder Plot* (London 1846)

J F Larkin and P L Hughes (eds.), *Stuart Royal Proclamations* (Clarendon Press, 1973).

N E McClure, *The Letters of John Chamberlain* (Philadelphia, The American Philosophical Society, 1939)

M Nicholls, *Investigating Gunpowder Plot* (Manchester University Press, 1991).

M Nicholls 'Strategy and Motivation in the Gunpowder Plot' (*Historical Journal* 50/4 2007)

O. Tesimond, *The Gunpowder Plot: The Narrative of Oswald Tesimond Alias Greenway translated from the Italian of the Stonyhurst manuscript, edited and annotated by Francis Edwards* (Folio Society, 1973).

INDEX